BLACK LEADERSHIP FOR SOCIAL CHANGE

Recent Titles in
Contributions in Afro-American and African Studies

BLACK LEADERSHIP FOR SOCIAL CHANGE

Jacob U. Gordon

Foreword by Samuel DuBois Cook

Contributions in Afro-American and African Studies, Number 200

GREENWOOD PRESS
Westport, Connecticut • London

Library of Congress Cataloging-in-Publication Data

Gordon, Jacob U.
   Black leadership for social change / Jacob U. Gordon ; foreword
by Samuel DuBois Cook.
      p. cm. — (Contributions in Afro-American and African studies,
ISSN 0069-9624 ; no. 200)
   Includes bibliographical references and index.
   ISBN 0-313-31396-2 (alk. paper)
   1. Afro-American leadership.   2. Social Change—United
States.   3. Afro-Americans—Politics and government.   4. Afro-
Americans—Social conditions.   I. Title.   II. Series.
E185.615.G666   2000
303.3'4'08996073—dc21   99–088483

British Library Cataloguing in Publication Data is available.

Library of Congress Catalog Card Number: 99–088483
ISBN: 0-313-31396-2
ISSN: 0069-9624

First published in 2000

Greenwood Press, 88 Post Road West, Westport, CT 06881
An imprint of Greenwood Publishing Group, Inc.
www.greenwood.com

Printed in the United States of America

The paper used in this book complies with the
Permanent Paper Standard issued by the National
Information Standards Organization (Z39.48-1984).

10 9 8 7 6 5 4 3 2 1

To the generations of African-American men and women who provided leadership for the redemption and renewal of the Soul of America

and

To all those who lived and died in the struggle for a fair and just society and in pursuit of the American dream.

Contents

Foreword

—————————————— *Samuel DuBois Cook*

As we begin a new century and millennium, problems of black leadership in the drama of the flux and flow of the American historical process loom large and deserve rigorous analysis and probing exploration. The stakes are high. This book by Dr. Jacob U. Gordon meets an urgent and timely need.

This is quite a book richly deserving of a wide audience. It is fascinating, imaginative, illuminating, challenging, learned, exciting, and thought-provoking. Indeed, it is magisterial, panoramic, wide-ranging, encyclopedic, and rigorous. It is a *tour de force* on black leadership.

Dr. Gordon explores the various dimensions of black leadership within the broad sweep, context, and conceptual scheme of American history and the dynamic and continuing struggle of blacks to achieve freedom, justice, equity, fairness, and equality. African-American leadership for what? The answer is to dislodge the cancer, albatross, and heavy yoke of racism and to pursue and realize full equality as citizens and as human beings. Black leadership is inextricably tied to social change, institutional reform, and structures and processes of power and influence.

The author asserts that, regrettably, "while much has been written about black leaders very little has been done about black leadership. A comprehensive book on black leadership is lacking. It is this gap in leadership literature that this volume attempts to fill."

Thus this book is a grammar of black leadership. While the author deftly discusses black leaders from the broad perspective of American history—from slavery to the contemporary scene—his chief focus is on the concept, philosophy, vision, and criteria of black leadership. Thus he roams far and wide. He wrestles with definitions, models, styles, strategies, tactics, dilemmas, ideologies, dialectics, diversities, multi-dimensionality, changes, continuities, typology, sources, foundations, black leadership in a variety of institutions—corporate America, education, community, religion, international relations, military—and the future.

What a broad reach and inclusive perspective!

Dr. Gordon's book is a rich and powerful contribution to the literature not only of black leadership, but also to the understanding of the black experience in the ebb and flow, the tragedies and triumphs, the heights and depths of the American historical, social, political, and cultural processes. This book is also courageous, engaged and inspiring. It deserves wide, thoughtful, critical, and constructive readership. It has creative and enduring utility. Dr. Gordon has plowed new ground and established significant scholarly foundations on which to build.

Note: Dr. Samuel DuBois Cook is President Emeritus of Dillard University and President of the Association for the Study of African-American Life and History, Inc.

Acknowledgments

This book is a reflection of my belief that a study of African-American leadership within the context of American history will reveal, among other things, some of the continuities and changes in African-American reactions to unremitting white racism and oppression. For the past ten years, I have been teaching an upper-class undergraduate course in black leadership to American and foreign students at the University of Kansas. Facing the paucity of a comprehensive text and especially the lack of black leadership theories in leadership literature has been a challenge.

Throughout my work on this volume I have tried to keep in mind the observation of Martin R. Delany in 1852:

Our elevation must be the result of self-efforts and work of our own hands. No other human power can accomplish it. If we but determine it shall be so, it will be so.

In putting together this book, I owe many debts to a number of people. First, to my wife Thelma and my four children who have given me the love and encouragement from start to finish. Second, I would like to thank my students in my black leadership classes for challenging me to write a text on this neglected area of the African-American experience. Third, I am grateful to my colleagues in the Department of African and African-American Studies at the University of Kansas for their intellectual stimulation. To my staff at the Center for Multicultural Leadership–Life Span Studies: Katie Woods, who served as my research assistant, and Bridgitt Mitchell, my special assistant, I am appreciative. Special thanks to my editor at Greenwood Press, and Mary Brohammer for preparing the manuscript. Finally, I am grateful to all who participated in our interviews and black leadership surveys. Without the assistance of all those whom we have touched and/or those who have touched us during the course of our research, this book would not have been possible.

Introduction: Black Leadership for Social Change

To talk about the need and the importance of Black leadership is something that affects not only African-Americans but the entire country. And the civil rights movement in the past, and I suspect in the future as well, has provided a lot of moral support and a lot of energy to the Women's Movement, to the Gay Rights Movement, to the Labor Movement, and to other important movements for equality and advancement. So the issue of Black leadership is really important to everybody in this country.

> William M. Tuttle, Jr.
> Professor of History
> The University of Kansas

For the past ten years I have been teaching courses in black leadership in America to American and international students. This decade saw growing scholarship and public interest in the role of black leadership in American history. No student of American studies can any longer be unaware of the development of black history in the historical profession and the broad outlines of this scholarship, or of the significance of the unresolved issues of race and class in America, and the world at large.

This book reflects my belief that any serious and meaningful consideration of American history requires an understanding and appreciation of African-American leadership. It reveals some of the continuities, changes, and contrasts in African-American reactions to unremitting white racism, bigotry, and sexism. The work draws from a large body of African-American historiography and my experiences as a student of Africa and the African Diaspora. It is also drawn from the suggestions of my students and colleagues in the Department of African and African-American Studies at the University of Kansas.

In the quest for human rights and racial advancement, African-Americans have managed throughout their history to draw their leaders from their own ranks. African-American leaders have always sought diverse ways to overcome the racial barriers and oppression that have pervaded American society. It should be noted that the scarcity of power, prestige, and ideological differences in the African-American community has resulted in the struggle for leadership that is often ruthless and ineffective. And although black leaders share a common destiny and values for the respect for human dignity, they differ markedly in ideologies, leadership styles, and tactics. A classic case in point are the differences between two great black leaders, W. E. B. Du Bois and Booker T. Washington.

Although much work has been done on African-American studies since the establishment of the Association for the Study of African-American Life and History by Carter G. Woodson in 1915, very little has been done on black leadership. This conclusion is based on the recurring appearance of theory, research, and practice in leadership literature. Of particular concern is that leadership theories and practices are usually Eurocentric. The purpose of this book and its investigation is to document African-American leadership roles in America's search for social change. The major area of investigation is threefold: (1) the impact of African-American leadership in America's search for social change, to ensure justice, fairness, equality, and the pursuit of happiness for all Americans; (2) an analysis of the enduring dilemma of black leadership, especially in light of the emergence of Louis Farrakhan as a possible political leader; and (3) the future role of African-American leadership in the twenty-first century.

This book is based on historical and contemporary contexts. Black leadership should be viewed as part of American leadership history. It should be noted, however, that black leadership is different from the American, "dominant culture" leadership. While the former grew out of the enslavement and oppression of African-Americans, the latter was, for the most part, an extension of European culture and values.

Black leadership and black social thought have traditionally been characterized as either liberal or conservative (but for the most part, liberal). Thus, the main thrust of this book is the examination of the impact of African-American leadership in American life, both from liberal and conservative perspectives. The book provokes several related questions:

1. How much power did various black leaders actually have?
2. What were the sources and limits of that power, and how did the leaders use that power or influence in seeking to attain their goals?
3. To what extent was that power derived from black support, to what extent from white support, and to what extent from an organizational base or from a position in government?
4. What tactics did individual leaders use to appeal to blacks and/or whites to achieve their aims?
5. To what extent did the leaders cooperate with each other, to what extent were they competing with each other, to what extent were their relationships marked by conflict, and

how in turn did such patterns of cooperation, competition, and conflict shape the course of their careers and the degree to which the cause of black advancement was hindered or promoted?

6. What were the different ways in which the style and strategies of the individual leaders were shaped by their personal backgrounds and the differing social contexts in which they operated?

7. To what extent were any of the leaders able to move beyond their role as leaders in the cause of black advancement, to become leaders prominent in other broader and predominantly white social movements as well?

8. What is the future of black leadership in America?

In order to adequately address these questions, the book has been organized into three parts: Part One—Theorizing Black Leadership; Part Two—Foundations of Black Leadership; and Part Three—Twentieth Century and Contemporary Black Leadership. The book concludes with a chapter on the future of black leadership.

For the purpose of clarity, relevance, and appropriateness, several terms have been used interchangeably throughout this book to refer to persons of African ancestry in the United States. The terms "black" and "African-American" are most commonly used; the latter is the official term used by the U.S. Census of 1990.

According to a survey of 1,003 African-Americans age fourteen and over (survey conducted from October to December of 1992 by Burrel/Yankelovich for the American Association of Retired Persons [AARP]), the most preferred term to describe this ethnic group is "Black" (38%), followed by "African-American" (30%), "Afro-American" (20%), "Negro" (4%), and "Other" (5%). Each generation of African-Americans has different preferences:

• Age 50+ prefer "Black" (49%)
• Age 30–49 moderately prefer "Black" (42%) versus African-American (31%)
• Age 21–29 are undecided (three choices are all within 31–32%)
• Age 14–20 strongly prefer "African-American" (46%)

Black/African-Americans are the largest ethnic group in the United States, making up 12.1 percent of the total population. Between 1980 and 1990, the black population increased by 13.2 percent compared with a 9.7 percent increase in the total population. About 80 percent of the black population reside in southern and industrial states, particularly in large cities (U.S. Census Bureau, 1990).

Like the other four major groups (American Indian/Alaska Natives, Asian and Pacific Islanders, Hispanic/Latino-Americans, and White/European Americans), the Black/African-American group is heterogeneous. During the twentieth century, members of this group have come from different countries, represented various cultures, languages and dialects, and included both native and foreign-born individuals. They also reflect a variety of skin colors, from "white" to "darkest black."

In sciendfic study of leadership in the United States, the concept of *leadership*, despite its obvious centrality in American politics, has not been sharply defined. Indeed, in reviewing the interdisciplinary scientific literature of leadership, the author concludes that there is a lack of explicit focus on leadership as a core concept. In the general social science literature, the concept of leadership has been used in such diverse ways to characterize the varied phenomena that there is a lack of agreement regarding even the basic properties of leadership. This ambiguity in the general concept of leadership is reflected specifically in black leadership literature. Here, there is a wide variety of definitions, implicit and explicit. It is even debatable as to whether there is such a thing as black leadership, let alone the notion of any academic inquiry of the subject.

Gunnar Myrdal (1944) wrote in his classic study, "We should not start from an attempt on *a priori* grounds to define the principle concept. . . . We have only to settle that we are discussing the role and importance of individual persons in the sphere of social action." Similarly, Ladd (1966) wrote that little effort was made at the outset to develop any full and precise definition of black leadership, because "the study as a whole is centrally concerned with defining it."

Writing about the crisis of leadership, a pioneer scholar of leadership, James MacGregor Burns (1978) writes, "If we know all too much about leaders, we know far too little about leadership. We fail to grasp the essence of leadership that is relevant to the modern age and hence we cannot agree even on the standards by which to measure, recruit, and reject it." He goes on to say that "one of the most serious failures in the study of leadership has been the bifurcation between the literature on leadership and the literature on followship."

In recent years, the scholarship in African-American studies has gained national recogrudon in American historiography. Regrettably, however, while much has been written about black leaders, very little has been done about black leadership. A comprehensive book on black leadership is lacking. It is this gap in leadership literature that this volume attempts to fill.

A brief review of selected major publications on black leadership should shed light on the subject. John Hope Franklin's (1982) *Black Leaders of the Twentieth Century* is an essential volume on the major accomplishments of fifteen twentieth-century black leaders—nationalist and integrationalist, the charismatic and the bureaucratic, and men and women who came from diverse walks of life, including religion, labor, business, the professions, and the arts. John White (1985) examines black leadership in America from 1895 to 1968 in a work of synthesis of five outstanding black male leaders' lives and their collective biographies. The book is the first attempt to examine the problems facing these men, their personal and ideological relationships, and the historical context in which they operated. He also examined such civil rights organizations as the National Association for the Advancement of Colored People, the National Urban League, the Southern Christian Leadership Conference, and the Nation of Islam. Some scholars have also explored the role of black leadership during the Reconstruction Era. Of special interest is the work of Howard Rabinowitz (1982), *Southern Black Leadership of the Reconstruction Era.*

Rabinowitz has assembled an anthology that transcends recent efforts to "rehabilitate" black leaders' reputations and that explores the larger question of how black leaders *"functioned* in Reconstruction politics and within the Republican party" (p. xviii). The combined studies of selected congressmen, individual state and local leaders, and the collective biographies of state and local figures provide a storehouse of information about black political leadership during Reconstruction. The purpose of this book, according to the author, is twofold: to make readily available "the fruits of recent biographical work" and to point the way toward future investigations (p. xx). Rabinowitz and his fellow authors succeed admirably in both efforts. They assemble an extended collection of biographical information that illuminates the crucial areas of black–white interdependence and divisiveness among blacks within the Republican coalition; for, as Rabinowitz notes in his introductory essay, without such information "neither the nature of black leadership nor the course and direction of Reconstruction can be properly grasped" (p. xix). The authors also raise a multitude of questions—particularly about the nature of black interactions with the white world—that could profitably engage the attention of Reconstruction scholars for years to come.

Reflecting careful conception and planning, the volume includes an introductory essay by Rabinowitz that traces the historiographical debate over the quality of black leadership; individual essays that are drawn from every state of the Confederacy and that explore every variety of black leadership; and a concluding chapter by August Meier that highlights the major themes and findings of the essays and underscores the need for further research in particular areas. The fourteen essays are consistently of high quality, and although they differ somewhat in interpretation, they all focus on the central question of how blacks functioned in Reconstruction politics—or in other words, how they "gained, maintained, and finally lost power . . ." (p. xviii).

August Meier notes in his conclusion that "one of the virtues of this volume is that it illuminates so well the complex and ambiguous ways in which late nineteenth century Black political leaders in the South functioned" (p. 401). One comes away from this volume, however, with something of an overdose of complexity and ambiguity, and grasping for another level of analysis of all this carefully assembled new information. Rabinowitz could have strengthened this volume and increased its usefulness and significance considerably by expanding his introduction to include an overview of the major findings of his contributors. Meier's afterword is helpful in this regard, and he draws a series of "tentative conclusions" based on the research presented within, but one is left with the unsettling impression that Rabinowitz has not quite completed the task at hand. His own reflections, in addition to Meier's, would have brought the project to a more successful conclusion. Although scholars in the field will find this a valuable compendium of biographical information and an important corrective to stereotypes both old and new, the overburdened scholar in related fields will probably not find the time to extract the essence of meaning from this volume.

Another attempt to document black leadership is an anthology edited by Georgia A. Persons (1993), *Dilemmas of Black Politics*. A reviewer noted, "Here at last is a major collection of writings on Black leadership and electoral politics in the post-Reagan era." The book focuses on recent high-profile elections; it assesses the strategies that are helping black candidates win an increasing number of political contests. What appears to have emerged from the collection is a clear evidence of a new strategy of "de-racialization," a major departure from the traditional agendas and assumptions of black politics in America.

In a recently published work on twentieth century black leadership, Manning Marable (1998) presents his family during slavery and Reconstruction, and their efforts to achieve full equality. In this compelling work, the author identifies three major traditions that have defined black American political culture: integration, nationalist separatism, and what he terms *democratic transformation*. At the heart of the book are critical portraits of four leaders whose legacies speak to the challenges of race, class, and power: Booker T. Washington, W. E. B. Du Bois, Harold Washington, and Louis Farrakhan. The author argues convincingly that the history of the black struggle for civil rights and political and economic equality in America is deeply tied to the strategies, agendas, and styles of black leaders. Professor Marable's book is undoubtedly one of the most exciting and important books on race and black leadership to appear in quite a while. It is by no means a comprehensive text on black leadership, nor was it intended to be one. Nevertheless, it is a valuable addition to the field.

While these publications are useful documents, the need for a comprehensive text in this increasingly important field cannot be overemphasized. It is also clear that the theoretical and practical knowledge of black leadership remains incomplete. However, I believe that the richness of the information in this volume provides a sound basis for a better understanding and a deeper sense of appreciation for the impact of black leadership in American life.

Although the aforementioned publications are useful documents, a comprehensive book in black leadership is lacking. It is this gap in leadership literature that this volume attempts to fill.

Part One

Theorizing Black Leadership

Movements of thought and social change cannot be fully understood without some sense of their relation to the theories and practices which explain the phenomenon of human behavior.

Jacob U. Gordon
Professor and Research Fellow
The University of Kansas

The key to understanding the idea of black leadership is to examine the subject within the literary context of leadership as a universal human experience. Equally important is an understanding of the role of black leadership in American life. Both contexts, the universal and the American, are critical to the understanding and appreciation of the contributions of black leaders to the American society and the human race.

In the quest for freedom, racial equality, civil and political rights, and economic and educational advancement, black Americans, both during and after slavery, responded to the proposals and rhetoric of leaders drawn from their own ranks. Yet, one of the anomalies in African-American history is the omission of blacks in American leadership literature. Leadership theories and practice have usually excluded black leadership.

The purpose of this part of the book is to fill this gap by examining such questions as: What is leadership? What is black leadership? Why black leadership? What are the foundations of black leadership? And finally, what are some of the theoretical and emerging concepts in black leadership?

1

Defining Black Leadership

The key to understanding leadership lies in recent findings of the origin and sources of leadership. Rigid hierarchies of coercion and deference would seem to bar leadership from animal life. However, extended observations by psychologists of primates (Willhoite, 1976) have suggested that animals indulge in various forms of leadership. In an experiment designed to answer the question whether leaders need followers, a chimpanzee was shown some food hidden under leaves and grass, then led back to rejoin his group. Soon he was trying to persuade the others to follow him to the food. He rushed from one follower to another, grimacing, tapping the follower on the shoulder, screaming, and sometimes grabbing a companion and dragging him or her toward the food. According to the observer (at the Delta Regional Primate Research Center), all this "suggested that group cohesion was strong and the 'leader' was as dependent upon the group for getting to the food as they were dependent on him in knowing precisely where to go."

A study of goal behavior (Stewart and Scott, 1947) concluded that the phenomena of dominance and leadership were not correlated, but the result of two separate learning processes. Studies of "imprinting" by Lorenz and others found that "following responses" are set at intervals early in an animal's life and tend to persist. "Finder" bees are known to communicate the location of food by indicating the nature and direction of the food through variations in buzzing and flower scents exuded from their body. Some of these behaviors are genetically determined, but others seem to be learning experiences based on recognizing leaders with dominant influence, as well as by knowing the right cues.

Another, quite different, biological emphasis in the study of leadership is the assumption of male leadership, especially at the higher levels of power. In this context, power may be defined as the ability to control what others want (Lassey and Sashkin, 1983). Researchers have noted that to lead successfully and permissively, a group member must have the power to impose restrictions on what other members are permitted to do, and must have the ability to know when such restrictions are necessary and when would be best to avoid such impositions.

Most leadership studies have been (and are) concerned with males—at least, male leaders. Gender, as an important aspect of the situation, has rarely been studied. Denmark and Diggory (1966) found, contrary to their hypotheses, that male leaders exhibit and find approval from followers for more authoritarian behavior than do women leaders. This is especially true when leaders use power to induce individual members to conform to group norms. The lack of the gender variable in studies of leadership points to the gaps in existing research and theoretical models.

In the scientific study of politics in the United States, the concept of leadership, despite its centrality in American life, has not been sharply defined. Indeed, early studies and definitions of leadership in the 1930s and 1940s were based on attempts to determine the traits and characteristics of leaders. Smith and Krueger (1933) surveyed the literature on leadership. Leadership methodology, as related to military situations, was reviewed in 1947 by Jenkins. Stogdill's (1948) studies included all studies bearing on the problems of traits and personal factors associated with leadership. It is important to note that these early studies appear to have little relationship with the problem of defining leadership. Except in few cases, the authors asked different groups of persons, usually business executives and members of the professions, to list the traits which they believed to be essential to leadership. Little uniformity was found among the items contained in such lists. Only intelligence, initiative, and responsibility were mentioned twice each among the top five items in the lists reported (Gowin, 1915; Heath and Gregory, 1946; Jones, 1938; and Starch, 1943). Other traits included in the studies were: age, height, weight, physique, energy, health, appearance, fluency of speech, scholarship level, knowledge level, judgment and decision skills, insight, originality, adaptability, degree of introversion–extroversion, dominance, initiative, persistence, ambition, dependability, responsibility, integrity and conviction, self-confidence, mood control, mood optimism, emotional control, social and economic status, social activity and mobility, bio-social activity, social skills, popularity and prestige, and so forth.

The following conclusions are supported by uniformly positive evidence from ten or more of the studies surveyed:

The average person who occupies a position of leadership exceeds the average member of his or her group to some degree in the following respects: (1) sociability; (2) initiative; (3) persistence; (4) knowing how to get things done; (5) self-confidence; (6) alertness to, and insight into, situations; (7) cooperativeness; (8) popularity; (9) adaptability; and (10) verbal facility.

In addition to the aforementioned, a number of factors have been found that are specific to well-defined groups. For example, athletic ability and physical prowess have been found to be characteristics of leaders in boys' gangs and play groups. Intellectual fortitude and integrity are traits found to be associated with eminent and natural leadership in maturity.

The items with the highest overall correlation with leadership are originality, popularity, sociability, judgment, aggressiveness, desire to excel, humor, cooperativeness, liveliness, and athletic ability, in approximate order of magnitude of average correlation coefficient.

In spite of considerable negatively correlated evidence, the general trend of results suggests a low positive correlation between leadership and such variables as chronological age, height, weight, physique, energy, appearance, dominance, and mood control. The evidence is about evenly divided concerning the relation to leadership of such traits as degree of introversion–extroversion, self-sufficiency, and emotional control.

The evidence available suggests that leadership exhibited in various school situations may persist into college and into later vocational and community life. However, knowledge of the facts relating to the transferability of leadership is very meager and obscure.

The most fruitful studies, from the point of view of understanding leadership, have been those in which leadership behavior was described and analyzed on the basis of direct observation or analysis of biographical and case history data.

The factors that have been found to be associated with leadership could probably all be classified under the general headings of *capacity, achievement, responsibility, participation,* and *status.*

The definition of leadership based on traits is troublesome. The process of analyzing the studies proved frustrating because each student of leadership created different definitions based on the particular selected sets of traits. Few characteristics could be universally identified as constituting leadership behavior. The requirements for leadership, characteristics of leaders, and definitions of what constitutes leadership varied widely, depending on circumstances. Therefore, analysis in recent decades has concentrated on examination of leadership behavior in various contexts.

In a review of leadership literature, several definitions can be summarized. Stogdill (1974) suggests eleven perspectives that define leadership as:

1. A function of group process
2. Personality or effects of personality
3. The art of inducing compliance
4. The exercise of influence
5. A form of persuasion
6. A set of acts or behaviors

7. A power relationship
8. An instrument of goal achievement
9. An effect of interaction
10. A differentiated role
11. The initiation of structure

Burns (1978) defines leadership as the reciprocal process of mobilizing—by persons with certain motives and values—various economic, political, and other resources, in a context of competition and conflict in order to realize goals either independently or mutually held by leaders and followers. Burns also defines leadership as a special form of power. He noted two essentials of power: motive and resource, and the possession of control, authority, or influence over others.

Hogan, Curphy, and Hogan (1994), in their search for what we know about leadership, have suggested that leadership involves persuading other people to set aside for a period of time their individual concerns and to pursue a common goal that is important for the responsibilities and welfare of a group. . . . Leadership occurs when others willingly adopt, for a period of time, the goals of a group as their own.

Bass (1973) observed that leadership is the observed effort of one member to change other members' behavior by altering the motivation of the other members or by changing their habits.

Lassey and Sashkin's (1983) study of leadership and social change defined leadership as a role that leads toward goal achievement, involves interaction and influence, and usually results in some form of changed structure or behavior of groups, organizations, or communities.

Writing on leadership, Gardner (1990) defined leadership as the process of persuasion or example by which an individual (or leadership team) induces a group to pursue objectives held by the leader or shared by the leader and his or her followers.

Finally, in their study of leadership as everybody's business, Lawson, Griffin, and Don (1976) defined leadership as "the process of influencing others in making decisions, setting goals and achieving goals . . . and, concurrently, it is the process of keeping the group voluntarily together."

At the time of writing, one of the world's most important leadership campaigns was underway in the United States. It was the re-election campaign of President Clinton in 1996. The bottom-line questions in this contest for the U.S. presidency were: Who among the candidates could *lead* the nation? Who would be the next *leader*?

While the words "lead" and "leader" are frequently used in conversations and media reports, they are used loosely—seemingly with an assumption that their meanings are static and universally understood. Carnahan, Smith, and Gunter, Inc. (CSG) (1996) as part of an ongoing effort to explore and understand the implications of the usage and meaning of these words, commissioned its news media study on the subject.

The news media was selected for such an exploration because they are the major source of popular knowledge in free-speech societies, such as the United States. While the media reflect the cultural behavior and attitudes of the societies covered, they also influence behavior and attitudes in the way they define and present the news.

Interestingly, the newspaper articles collected for the CSG study contained very little substantive discussion on—and description of—what constitutes leading or being a leader, whereas detailed descriptions of what appears to be a radical shift in the notion of business leaders and leadership styles dominated the magazine articles studied.

It should be noted that the attributes of business leaders used in the magazine articles were, when spelled out, similar to those used in the newspaper articles about all sorts of leaders; such attributes included "visionary" and "experienced." The differences were found in the function descriptors, or the leadership skills, required. In the past, a hierarchical leadership style relied on "command" and "control" or "top-down" decision-making. The main leadership skills emphasized in the magazine articles in this study were: facilitation, negotiation, empowerment of employees to make decisions (that is, *to lead*), and mentoring. The following sections briefly discuss the study findings. Their implications call for further exploration and dialogue.

KEY FINDINGS

- In the newspaper articles examined, *leader* was sometimes used as a job title or a function; other times it was used as an attribute.
- Used either way, in the publications studied that were geared to general audiences, *leader* was predominantly applied to white males, and infrequently to others.
- One of the most glaring examples of the aforementioned was found in the articles about Ron Brown, U.S. secretary of commerce, after he died in a tragic plane crash. Although the adjectives used *to* describe him were typical of those applied to *leaders* in articles that included function descriptors, 87 percent of the articles about him were devoid of such terms as *leader, leadership, lead,* and the like.
- Although 1996 was a major U.S. political campaign year in which people from the local to the national level sought elective office (that is, key cultural *leadership* positions), there was little discussion in the newspaper articles of what constitutes a *leader* or the requisite *leadership* skills needed for these jobs. While there was considerable discussion in the business magazine articles about *business* leaders and leadership styles, there was very little discussion about *political* leaders and leadership styles, and the implications for business of either or both.
- In the hundreds of articles about the main political contenders for the U.S. presidency that appeared in the general-interest newspapers examined, the term *leader* was seldom used and its meaning discussed even less. When used, it was mostly the congressional job title of the presumptive Republican candidate who was the Senate majority *leader.*
- The term *leader* was used in the newspaper articles in reference to politicians (world leaders), warriors (rebel leaders), cultists (militia leaders), criminals (ringleaders), artists (leading man), chief executive officers and other business managers, heads of religious organizations, educators, community organizers, and others. There were no articles in

the publications examined that discussed whether or not there were differences in the requirements for or attributes of *leaders* or *leadership* skills in the varied list.

- Similarly, there was minimal discussion of *leadership* styles or qualities required for various environments. For example, are business leadership skills interchangeable with military or political leadership requirements?
- Vision, experience, education, accomplishment, action, being a risk taker, creativity, being trusting/trustworthy, intelligence, and popularity were the top ten attributes mentioned in newspaper articles examined that described a *leader* in more detail. Similar attributes were found in the magazine articles.

NEWSPAPER FINDINGS

Six geographically diverse, general-interest newspapers were selected for the CSG study conducted in April 1996. Articles containing key words such as *lead, leading, leader,* and *leadership* were culled for the analysis. The research focused on the context in which these words were used, the articles in which they were found, the placement and location of the articles, and the frequency and application of these and related terms. The newspapers studied were the *Atlanta Journal-Constitution,* the *Los Angeles Times,* the *New York Times,* the (Portland) *Oregonian,* the *Seattle Times,* and the *St. Louis Post-Dispatch.*

With the exception of sports and comics pages, all sections of the selected papers were searched for articles or commentaries that contained the key "leader" words. Duplicates (wire stories and syndicated columns that were carried in several publications) were eliminated.

Articles that did not include the key leader words, but did include words normally ascribed to leaders as found in CSG's 1994 study, such as *visionary, pioneer,* and *accomplished,* were also culled for review. This brought the total number of newspaper articles examined for the CSG study to slightly more than 800.

Passing References

Sixty-four percent of the newspaper articles that contained the word *leader* were found primarily in political stories; secondarily, in war and mayhem stories. Of these, most (88 percent of political stories; 91 percent of war/mayhem items) were passing references with no further descriptors or discussion as to why these individuals were referred to as "leaders." The references were to world leaders, political leaders, ringleaders, military leaders, cult leaders, guerilla leaders, and rebel leaders.

Some examples of actual passing references include:

- "Russian leader's blast against illegal immigrants and hint at delayed resolution of border dispute are tied to election politics." (*Los Angeles Times*, 4-25-96)
- "Senator Roosevelt was the leader of twenty-one Democratic lawmakers who were willing *to* take their political future in their hands. . . ." (*New York Times Magazine*, 4-14-96)

- "Senator Majority Leader Bob Dole (R-Kan.), who is assured of being the GOP presidential nominee. . . ." (*Atlanta Journal-Constitution*, 4-28-96)
- "Sinn Fein leader Gerry Adams said the statement was not all doom and gloom." ([Portland] *Oregonian*, 4-5-96)

By implication, these leaders were designated as such possibly because they a) represented their respective communities; b) made the final decisions; or c) were the appointed spokespersons for their groups; or because the term "leader" simply indicated their position or job title.

Stories that contained reference to business, religious, arts, academic, and other miscellaneous *leaders* followed the same trend. Eighty-two percent of these were passing references.

Attributes

Of the many attributes that were listed in the newspaper articles that did describe a leader in more detail, the top ten were:

- Visionary
- Experienced
- Educated
- Accomplished
- A doer
- Trusting/trustworthy (good character)
- Risk taker
- Innovative
- Intelligent
- Likable

One of the best examples of the relevance of *vision* as a leadership attribute was found in "Voters Look for Glimpses of presidential Candidates' Vision" ([Portland] *Oregonian*, 4-28-96). Writer Jodi Enda said that "people . . . want signs that potential leaders have a sense of direction," a vision for the future. The lengthy article contained a quotation from Roger Simon, a syndicated columnist and author who at the time was writing a book on the 1996 presidential election. Simon said:

They [the voters] are genuinely looking for somebody who embodies American ideals or American myths. They want someone to represent what is good about America, a person who has a clear vision of what America's aspirations should be, and who can at least give a reasonable blueprint about how he or she intends to achieve those aspirations. . . .

Less frequently but consistently used *leader* descriptors included "reformer/change agent," "influential," "role model," "energetic," "mentor," "decision-maker," "bold," "passionate goal/job/responsibility," "compassionate," "confident," "communicator," "trail blazer," "guiding force," and "dependable."

To illustrate: "Reflection on Ironies of an Activist's Life" by George Ramos (*Los Angeles Times*, 4-17-96) described Victoria Castro as a "leader" of university reform, bright and promising, an activist, "a force to be reckoned with," educated, and passionate about her cause.

Diversity

Ninety-nine percent of the political leader references were to males; 83 percent to white males. To illustrate the propensity to refer to males as leaders while using other terms for their female counterparts, consider the following two examples:

- The *New York Times* (4-8-96) carried three obituaries on the same page (B12). Ilka Payan, an actress and successful social activist, was described as a *champion*. Barbara McLean, one of the first women to work as a Hollywood film editor with extensive influence far beyond the cutting room, was referred to as a *pioneer*. Raymond S. Rubinow, a social activist, was called a civic *leader*.
- The [Portland] *Oregonian* (4-18-96), in its lead editorial that day, talked about and endorsed three local political candidates, *two* women and one man. The term *leader* was used only for the man.

There were no female *leaders* mentioned in any of the war/mayhem stories. Of the miscellaneous leader stories, only 18 percent referred to female leaders.

The racial/ethnic breakdown was better in the miscellaneous category (business, religious, arts, academia, and the like). Twenty percent of the leader references were to people of color. Of the political stories, however, only 13 percent of the leader references were to people of color (primarily Asian, Asian-American, and African-American). In the war/mayhem category, 9 percent were to people of color. It should be noted that only those individuals whose gender and racial/ethnic background could be identified were counted. Where there was question, the individuals were tallied in an "unknown" category.

Undesignated Leaders?

The news articles collected in this category contained attributes normally ascribed to leaders, but did not actually use the word *leader*. It is here that women and people of color dominate as the central focal point.

Ron Brown

The tragic death of U.S. Secretary of Commerce Ron Brown generated a large number of articles about this outstanding man. He was the subject of banner headline news, editorials, commentaries, news analyses, and daily news stories. Writers of both genders and of varied racial and ethnic backgrounds sang Brown's praises. The president's eulogy in part and whole was carried in newspapers around the country.

Brown was described as a "first" in many of his endeavors, a talented bridge builder, a mover and shaker, a confident man with a can-do spirit, a role model, a visionary who was passionate, determined, accomplished, and charismatic. He was credited in his latest, and last, job as having won more foreign business for America than anyone else before him. In his eulogy, President Clinton paid the gifted Ron Brown the highest compliment: "If it weren't for you, I wouldn't be here."

Yet, in all of this high praise, seldom was the word *leader* used in reference to Brown by male or female writers, neither by African-American nor by other racial and ethnic sources. Eighty-seven percent of the articles about Brown did not mention the word *leader.* However, business professionals who died in the same plane crash with Brown were often referred to as *leaders.*

Marj Carpenter

Another example of articles collected in this category was an almost full-page one entitled "Marj on a Mission" by Mike Cochran (AP, the *Atlanta Journal-Constitution,* 4-13-96). Marj Carpenter was described as "tough, brash, wily, witty," "the highest elected official of one of America's most socially conscious mainstream denominations," "goodwill ambassador for the denomination," "indomitable," accomplished, and more. Never was she described as a *leader.*

U.S. President

To a far lesser degree, but significant nonetheless, articles in this category about the president and presidential candidates which lacked discussion of leadership as well as even passing references to the word *leader.* An example of such an article was found in the *New York Times* (4-1-96). Entitled "Can the President Capitalize On the Economy's Strength?" it talks about Clinton's accomplishments as the "guy . . . in charge," and the "central figure in Government," not *leader.*

Family Values

Family values is a term that came into popular use after the Republican Congressional electoral victories in 1994. Like *leader* and *leadership, family values* is a term commonly used, seldom explained, and assumed to be defined universally in the same way.

Families remain the basic unit of society. It is there that most people, as children, are imbued with a basic value system. Articles that mention *family values* were included in this study about *leaders* and *leadership* in order to begin an exploration of the possible relationship between family values and leadership, as well as to see if, in defining family values, more could be discerned about society's concept of leaders and leadership.

Most of the articles collected merely mention *family values* in passing. Of the descriptors ascribed to family values that were found in these articles, those that predominated included getting married and having children, being peaceful, taking personal responsibility, being grounded in religion/spirituality, having good character/morality, being respectful, being hardworking, doing good deeds, and being compassionate. If not the same, many of these descriptors are similar to those used to describe leaders and leadership skills.

The terms *leader* and *family values* mixed company in several news articles about presidential contender Bob Dole's effort to portray himself as trustworthy. "When Did the Presidency Turn into a Dads' Contest?"—an editorial written by syndicated columnist Ellen Goodman (*Seattle Times,* 4-19-96) provides a good illustration of this, with meanings ascribed to both terms. Goodman wrote:

And you thought that Bob Dole and Bill Clinton were running for president. Instead, it turns out that these two men are in a race to become Father of their Country . . . Dole was raising the Big Daddy issue as a test of character . . . who do you trust . . . It's Papa Bob versus Daddy Bill. . . . Any kid in trouble with Bob would get a lecture, a list of virtues, and some character-building chores. Bill on the other hand would force her into a marathon discussion of her motives, his pain, and sentence her to a timeout. Or a therapist. The emergence of the dads' competition . . . is based on the assumption that the country is on an all-points search for a national father-figure. . . . Dole comes across as a dad of his time, caring but distant. Clinton is the baby-boomer father who doesn't always know best but is on the case. Around kids, Bob goes by Robert's Rules of Order; Bill is a natural. Bob is the authority figure; Bill the parenting partner. . . .

Referring to *American values* rather than *family values,* an article in the *New York Times* (4-16-96) talked about what some of those values are: trust, honesty, decency, self-reliance, responsibility, and being willing to institute change or being a reformer. Dole was quoted as saying that these values are what is needed in a president—the country's most noticeable *leader.*

The strong similarity in family value attributes and leader/leadership attributes prompts many questions, such as: Assuming two individuals exercise the same value system, what makes one individual a leader and the other simply a good person? By discerning family values, have we come any closer to understanding what a leader is and why leadership is important?

MAGAZINE FINDINGS

As a counterbalance to the general-interest newsprint media, three special-interest publications were included in the CSG study. Because leaders and leadership are frequently the focus of business conversations, three business magazines were reviewed.

Using the same criteria as for the newspapers, slightly more than 100 articles were culled from issues published between May 1995 and April 1996. The magazines reviewed were *Black Enterprise, Harvard Business Review,* and *Inc.*

In the 1994 CSG leadership study, a great disparity was found in the application of the term *leader* to individuals other than white males. Because of this finding, it was decided in this more recent study to include a publication that was aimed specifically at a racial minority audience, to see if there were differences in the application and use of the terms *leader* and *leadership*.

Business Leaders and Leadership

The magazine articles, although focused on *business leaders* and *business leadership*, provided much more substantive information regarding the meaning of these terms than did the newspaper articles. Common to all three magazines was the overriding notion that traditional hierarchical management (that is, *leadership*) is out. Its replacement in a variety of forms is basically decentralized decision-making, wherein employees are empowered to shoulder more of the responsibility for *leading* the company. The most popular of these forms seems to be "open-book management," under which employees are trained to think and act like business owners.

In a special report on open-book management, David Whitford *(Inc.,* June 1995) wrote that this technique works because it "transforms human behavior. It gives individuals reason to care, knowledge to work with, and the power to act. It connects every worker with the ecstatic buzz of business and enables ordinary people to perform better than anyone ever expected." The system, says Whitford, requires trust and respect. It enhances confidence and self-esteem. It encourages creativity, initiative, personal responsibility, and dependability.

In short, it expands the pool of *leaders* by supporting the acquisition and implementation of leadership skills by all employees. "The old top-down, chain-of-command style of management is out; today's boss is supposed to walk around, involve the troops, and encourage participation. . . . Workers are now supposed to take on big responsibilities—to solve problems, cut costs, and reduce defects. The language of business reflects the new ideas. Trendy companies don't have employees, they have *associates.* They don't have managers, they have *coaches"* *(Inc.,* June 1995; article adapted from a recently published book entitled *Open-Book Management: The Coming Business Revolution,* by John Case).

Attributes

Whether applied to chief executive officers as "leaders" or about their "leadership" style or likewise applied to "empowered" employees in reformed labor environments, the attributes listed in the business magazine articles were similar for each group. They were similar, as well, to those found in general-interest news publications. *Visionary, change agent/reformer, educated, experienced/ accomplished active, team builder, risk taker, innovative, trusting/trustworthy,* and *mentor* led the list.

Entrepreneurial was another frequently used attribute in the business magazine articles. It was applied to both business owners and top managers, as well as to the general labor force. Describing the innovative building of a new company, one of its executives commented on the company's employee research (*Inc.,* November 1995, "Breaking Away" by Alessandra Bianchi). The executive said her business was "looking for people who were entrepreneurial by nature—who didn't need a lot of supervision or support staff, who were flexible, willing to learn and try new things and chip in to get the job done."

Other attributes used frequently in describing leaders and leadership style included *commitment, pioneering, first, charismatic, passionate about goal, motivator,* and *energetic.* Lloyd Ward, Frito-Lay Central Division president, was selected as *Black Enterprise* magazine's executive of the year in 1995. In a June article about him in the magazine, he said about his leadership, "I am committed and passionate. . . . I am interested in being something and leaving something. I am motivated to—absolutely, positively every day, every moment—be the best that I can be. And I am committed to creating an environment and a culture where others can achieve the same."

In their August 1995 issue, *Black Enterprise* magazine selected twenty-five people (fifteen men and nine women) as future leaders to watch. Selected because they "personify leadership," the article about them said they were all "bright, driven, accomplished, independent, and committed—not just to their own success, but to the success of the larger black community."

Helen Rheem, writing in the May-June 1995 issue of *Harvard Business Review,* notes that effective leadership requires helping employees reach their full potential. "An organization's success depends on the people who work for it," she said.

"Sometimes what a company needs is a group that a manager can't control," said writers Harold J. Leavitt and Jean Lipman-Blumen in the July-August 1995 issue of *Harvard Business Review.* A "hot group" is a "lively, dedicated group, usually small, whose members are turned on to an exciting and challenging task." The authors noted, too, that leadership may also shift from one member to another as the situation dictates."

It should be noted that this was one of the few examples found in all of the articles examined during the study where the word *control,* or something similar, was used to describe an attribute or function of a manager or *leader.* Another rarity was found in the latter aforementioned quote: the suggestion that different situations require different leaders or leadership styles.

Gender Diversity

Racial and ethnic diversity was not tabulated for the magazine articles, because one of the magazines was targeted at a specific minority group. Gender diversity was reviewed, however.

In this arena, the magazine and newspaper articles were similar: Males dominated when it came to articles about leaders or leadership. Eighty-six percent of the individuals profiled in the articles culled from the three magazines for review were men (this includes both those referred to specifically as *leaders* as well as those whose listed attributes matched those in the *leader* category).

One of the more extreme examples of male dominance was found in a May-June 1995 article in the *Harvard Business Review.* Entitled "Changing the Role of Top Management: Beyond Systems to People," all of the images (artwork, photographs, and cartoons) portrayed males. Of those referenced or quoted in text, fifteen were men and only one was a woman. It should be noted that nationally, women own one-third of U.S. businesses and represent the fastest-growing sector in the business community.

KIDS TALK ABOUT LEADERSHIP

The Women's Leadership Institute of Wells College released a study entitled "Kids Talk About Leadership" in September 1995. In their introduction to the findings, the authors make two significant points. The first is that children's perceptions, such as those regarding stereotypes and myths, often mirror those of adults. The second concerns the need to understand children's ideas before constructing programs to influence their thinking—or to train them to be leaders in their chosen fields of endeavor. Eighty-five fourth and fifth graders from upstate New York were interviewed for the study.

Consider some of the key findings, in light of the findings from the media study on leaders and leadership:

- The children defined *leadership* in terms of traditional characteristics—command and control.
- Leaders were depicted as physically out of touch with people they are leading.
- The children believed more inclusive leadership is desirable.
- The children thought that leaders are necessary, because without them there would be "catastrophic consequences."
- Children are not receiving supportive messages about their own leadership potential.
- Children listed more frequently their characteristics that would hinder their ability to lead, rather than those that would enhance such capability.
- Children obtain their leadership models primarily from government and politics, secondarily from family and school.
- While they unanimously agreed that women could be leaders, over 40 percent of the students interviewed could not name a female leader.
- Both boys and girls depicted their own gender as leaders, but boys did so at twice the rate of girls.

WHO LEADS?

Many people lead in many fields in many ways, obviously; but who they are, where they are in their respective arenas (are they the CEOs or empowered employees? housewives or entrepreneurs? athletes or coaches?) and what skills and attributes they need and use are less obvious. As previously stated, in this study of fourth and fifth graders, what is meant by the terms *leader* and *leader-ship* has been explored via a selection of general-interest newspapers and special-interest business magazines.

The findings imply that there is no specific definition of what a "leader" is, who the "leaders" are, what "leadership" is, or even if it is necessary to define these terms in only one way. Perhaps it is not. Outside of the study, there also appears to be an assumption of a common understanding of what a *leader* is and what skills and characteristics are needed for *leadership*. If there is such an under-standing, it was not apparent in the material reviewed during the study.

This media study found some discernible patterns in the application of the term *leader* by general-interest newspaper journalists. First, the word *leader* was most often used in reference to politicians, military officials, and persons (such as ter-rorists) connected with "mayhem" stories as opposed to individuals in other fields, like education, arts, science, and religion. (Oddly, the term *leader* was sel-dom applied to the sitting U.S. president and his primary opponent.) Second, *leader* was most frequently used in reference to white males in both the general- and special-interest publications examined. Third, *leader* was used most fre-quently to imply function or position held, rather than an attribute.

While there were many commonly used attributes ascribed to leaders in many of the articles reviewed—again, in both the general- and special-interest publications—one consistent set was not applied. These attributes were found in many other arti-cles referring to a variety of people, but the word *leader* was not included.

This report is part of an ongoing effort by Carnahan, Smith and Gunter, Inc. to distill information about who leads, their characteristics and styles as one way to discern what is needed to recognize and develop leaders for tomorrow. Identifying leadership potential depends largely on how *leader* and *leadership* are defined.

Experience has often been used as a primary criterion on which to judge potential leadership capability, but what kind of experience is relevant? The type that requires the autonomous control of traditional hierarchies or the variety that facilitates the dispersed decision-making of collaborative environments, or some variation?

What about performance, another commonly used criterion? Is solid perfor-mance enough, or must it be accompanied by willingness to learn new things, to take risks, to recover from failure, to be flexible?

How much does the task dictate the type of leader or leadership style? For example, can a nation be led the way a business is? Does a leader of a military operation need the same attributes as a leader of a church?

Tom Richman, writing in the November-December 1995 issue of the *Harvard Business Review,* reported on the work of three professors from the University of Southern California's School of Business Administration. Their research showed that traditional leadership-screening based on demonstrated skills is insufficient. They have suggested a new model relying on other assumptions:

a) The future will require different skills from the past;

b) "Successful executives aren't born that way but develop with experience"; and

c) Leaders need a variety of characteristics to be effective.

If leaders are made, not born, and if we are not certain how to define current leaders, how can we develop future ones?

The purpose of this study is to examine public dialogue about leaders and leadership by using the media as an indicator. What can be learned from these media reflections of American society, both by the public and the media itself? This 1996 study explored the question, Who Leads? While no conclusive answers were found in the publications reviewed, the implications were many and varied.

It is important to understand these implications and the assumptions behind them. Knowing who leads now and having a clearer understanding of what it is that is needed and wanted in leaders will make it easier to help develop and select leaders for the future. In the meantime, how do we define *black* leadership and to what extent is it different from our present understanding of leadership in general? First we must attempt to define black leadership within the context of our current debate on what *leadership* means, and even sometimes what it does not mean. We must also define black leadership as a product of the varied experiences of black Americans in American history. It can also be argued that the African background of black Americans is a relevant consideration. Thus, *black leadership* may be defined within the context of American and African history as: a group reaction of peoples of African descent in America to their oppression, engendered by the psychology of slavery. Their desire to be free human beings in the world's greatest democracy was their driving force.

2

Concepts in Black Leadership

Leadership is exercised in numerous variations in widely divergent social units, and certain basic patterns of leadership appear to have widespread applicability. These patterns or characteristics may be referred to as "basic concepts"; they will help to establish the knowledge base that is necessary to understand the more specific and more complex explanations in later chapters. Fundamental to these concepts is an understanding of two basic characteristics of human nature: the *rational tendency* and the *emotional need*. Individuals and social groups require structure and a sense of order for the achievement of goals, and also demand to be treated with concern and respect. These two factors are critical to an understanding of why some leaders are effective while others make the effort but fail. A leader must balance attention to personal feelings against the need for achievement of individual and group tasks. This conclusion is based on the recurring appearance in the reports of two primary sets of activities in the report of theory, research, and practice; these two sets of functions have in fact been identified by Benne and Sheats (1948) as critical: *task functions* must be executed to rationally select and achieve goals; *maintenance functions* associated with emotional satisfaction are required to develop and maintain group, community, or organizational viability.

TASK FUNCTIONS

Initiating activity: proposing solutions; suggesting new ideas; providing new definitions of the problem, attacking problems in new ways, organizing material.

Information seeking: asking for clarification of suggestions; requesting additional information or facts.

Information giving: offering facts or generalizations; relating one's experience to group problems as illustration.

Opinion giving: stating an opinion or belief about a suggestion (or one of several suggestions), particularly concerning its value rather than its factual basis.

Elaborating: clarifying by giving examples or developing meanings; trying to envision how a proposal might work if it were adopted.

Coordinating: showing relationships among various ideas or suggestions; trying to pull ideas and suggestions together; trying to draw together activities of various subgroups or members.

Summarizing: pulling together related ideas or suggestions; restating suggestions after the group has discussed them.

Testing feasibility: making application of suggestions to real situations; examining practicality and workability of ideas; evaluating possible decisions.

Evaluating: submitting group decisions or accomplishments for comparison with group standards; measuring accomplishments against goals.

Diagnosing: determining sources of difficulties, appropriate steps to take next, and primary obstacles to progress.

MAINTENANCE FUNCTIONS

Encouraging: being friendly, warm, and responsive to others; praising others and their ideas; agreeing with and accepting the contributions of others.

Gatekeeping: trying to make it possible for another member to make a contribution to the group; suggesting a limited talking time for each member so that everyone will have a chance to be heard.

Standard setting: suggesting standards for the group to use in choosing its content or procedures or in evaluating its decisions; reminding the group to avoid decisions that conflict with group standards.

Following: going along with the decisions of the group; passively accepting the ideas of others; serving as an audience during group discussion and decision-making.

Expressing group feelings: sensing and summarizing group feelings; describing group reactions to ideas or solutions.

Consensus taking: tentatively asking for group opinions in order to find out if the group is nearing consensus on a decision; sending up "trial balloons" to test group opinions.

Harmonizing: mediating; conciliating differences in points of view; making compromise solutions.

Tension reducing: draining off negative feelings by jesting or "pouring oil on troubled waters"; putting a tense situation into wider context.

NONFUNCTIONAL BEHAVIOR

Some participants in groups regularly deter achievement. The more common types of nonfunctional behavior include:

Aggression: working for status by criticizing or blaming others; showing hostility against the group or some individual; deflating others.

Blocking: interfering with the progress of the group by going off on a tangent; citing personal experiences unrelated to the problem; arguing too much about a point; rejecting ideas without consideration.

Self-confessing: using the group as a personal sounding board; expressing personal feelings or points of view that are not related to the group.

Competing: vying with others to produce the best ideas, talk the most, play the most roles, or gain favor with the leader.

Seeking sympathy: trying to induce other group members to be sympathetic to one's problems or misfortunes; deploring one's own ideas to gain support.

Special pleading: introducing supporting suggestions related to one's own concerns or philosophies; lobbying.

Horsing around: clowning; joking; mimicking; disrupting the work of the group.

Recognition seeking: attempting to call attention to one's self by loud or excessive talking, extreme ideas, or unusual behavior.

Withdrawing: being indifferent or passive; resorting to excessive formality; daydreaming; doodling; whispering to others; wandering from the subject.

When functional or nonfunctional behaviors occur in settings in which leadership is under study, then can be recognized quickly. Understanding behaviors that help or hinder achievement helps the individual to appreciate how improved performance on the part of the leader can increase the effectiveness of a group, organization, or community.

The foregoing may be diagrammed as follows in Figure 2.1.

Figure 2.1 Functional Dimensions of Leadership

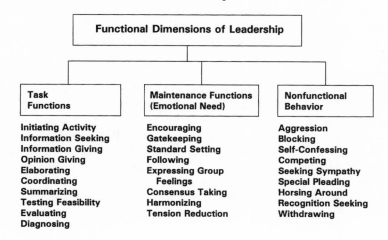

As Smith noted in his study of black leadership, the ambiguity in the general concept of leadership is reflected in the black leadership literature. This has lead to a wide variety of definitions of black leadership, implicit and explicit. For example, Myrdal (1944, 1962) writes, "We should not start from an attempt on *a priori* grounds to define the principal concept. . . . We have only to settle that we are discussing the role and importance of individual persons in the sphere of social action." In the same vein, Ladd (1966) writes that little effort was made at the outset to develop any full and precise definition of black leadership because "the study as a whole is centrally concerned with defining it." However, Ladd agrees that black leaders are considered to be "persons able to make decisions affecting the choice of race objectives and/or the means utilized to attain them." Matthews and Prothro (1966) provide an operational definition: "those persons most often thought of as Negro leaders by Negroes." Wilson (1960) understands black leaders to be "civic leaders—persons who acted as if the interests of the race or community were their goal." Thompson (1963) uses what he calls a "functional approach to leadership," designating the individual actor as a leader "who for some period of time overtly identifies with the Black effort to achieve stated social goals." In the most parsimonious definition, Burgess (1962) defines a leader as an individual whose behavior affects the patterning of behavior within the black community at a given time. Cox (1965), in his neo-Marxist historical analysis of the development of black leadership, adds another perspective to the debate on the definition of black leadership. He writes:

But the common cause of the Negro in the United States is not fundamentally limited to Negroes. It is in fact an aspect of the wider phenomenon of political–class antagonism inseparably associated with capitalist culture. A principle involved in the process of democratic development is at the basis of the Negroes' cause, and for this reason leadership among Negroes is likely to be as effectively white as Black.

Similarly, Holden (1973) understands black leadership generally to mean "those who seek (or claim to seek) the interests of the whole black population. He adds that such persons purport to lead by defining for blacks how they should relate to whites. More specifically, Holden suggests that it is appropriate to regard as a leader anyone who holds a key position in any of the major black socioeconomic institutions. Thus, the leadership concept as developed by Holden concerns persons (black or white) seeking or claiming to seek the interests of blacks as a whole in their relationship to whites. In contrast, Higham's (1978) view of ethnic leadership has to do with internal processes of community development and symbolic expression. In the same vein, Hamilton (1981) defines a black leader as "one who is racially black in a leadership role and who speaks and acts on matters of specific (but not necessarily exclusive) concern to Black people as a direct purpose of occupying that role." He argues that if one were racially black and, say, mayor of an all-white city and never spoke or acted on issues of specific concern to blacks as such, it would not be proper to designate such a mayor as a black leader. Similarly, with regard to black appointed officials, Smith (1981) raises the question, 4 under what conditions and circumstances should Black appointees be viewed as Black leaders?" The important point, he said, is that black officials of the government or other major American institutions—for example the Ford Foundation—do not necessarily represent black leadership. In other words, black appointed officials cannot be automatically viewed as black leaders. Their role in black leadership is a matter to be explicitly demonstrated rather than implicitly assumed.

While there is no consensus about the definition of black leadership among scholars, their varied definitions of the term are not only comprehensible but empirically relevant. It should also be noted that while agreement on the meaning of black leadership is far from universal, it is possible to discern critical elements of agreement among most scholars in the field: (1) black leadership has to be viewed within the context of American leadership in general; (2) black leadership involves interaction on three levels (within the black community, the American society in general, and the international community); (3) black leadership involves goal setting, goal achievement and group organization; and (4) black leadership focuses on the advancement of the black race, ranging from the struggle for freedom to civil rights and economic self-sufficiency.

Thus, black leadership may be defined as the process of black self-determination, a search for the realization of the "American Dream" for all black Americans. Black leadership may also be defined as a movement; if you will, a black *nationalist* movement. As Bracey, Meier, and Rudwick (1970) define *black nationalism,*

the term black nationalism has been used in American history to describe a body of social thought, attitudes, and actions ranging from the simplest expressions of ethnocentrism and racial solidarity to the comprehensive and sophisticated ideologies of Pan-Negroism or Pan-Africanism.

Between these extremes lie many varieties of black nationalism, of varying degrees of intensity: racial solidarity, cultural nationalism, religious nationalism, economic nationalism, bourgeois reformism, emigrationism, territorial separation, and Pan-Africanism.

Racial Solidarity

The simplest expression of racial feeling that can be called a form of black nationalism is *racial solidarity*. It generally has no ideological or programmatic implications beyond the desire that black people organize themselves on the basis of their common color and oppressed condition to move in some way to alleviate their situation. The concept of racial solidarity is essential to all forms of black nationalism. The establishment of mutual aid societies and separatist churches in the late eighteenth century had little ideological justification beyond that of racial solidarity.

Cultural Nationalism

A more pronounced form of black nationalism is *cultural nationalism*. Cultural nationalism contends that black people—in the United States or throughout the world—have a culture, style of life, cosmology, approach to the problems of existence, and aesthetic values distinct from that of white Americans in particular and white Europeans or westerners in general. Mild forms of cultural nationalism say merely that the Afro-American subculture is one of many subcultures that make up a pluralistic American society. The militant cultural nationalists assert the superiority of Afro-American culture—usually on moral and aesthetic grounds—to Western civilization. Programmatic or institutional manifestations of cultural nationalism include the development of a body of social-science literature—history, philosophy, political science, and the like—written from the Afro-American point of view; the unearthing and publicizing of all the past glories of the race; the development of a distinct Afro-American literature, art, and music; the formation of appropriate vehicles for the transmission of Afro-American culture—newspapers, journals, theaters, artistic workshops, and musical groups; and the assertion of a distinct lifestyle and world view in such ways as assuming African or Arabic names, wearing African clothes, and speaking African languages.

Religious Nationalism

Closely linked in form and function to cultural nationalism *is religious nationalism*. Within the theological boundaries of Christianity are such black nationalist assertions as that blacks should establish and run churches of their own, for their own people; that God, or Jesus, or both were black (the "Black Messiah" theme); that Afro-Americans are the chosen people. Religious rationalism has also taken non-Christian forms, as can be seen in such twentieth-century groups as the Nation of Islam, the Moorish Science Temple, the several varieties of black Jews, and the Yoruba Temple. A milder expression of religious nationalist feeling is manifested in the recent formation of black caucuses within the major Christian denominations. In Chicago in 1968, black Catholic priests conducted a "Black Unity Mass" to the beat of conga drums; they wore vestments of colorful African cloth and shared the altar with, among others, a Baptist preacher.

Economic Nationalism

Economic nationalism includes both capitalist and socialist outlooks. The capitalist wing, or the bourgeois nationalists, advocates either controlling the black segment of the marketplace by attempting to establish black businesses and by "buy-black" campaigns, or establishing a black capitalist economy parallel to the economy of the dominant society. Slightly to the left of the bourgeois nationalists are those who contend that formation of producer and consumer cooperatives is necessary. Further to the left are black nationalist socialists who feel that abolition of private property is a prerequisite for the liberation of black people. (Such socialists should be distinguished from black integrationist socialists like A. Philip Randolph and Bayard Rustin.) At the opposite extreme are those who call for the reinstatement of preindustrial communalism. Black nationalist socialists tend to coincide with revolutionary nationalists, who apply Marxian theory to the experience of Afro-Americans, whereas those who favor preindustrial African economic forms tend also to be militant cultural nationalists. Negro capitalists tend to be bourgeois in their political and cultural outlooks, as well.

Bourgeois Reformism

In the area of *politics,* black nationalism at its mildest is *bourgeois reformism,* a view that assumes that the United States is politically pluralistic and that liberal values concerning democracy and the political process are operative. Programmatic examples of such a view are the slating and supporting of Negro candidates for political office; the drive for black political and administrative control of local and county areas where Negroes predominate; and the formation of all-black political parties. In contrast, *revolutionary black nationalism* views the overthrow of existing political and economic institutions as a prerequisite for the liberation of black Americans, and does not exclude the use of violence.

Emigrationism

A most significant variety of black nationalism is *emigrationism.* From the earliest attempts of slaves to capture the ships bearing them to the New World in order to steer them back to Africa, a substantial number of black people have wanted to return to the ancestral homeland. However, to emigrationists for whom Africa is too far away in time and space, or unacceptable for other reasons, the West Indies, South America, Mexico, Canada, and even the island of Cyprus have been touted as potential homelands.

Territorial Separatism

Related to emigration is what we may call *territorial separatism,* a term best applied to the view of those blacks who wanted a share of the country that their labor had made so prosperous but who had no illusions about living in peace and equality with white Americans. Territorial separatists advocated the establishment of all-black towns, especially in the South and Southwest, all-black states, or a black nation comprising several states. Recent and milder forms of territorial separatism are often linked to the concept of political pluralism and advocacy of "black control of the black community."

Pan-Africanism

Implicit in many of these varieties of black nationalism is the international extension of racial solidarity in the doctrines of *Pan-Negroism,* or *Pan-Africanism.* Both foster the belief that people of African descent throughout the world have common cultural characteristics and share common problems as a result of their African origins, the similarity of their political oppression and economic exploitation by Western civilization, and the persistence and virulence of racist theories, attitudes, and behavior characterizing Western contact with people of African descent. Afro-American advocates of Pan-Negroism historically assumed that Afro-Americans would provide the leadership for any worldwide movement. Only recently, with the political independence of African nations, have Afro-Americans conceded that Africans themselves might form the vanguard in the liberation of all peoples of African descent.

The varieties of black nationalism are often not sharply delineated, nor are they mutually exclusive categories. Any one individual may assume any number of combinations of black nationalism. Moreover, nationalism and racial integration as ideologies or as programs have often coexisted in organizations, in theories, and in the minds of individual black Americans. To deal exclusively with the varieties of black nationalism in American history is not to suggest that only black nationalism existed. In fact, a book of documents on black nationalism is needed to correct the more generally held view that integration and assimilation had an undisputed reign on the minds of black Americans. Perhaps this book can serve to remind the reader that the problems of the complexities of human behavior are no less formidable where black folks are concerned.

3

Toward a Theoretical Framework

Perhaps the greatest weakness in the study of black leadership is the lack of clearly identified theoretical models scholarly inquiry. Much of what we know in black leadership literature has, for the most part, been based on the case method. This reliance has several shortcomings. In general, the case method is limited and static in its character (Froman, 1948; Kaufman, 1958). In the age of systematic quantitative and qualitative research, the case method is an inadequate approach of inquiry. First, it is difficult if not impossible to make reliable generalizations on the basis of a single or even several cases. Logical inferences require information from random samples of all cases. Second, case studies are almost always *static*, dealing with only a single point in time. Finally, the case method makes it difficult to check the reliability of the findings, because it is extremely problematic and time-consuming to replicate a case study precisely. There are several examples of the case study approach in black leadership studies. John Hope Franklin and August Meier's book (1982) is perhaps the most comprehensive. Franklin and Meier analyze the careers of fifteen nationally known twentieth-century American black leaders who sought in diverse ways to advance the race and overcome the racial barriers and oppression that have pervaded American society. The leaders are: Booker T. Washington (1856–1915); T. Thomas Fortune (1856–1928); Ida B. Wells-Barnett (1862–1931); W.E.B. DuBois (1868–1963); James Weldon Johnson (1871–1938); Marcus Garvey (1880–1940); A. Philip Randolph (1889–1979); Charles Clinton Spaulding (1874–1952); Mary McLeod Bethune (1875–1955); Charles Hamilton Houston (1895–1950); Mabel K. Staupers (1890–1989); Adam Clayton Powell, Jr. (1908–1972); Martin Luther King, Jr. (1929–1968); Malcolm X (1925–1965); and Whitney M. Young, Jr. (1921–1971). Essentially, Franklin and Meier presented the contemporary state of knowledge in the field and thus prepared the way for deeper and more systematic study of the subject of twentieth-century black leadership. An earlier publication by Lerone Bennett, Jr. (1968), *Pioneers in Protest,* provides a portrayal of the lives of twenty men and women, black and white, who pioneered black protest.

Several other studies include: Morrison's (1990) *Intragroup Conflict in African-American Leadership;* Rabinowitz's (1982) *Southern Black Leaders of the Reconstruction Era;* McFarlin's (1976) *Black Congressional Reconstruction Orators and their Orations*; and several journal articles. The journal articles include the following: Samuel Shapiro, "A Black Senator from Mississippi: Blanche K. Bruce (1841–1898)," *Review of Politics,* 1994; Richard Lowe, "The Freedmen's Bureau and Local Black Leadership," *Journal of American History,* 1993; Euline W. Brock, "Thomas W. Cardozo: Fallible Black Reconstruction Leader," *Journal of Southern History,* 1981; Minion K.C. Morrison, "Intragroup Conflict in African-American Leadership: The Case of Tchula, Mississippi," *Society for Comparative Study of Society and History,* 1990; Kenneth Eugene Mann, "Blanche Kelso Bruce: United States Senator Without a Constituency," *Journal of Mississippi History,* 1995; and Richard Lowe, "Local Black Leaders During Reconstruction in Virginia," *Virginia Magazine of History and Biography,* 1995.

Most of the serious works in black political experience in the United States are studies in leadership (Jones, 1972; Morris, 1975). Ladd (1966) writes that to ask questions about "Negro leadership" is to ask some basic questions not only about the nature of that leadership but also about the larger subject of black politics. Jones also argues that much of the research on black leadership in America "proceeds in a theoretical manner." Consequently, what is needed is the development of some fundamental categories of a theory of black leadership in America.

In 1985, an unpublished monograph by Robert C. Smith at Howard University surveyed theoretical concepts in black leadership. Among other things, Smith's study of black leadership theoretical concepts has produced several typological schemas and labels: accommodationism; protest; "conservative," "liberal," "moderate," and "radical"; "Uncle Tomism," "race men" and "race diplomat"; "militant"; and traditionalism.

Another approach that has received frequent criticism in black leadership literature is the *militancy construct.* This concept has been basic to discussions of the leadership phenomenon among African-Americans. Its basic premise is that black leadership is militant in approach and substance. Some of the major critics of this concept (Cole, 1976; Scoble, 1968; Smith, 1976; Holden, 1973; Hamilton, 1973; and Forsythe, 1972) have contended that the concept is so characterized by ambiguities that it is rendered invalid as a tool of inquiry. An empirical study investigating the utility of militancy as an analytic concept and as a practical way to engage black political leaders in Washington, D.C., in 1968–1969 found that it was extraordinarily difficult to apply the concept consistently. This was because the definition of the term was dependent upon one's frame of reference. That is, one cannot be militant in isolation. Rather, one has to be militant in relation *to* something, and that something in this context is white behavior toward blacks.

Forsythe (1972) points out that the major problem with the concept is its focus on means rather than ends, and its failure to capture the reality that leadership types can best be understood only when their stated goals are examined. Of course, to a considerable extent the militancy concept was more often tied to means or methods than to goals or beliefs, because much of the cleavage observed in the black leadership stratum (1995) revolved around methods rather than goals. That is, the basic belief or goal of black leadership—elimination of the system of caste-segregation—was by and large accepted by all leadership types. Thus, leaders were empirically distinguishable, not in terms of their goals, but in terms of their means, methods, or styles of pursuing the generally accepted goal of eliminating caste. Militants, moderates, conservatives, Uncle Toms, race men, and so forth were thus typed on the basis of their methods and styles of opposition to the caste system, because this generally was the observed empirical regularity.

However, the critics make an important point when they argue that, in classifying leaders, means should be subordinate to ends. Unless political methods determine political beliefs (which to some extent may be the case for black leadership), then in political praxis as in political science a preoccupation with methods narrows rather than enlarges our understanding of the political world. For political and political leaders, methods should be the tools of one's work and should not be substituted for substantive goals. Thus, to be a viable concept the ends–means components of militancy must be specified.

This was done in the review of the black leadership literature. The leadership typology was disaggregated into its three constituent elements—*beliefs, methods,* and *rhetoric*—and applied fruitfully to the available data on black leaders, thereby permitting the distinguishing of leadership militancy on the basis of each of the cements. Leaders are classifiable as "militant" or "moderate" in terms of their goals, methods, and rhetoric, or some combination thereof. "Militancy" is defined as the extent to which leaders' beliefs, methods, or rhetoric depart, at any given time or place, from the beliefs, methods, and rhetoric of dominant whites.

Looking at what can be learned from the new literature on black leadership compared with the literature of old black leadership, one is disappointed. While the case study approach is now generally avoided, there are really few studies of the new black leadership that are of the depth and sophistication of studies pertaining to the old black leadership. Rather, there is almost exclusive preoccupation with descriptive research on various phenomena associated with black elected officials to the exclusion of black caucus-type organizations, and especially nationalist and leftist leadership. There is also little effort to develop formal leadership typologies or to put the research findings in even the most elementary of theoretical constructs. Thus, one learns relatively more from the old black leadership studies in spite of their limitations than one does from the most recent research on black leaders.

Putting these bodies of research together, one notes the emergence of a sizeable number of black elected officials (and leading blacks in the executive branch, the judiciary, and other societal control institutions, such as corporations, universities, and foundations); a decline in "glamour" personality leadership; and the emergence of new caucus and community-based organizations. However, aside from—and perhaps in spite of—these important changes of the 1960s, there appears to be more continuity than discontinuity in Negro and black leadership in terms of social background, organization, power structure, ideology, and the designated roles of preachers, whites, and the masses. For example, the evidence shows continuity in terms of the militancy–moderate cleavage. Contemporary moderates tend to adhere to liberal, integrationist beliefs and conventional methods and rhetoric, while militants tend toward socialist or nationalist beliefs, and unconventional methods and rhetoric. Militants also tend to be more predisposed toward involvement with and support of mass action than do moderates. There is, of course, some overlap. Some leaders who are moderate in their beliefs favor militant methods and mass action, and some leaders who are militant in their beliefs are moderate in their methods, if not also in their rhetoric. However, these are exceptions. In general, the pattern is one of consistency along all three dimensions of typology, and a profile of the leadership types today resembles in many ways the profile drawn by Myrdal more than 50 years ago. Looking back on the important transformations of the 1960s, one might say that in black leadership the more things change the more they seem to remain the same.

RELATED CONCEPTUAL ISSUES

The complex William Edward Burghardt (W.E.B.) Du Bois remains to this date a towering figure in the pantheon of black twentieth-century leaders. Both his thinking and the extent to which he functioned as a leader in the struggle for race advancement underwent marked transformations over the years. Historically, Du Bois' fame rests mainly on his brilliant articulation of black protest, and particularly on the key role he played early in the century. His contribution to black leadership went beyond his personal leadership responsibility. He also made significant contributions to concepts in black leadership. In his book The *Souls of Black Folks* (1903), Du Bois postulated his theory of "twoness" when he wrote:

One ever feels his two-ness—an American, a Negro; two souls, two thoughts, two unrec-onciled strivings; two warring ideals in one dark body, whose dogged strength alone keeps it from being torn asunder. The history of the American Negro is the history of this strife—this longing to attain self-conscious manhood, to merge his double self into a better and truer self. In this merging he wishes neither of the old selves to be lost. He would not Africanize America, for America has too much to teach the world and Africa. He would not bleach his soul in a flood of white Americanism, for he knows that Negro blood has a message to teach the world.

The concept of "twoness" helps to examine the dilemmas of black leadership. For example, it raises the question as to whether a black leader who represents a predominantly white jurisdiction is a black leader with two souls, one white (American) and the other, his own African black soul.

Du Bois also postulated the idea of the "Talented Tenth" and its role in black leadership. Six positions taken from Du Bois' articulation of the Talented Tenth are: (1) leadership is solely the responsibility of the college-educated; (2) teachers, or at the very least, teachers of teachers, are, *ipso facto,* part of the black leadership structure; (3) college or classroom teaching is primarily a leadership function; (4) leaders are particularly prepared to guide and direct the African-American masses; (5) African-American leaders must think in terms of racial uplift; and (6) African-American leadership—as distinct from other American leadership—has a specific role in dealing with the particular problem faced by African-American people. It is worth noting that the last two positions have no place in a politics of de-racialization. Persons' (1993) study compared these ideas with the views of California's black legislators.

The comparisons show that on the first of the positions—leadership is solely the responsibility of the college-educated—the legislators are unanimous, explicitly in complete *dis*agreement with Du Bois. Although on the second and third positions concerning the roles of teachers, or teachers of teachers, the legislators do not directly address these points, by implication they disagree with Du Bois. On the fourth position, that leaders are particularly prepared to guide and direct the African masses, the legislators' comments varied across three positions: (a) not responsive to the question; (b) disagreement; and (c) agreement. On the sixth position, that African-American leadership—as distinct from other American leadership—has a specific role in dealing with the particular problems faced by African-Americans, two-thirds agreed and one-third disagreed, although the explanations of disagreement tended to minimize the degree of disagreement. *De-racialization, it seems, is problematic at best for these leaders.* On the fifth position, that African-American leaders must think in terms of racial uplift, the legislators were unanimously in accord with Du Bois. *And this position today has no place in de-racialized politics.*

The comparisons show that between Du Bois and the legislative leaders there are more points of disagreement than agreement on the six positions. The major points of disagreement concern the role of the educated and the role of teachers of teachers, or teachers, as principal elements of black leadership. There are minor points of disagreement on the unique role of black leaders *qua* leaders, and the specific responsibilities of black leaders.

The points of agreement, however, are more critical. They are: the role of leaders in racial uplift, the specific role of black leaders in dealing with the particular problems of black people, and, to some degree, the unique role of black leaders *qua* leaders.

All three of the major points of disagreement can be directly related to changes in the conditions of the black population between Du Bois' and the legislators' two periods. Thus, Du Bois must be viewed in the context of his generation vis-à-vis the setting of contemporary visions of black leadership.

THEORY

The consensus that clearly emerges from the literature reviewed here, both the old and new but especially the old, is that the most appropriate general theory for the study of black politics and leadership is some variant of the race dominance–power approach. In one form or another, nearly all the students who sought to explain black leadership theoretically did so in terms of the subordinate power position of blacks relative to whites.

Salamon (1973) satisfactorily demonstrated the utility of the "modernization perspective" in his study of the emergence of a black-politician stratum in Mississippi. But, in general, the modernization approach lacks the grounded specificity of the race dominance framework, and isomorphism with the political experience of the peoples of the black world (Jones, 1972). And "although the process of modernization, particularly industrialization, has implications for race relations, the evidence suggests that its role is at best indirect. It creates some conditions that are conducive to securing changes in race relations, but does not independently alter highly developed patterns of race relations" (Morris, 1975). Thus, the modernization approach is probably less appropriate as a general theory than is the race dominance framework.

Jones (1972) made the most clear-cut contribution toward developing the basic concepts and hypotheses of the power–race dominance approach as a systematic framework to order inquiry on black leadership. His most basic assumption is that "a frame of reference for [B]lack politics should not begin with superficial comparison of [B]lacks and other ethnic minorities . . . [but rather] it should begin by searching for those factors which are unique to the [B]lack political experience, for this is the information which will facilitate our understanding of [B]lacks in the American political system."

Given this assumption, Jones, building on the earlier work of Roucek (1956), argues that black politics should be conceptualized as "essentially a power struggle between [B]lacks and whites, with the latter trying to maintain their superordinate position vis-à-vis the former." But in order to clearly distinguish "Black political phenomena" from other extensions of the universal power struggle, the stipulation that the "ideological justification for the superordination of whites is the institutionalized belief in the inherent superiority of that group" (Jones, 1972) is added as a necessary specifying condition. Finally, Jones presents five black "goal directed patterns" of activity (integration, accommodation, black consciousness, black nationalism, and revolution) that can, with modifications, be usefully applied to "advance explanatory propositions" regarding black leadership. Although Jones in this initial formulation develops only the basic concepts of the framework, in a subsequent case study (Jones, 1978) he applies it with modest success to an analysis of the emergence of the first black-led governing coalition in Atlanta.

In addition to Jones, Katznelson (1971) has argued that power must be the central construct in the reformulation of race relations research within the discipline. More recently, Greenberg (1980) in a cross-cultural study case uses the concept of "racial domination" in his research findings on race politics in the United States and three other advanced capitalist societies. Thus, from the black leadership literature and from the more recent work of students of race politics, the racial domination approach emerges as the most *basic*—but not the sole—frame of reference for the study of leadership and politics in racially stratified societies.

A number of students of black leadership have argued that, in addition to racial domination, a secondary factor in explaining patterns of leadership in black politics in the United States is the structure of particular racial environments. Walton (1972) has, perhaps, been clearest on the theoretical import of this factor:

Basically speaking, [B]lack politics springs from the particular brand of segregation practices found in different environments in which [B]lack people find themselves. In other words, the nature of segregation and the manner in which it differs not only in different localities but within a locality have caused [B]lack people to employ political activities, methods, devices and techniques that would advance their policy preferences. *In short, [B]lack politics is a function of the particular brand of segregation found in different environments in which [B]lack people find themselves.* And the politics of [B]lacks differ significantly from locality to locality. Although there are many striking similarities between the political activities of [B]lack Americans in different localities, there are differences far greater than geography can explain. Basically, the differences lie in the variety of forms that segregation and discrimination have taken in this community. [emphasis in text]

It should be clear that Walton does not deny the central theoretical importance of racial domination. Instead, Walton suggests that racial domination the United States has been particularized, and that this particularity has to be taken into consideration in understanding and explaining black politics and leadership.

The foregoing factors, which are essentially exogenous, suggest that, fundamentally, black leadership behavior is a function of factors external to the community. Two endogenous factors—*class* and *culture*—are also theoretically suggestive.

Class is thought to be theoretically significant because of two factors. The first pertains to the black class structure itself—the relatively lower class, or as it is appropriately called today the *underclass*, a stratum increasingly isolated from the opportunities of modern society (Glasgow, 1980; Wilson, 1972). The second factor is the largely middle-class readerships' unwillingness or inability to make rapid and sustained progress toward the amelioration of the terrible problems of the underprivileged. These two factors give rise to what are variously referred to in the literature as class "tensions," "conflicts," or even "antagonisms" between the black leadership and the masses.

Evidence and arguments presented in Chapter 8 show that class conflict in the black community declined in the 1960s as a result of the civil rights revolution, the growth and diversification of the middle class, and the black power movement. Yet, in both popular and scholarly media one reads today of an unprecedented class conflict between the relatively secure new black middle class and the marginal black underclass (Bolce and Gary, 1979; Delaney, 1978). However, when viewed in the light of the pertinent data, such assertions appear to be without scientific foundation. There is some evidence of a leadership–mass cleavage on the subject of political methods, with the masses favoring more militant actions. But in terms of basic beliefs and policy preferences, there is a fundamental unity in the black community at all class levels, and between the leadership and the masses, in support of the ideology and policies of liberal integration.

Thus, the theoretical significance in black politics is limited. This is not to deny that there are differences of sentiment, ethos, and opinion in black America between the leadership and the masses. Rather, it is to suggest that these differences do not constitute class "antagonisms." Indeed, the class factor in studies of black leadership may be best construed as an aspect of culture. While specialists disagree as to whether the black community constitutes a separate and distinct subculture (Morris, 1975), the data are unmistakable that there are significant differences between black and white Americans in terms of their level of support for the system, their level of trust in the system, and political knowledge and efficacy (Morris, 1975). These aspects of the black "subculture," together with the reality of continued racial oppression, powerlessness, and economic deprivation, give rise to a series of characteristics identified by Holden (1973) as creating a culture adverse to effective leadership, because it results in very high demands on the leadership but relatively low support.

These cultural characteristics take the form of class tensions, manifested in the ritualistic condemnation of black leaders as "Uncle Toms" or "sell-outs" who have lost touch with the masses. These rituals of black culture have always been—and, in the nature of the black person's lot in this country, probably always will be—an aspect of the relationship between black leadership and followership. This is in spite of the fact that "it would be difficult to document a belief that any major [B]lack leadership group purposefully sought to retard the advance of the race as a whole" (Hamilton, 1981). Yet, because the masses are understandably disappointed with the pace of improvement of their life chances, there is extant in the community a relatively low level of trust in the leadership, and a tendency to blame the leadership for the society's failure to respond to the demands for racial justice. This is a *cultural* rather than a *class* phenomenon.

To conclude, contrary to the often-stated allegation, the literature on black leadership is not atheoretical. Rather, a basic frame of reference and two useful subconstructs of theoretical value are present in the literature. At this point, these fragments of theory cannot be regarded as a coherent set of propositions from which hypotheses for empirical research can be deduced. Yet, the recent research on black elected officials has tended to ignore even these fragments, in favor of descriptive and/or exploratory research. While exploratory research is appropriate in an emergent subfield as a means by which to lay the groundwork for theoretical exegesis, we now have enough historical and scientific research about the black leadership phenomenon to begin to translate available theoretical schema into testable propositions to guide and structure inquiry in the subfield.

BLACK LEADERSHIP TYPES

As pointed out earlier, the most persistent and common basis of classifying black leaders has been in terms of some variation of the militancy concept. Yet this method of classification has also been the source of the most common and persistent criticisms of the literature. It should be noted that as far back as 1944, Myrdal typed black leaders in terms of their propensity for accommodation or protest. This basic typology has persisted through the years in one form or another in studies of black leadership. Higham (1978) argues that in one way or another, the choice between a leadership of protest and a leadership of accommodation has also been characteristic of nearly all other ethnic groups in the United States.

While the number of types of leaders has varied from Myrdal's (1944, 1962) basic twofold construct to Burgess's (1962) and Thompson's (1963) fourfold ones, the variables used in categorizing leaders have basically been structured in terms of acceptance or rejection of the extant race system, style or method of opposition to the race system, or style or method of race advancement activity.

Myrdal's classic formulation is based on the "extreme policies of behavior on behalf of blacks as a subordinate caste: *accommodation or protest.* That is, because of their subordinate caste position, blacks find all their power relations confined to the narrow orbit of accommodation or protest, or to some compromise between accommodation and protest" (1944, 1962). Thus, the typology is based on observed empirical regularities in the behavior of black leaders, rather than on some abstract preconception.

Accommodation is described by Myrdal as historically the "natural," "normal," or "realistic" pattern of leadership behavior among blacks, especially in the south. Accommodation requires acceptance of the caste system; thus, leaders "lead" only in that context. That is, they seek modifications in the life conditions of blacks that do not affect the caste structure. Protest involves a rejection of the caste system. Behaviorally, the pattern consists of lobbying, litigation, and nonviolent protest in deference to law, the American creed, and the tenets of Christianity. The protest leader is most often observed in the north, because the less rigid system of racial oppression in many northern communities provides the opportunity for protest to exist. This variable—the nature of the localized system of racial oppression—is often central to the classification of leaders in this literature.

Examining briefly the other typologies, Burgess (1962) developed a fourfold typological schema in her study of Durham: (1) the *conservatives* are defined as those persons who are least likely to voice opposition to caste, conforming closely to Myrdal's accommodation pattern of "pleading to whites"; (2) the *liberals,* the most numerous of the types, are distinguished by their use of conventional political methods (for example, voting, lobbying, and litigating) to protest caste; (3) *moderates* are characterized as functional leaders who subordinate their role as race leaders to their role as leaders in the community generally; and (4) *radicals,* who are distinguished on the basis of their identification with the masses, mass demonstrations, and the approach of Martin Luther King, Jr. Thompson (1963) also identified four types of leaders in New Orleans: (1) *Uncle Toms,* who accept the caste system; (2) *race men,* who militantly reject the caste system and engage in overt forms of nonviolent protest; (3) *liberals,* who also reject the caste system, but who rely on moral suasion and appeals to the national government; and (4) the *race diplomats,* who through reliance on education and persuasion strike a middle ground between race men and Uncle Toms to incrementally change the system. Matthews and Prothro (1966) in their study of four southern communities identified these types of leaders: (1) *traditionalists,* those persons who engage in meliorative action within the context of caste; (2) *moderates,* who are defined as those persons who favor "welfare goals" and gradual change in the system through the use of conventional political methods; and (3) *militants,* who are characterized as those persons who favor "status goals"—that is, the immediate abolition of caste through direct action and mass protest. Ladd (1966) identified three types of leaders in Winston-Salem, North Carolina, and Greenville, South Carolina: (1) *conservatives,* functional equivalents of Myrdal's accommodating leader, depending for success on access and acceptability to whites; (2) *militants,* who are followers of Martin Luther King, Jr.'s approach of seeking "status goals" (that is, the immediate abolition of caste) through mass protest; and (3) *moderates,* who are considered to be those persons who seek the middle ground between "status" and "welfare" goals, relying upon negative inducements effected through conventional political methods. Finally, Wilson (1960) labeled black leaders in Chicago as *moderates* or *militants* in terms of whether they sought "status" or "welfare" goals; whether they tended to seek racial explanations for apparent anti-black acts; whether they tended to agglomerate or disaggregate issues; and whether they relied upon mass protest and politico-legal remedies or persuasion, education, and behind-the-scenes bargaining. In general, the moderates, the most numerous group in Chicago, preferred "welfare" to "status" goals (that is, immediate, tangible benefits rather than the more abstract goal of integration) and tended to seek nonracial explanations for apparently anti-black acts, to disaggregate issues, and to have less confidence in mass protests or legal-political solutions.

The foregoing brief sketch of the principal leadership typologies obviously cannot do justice to their subtleties and nuances. In trying to summarize the various approaches here, one should be aware that the typologies reviewed above were developed by scholars with different purposes and approaches. Thus, selecting commonalities among these typologies may do violence to the authors' original intents. Wilson, for example, is particularly adamant on this point. He writes that the labels "militant" and "moderate" were used "with the greatest misgiving," because of the tendency to "read substantive content into these words apart from the specific substantive material for which they are mere rubrics." However, in using sham, he stresses that they "have no normative implications" and have "no connection with the kinds of leaders mentioned by other authors writing on black leadership" (1960).

However, Wilson protests too much. There is a connection between his work and that of others writing on black leadership. This connection is, perhaps, clearest in Ladd's work, the last and most sophisticated of the black leadership studies. Fundamentally, the black leadership typologies appear to be based on a composite of goals, methods, and rhetoric. These variables are the explicit constituent elements of Ladd's leadership typology. The factor that determines the location of a particular type on what Ladd properly views as a leadership continuum is the degree of that particular type's acceptability to whites (Ladd, 1966). In other words, Ladd is saying that the goals, methods, and rhetoric of militants are less acceptable to the dominant group of whites than are those of moderates. Consequently, the goals and so forth of moderates are less acceptable than are those of the conservatives. Or, put another way, in the literature, leaders are more or less "militant" to the extent that their goals, methods, and rhetoric diverge from the conventional goals, methods, and rhetoric deemed appropriate by the dominant-class whites.

Ladd's leadership continuum allows us to see continuity in the literature because it enables one to compare the content of different styles in different times and places. As Ladd (1966) writes, "The limits and contents of the styles are determined by prevailing patterns of race relations which vary with time and place."

Part Two

Foundations of Black Leadership

The American Dream is one big tent of many cultures, races, and religions. Under that tent, everybody is assured equal protection under the law, equal opportunity, equal access, and a fair share. Our struggle demands that we open closed doors, extend the tent, and even the playing field.

Rev. Jesse L. Jackson, Sr.
President, Rainbow/Push Coalition

Black leadership in America is a product of the black experience in American history. It has its roots in Africa, the continent of origin of peoples of African descent. A review of the journey of African-Americans from freedom in Africa to slavery and emancipation in America suggests, at the very least, six sources as foundations of black leadership: (1) the African background; (2) the institution of slavery; (3) the development of an intellectual/ideological foundation; (4) religious and mutual benefit societies; (5) the Revolutionary philosophy and the American Constitution; and (6) the black press. These sources are the subject of discussion in this part of the book.

4

Sources of Black Leadership

THE AFRICAN BACKGROUND

From the very beginning, it was commonplace in the New World for peoples of African descent to speak and write sensitively of the land of their ancestors. While some of them could refer to the vast continent of Africa in the vaguest terms, others, such as Alex Haley (1976), could focus quite precisely on the specific areas from which most of their ancestors had come. The independence of most African countries in 1960 evoked a deeper sense of identification, even though the new nations had little connection with those nation-states of several centuries ago.

From the seventh century A.D. until the sixteenth century several powerful African states evolved. Of central importance were the nations of Egypt, Ghana, Mali, Kush, Meroë, and Songhay (Franklin, 1994; Davidson, 1970). These powerful kingdoms, like many other African states, were to some degree influenced by Islamic traditions and institutions; likewise, each kingdom influenced both the Arab people and other African people to the north, east, and south.

On the eve of the sixteenth century, Africa teemed with a rich diversity of cultures. Across the continent could be found stable political structures, diversified economies, and cohesive social institutions. Whether the states were great empires or modest political entities, they were generally well organized and able to maintain law, order, and social harmony. This political stability both within and among the African states was conducive to healthy economic development. The Africans, whether farmers or artisans, displayed remarkable versatility and a variety of talents and tastes.

Most impressive in the consideration of the social institutions of Africa was the cohesive influence of the family. The immediate family, the clan, and the tribe undergirded every aspect of life. The influence and hold the patriarch had over the members of the family was largely responsible for the stability characteristic of the area. The deep loyalty and attachment of the individual to the family approached reverence, and indeed, was the basis for most religious practices. Thus the world "discovered" by fifteenth century Europeans was already highly civilized.

For centuries some indigenous peoples had no interest in organizing themselves into states, perhaps seeing no need or advantage in erecting political institutions. Others, however, had different attitudes or needs, and therefore set out to build governments to meet those needs. Indeed, many well-developed political states had risen and fallen before any lasting contact was established between West Africa and the Near East. These states sprang up in more or less the same general region, from the Mediterranean southward to the Gulf of Guinea and from the Atlantic eastward almost to the Nile.

Scholars in African and American studies have discussed for many years the question of the extent to which African cultures were transplanted and preserved in the New World. A considerable number of scholars and students formerly contended that nothing existed in Africa that approached civilization and that, therefore, Africans brought nothing with them to the New World. Sociologists like E. Franklin Frazier and Robert E. Park failed to see anything in African-American life that can be traced to the African background. But as evidence to the contrary began to pile up, this position was no longer tenable. Questions still remained as to whether Africans continued to be Africans in ways other than color, and whether any substantial elements of Africa became part of the general acculturative processes taking place in America. Scholars like Carter G. Woodson, Melville J. Herskovits, Lorenzo Turner, John Blassingame, Jacob U. Gordon, and Albert Raboteau have insisted that the African cultural heritage can still be seen in many aspects of American life. Africans that were brought to America, either as indentured laborers or slaves, came to America with skills, spirituality, native abilities, aesthetics, music, values, and, in fact, their humanity. In the Americas, successful slave revolts made possible the transplantation, to a considerable degree, of African ways of life. African survivals in the New World have also been documented in African languages, including such words as "yam," "goober," "canoe," and "banjo." In literature, the persistence of African culture can be seen in the folk tales that have been recorded in recent years by American writers. In religion, here are divinations and various cult practices, some of which have been traced to the African background. In work, in play, in social organizations, including the African extended family structure, there is some evidence of African culture. These values are integral parts of the sources of black leadership in America.

THE INSTITUTION OF SLAVERY

The dispersion of Africans into the Americas and the leadership that emerged was conditioned both by environmental factors and by the psychology by the system of slavery. As Thompson (1993) put it, "for Africans enslaved in the Americas, many of whom previously enjoyed the status of free people in their continent of origin and enjoyed the benefits of liberty, their enslavement was not only a calamity but the experience must have posed many dilemmas for them." Many African-Americans who were enslaved were capable of working out stratagems to upset the system that held them in thralldom. They undermined, cheated, and ensured a defeat of the system. But if the cruel treatment of slaves was designed to prevent uprisings and running away, it was eminently unsuccessful. This was particularly the case in the Caribbean. On almost every Caribbean island there is a record of some serious revolt against the plantation system, and everywhere there is evidence of constant running away. When the British took Jamaica in the middle of the seventeenth century, most of the slaves promptly escaped to the mountains, where they were frequently joined by other fugitives. These runaways, called *Maroons*, continuously harassed planters by stealing, trading with slaves, and enticing them to run away. By 1730, these ex-slaves, under Cudgo, their powerful leader, had terrorized whites to such an extent that England was compelled to send out two additional regiments to protect the planters.

Haiti also had its Maroons as early as 1620, and the outlawed colony grew to such proportions that the colonial government recognized it in 1784. It is conceded that Haitian Maroons were largely responsible for the Haitian uprisings of 1679, 1691, and 1704. In the middle of the eighteenth century, the recalcitrant blacks of Haiti found a peerless leader in Macandal, a native-born African, who announced that he was the black Messiah sent to drive the whites from the island. In 1758 he carefully laid his plans for a coup d'etat. The water of Le Cap was to be poisoned, and when the whites were in convulsions the blacks, under the leadership of Macandal and his Maroons, were to seize control. By accident, the plot was discovered, and the fear-stricken planters hunted down Macandal and executed him. At the time of his execution he warned his enemies and comforted his friends by telling them that one day he would return, more terrible than before. Many blacks, and perhaps some whites, were later to believe that Toussaint L'Ouverture was the reincarnation of Macandal.

The trouble in Haiti was a source of motivation to slaves on the American plantations. In fact, it helped produce a number of black leaders who led slave revolts and insurrections in the nineteenth century.

INTELLECTUAL AND IDEOLOGICAL FOUNDATIONS

Black intellectuals and their ideological differences are products of the American tradition. The era of the American Revolution was a pinnacle of antislavery sentiment and racial egalitarianism. Largely influenced by the egalitarian ideology of the Revolution, Northern States took steps to free their slaves.

As Franklin (1994) has thoroughly documented, one of the first blacks to make the search for intellectual and spiritual independence was Jupiter Hammon, a slave on Long Island. Growing into manhood during the years when the Wesleyan revival was strong both in England and America, Hammon was greatly influenced by the writings of Charles Wesley and William Cowper. In 1761 he published "An

Evening Thought. Salvation by Christ, with Penitential Cries." In 1778 he published a twenty-one stanza poem, "To Miss Phillis Wheatley." Other poems and prose pieces appeared in the next two decades. In "An Address to the Negroes of the State of New York," published in 1787, Hammon showed that he felt it his personal duty to bear slavery patiently, but at the same time said that it was an evil system and that young blacks should be manumitted. He lived to see his master write a will ordering that certain of his slaves be set free at the age of twenty-eight, and in 1799, the year before his death, Hammon could rejoice that the state of New York had enacted legislation looking toward the gradual emancipation of all slaves within the state.

The individual strivings of Jupiter Hammon, Phillis Wheatley, Gustavus Vassa, Benjamin Banneker; and Paul Cuffe not only represented the effort of blacks to secure a measure of independence for themselves in the post-Revolutionary period, but also are examples of the movement of Americans toward intellectual and economic self-sufficiency, so characteristic of the period. Indeed, it can be said that these African-Americans were, in a sense, leading the way, given that they overcame both the degraded position of their race and the psychological and intellectual disadvantage that all Americans of the period suffered. Their search for independence was matched only by the efforts of groups of blacks, who found it necessary to forge separate institutions for their people during the same period.

In their efforts to elevate themselves intellectually in the post-Revolutionary period, blacks from the general trend to establish and improve schools in the new republic. There was also sentiment—which the various abolition and manumission societies expressed before the turn of the century—in favor of educating blacks. The New England and Middle Atlantic states were especially active in this area. Whites in Boston were teaching black children both privately and in public institutions. In 1798, a separate school for black children was established by a white teacher in the home of Primus Hall, a prominent African-American. Two years later, blacks asked the city of Boston for a separate school, but the citizens refused. The blacks established the school anyway, and employed two Harvard men as instructors. The school continued to flourish for many years. Finally, in 1820, the city of Boston opened an elementary school for black children.

One of the best-known schools for blacks during this period was the New York African Free school, established in 1787 by the Manumission Society.

Black urbanization and northward migration, the flowering of the jazz idiom, the Garvey Back-to-Africa movement, the burgeoning of black literature and art, the expanding work of the Urban League, and the anti-lynching campaign and other activities of the National Association for the Advancement of Colored People (NAACP) were developments that collectively attracted considerable attention. And when *Survey Graphic* issued its "Harlem" issue in 1925 (revised and published in book form as *The New Negro*), it seemed that a "New Negro" had matured and that a "Harlem Renaissance" was under way. Few inquired into his antecedents, but many welcomed the race-conscious, assertive, race-proud

New Negroes, who were "digging up [their] past," achieving middle-class status and creating an artistic expression of their separate group life while aiming at integration into American society.

The editor of the *New Negro* volume was the Harvard Ph.D. and Rhodes scholar, Alain Locke. He wrote feelingly of the new cultural expression, comparable to "those nascent movements of folk-expression and self-determination which are playing a creative part in the world today. . . . As in India, in China, in Egypt, Ireland, Russia, Bohemia, Palestine, and Mexico, we are witnessing the resurgence of a people." In fact, black Americans felt themselves to be "the advance-guard of the African peoples." To Locke, the "old Negro"—the "Uncle" and the "Mammy"—had long been something of a myth, having given place to a New Negro with "a spirit to seize, even in the face of an extortionate and heavy toll, a chance for the improvement of conditions." So independent and self-directed was the New Negro that he and she more than fulfilled the dreams of the racial leaders of twenty years before, who spoke of developing race pride and stimulating race consciousness, and spoke of the desirability of race solidarity as well. American democratic ideals were the objectives of the black's outer life, but those of his inner life, resulting from "an attempt to repair a damaged group psychology and reshape a warped social perspective," took the form of a more positive self-respect and self-reliance, so that there had occurred a "rise from social disillusionment to race pride." The mainspring of black life in the post-war generation was a "belief in the efficiency of collective effort, in race cooperation." Yet, Locke insisted that the ultimate success of blacks in "this forced attempt to build his Americanism on race values" was possible "only through the fullest sharing in American culture and institutions."

Other writers in the volume developed the details of this broad theme, especially in literature and the arts. Arthur A. Schomburg, a propagandist for black history, declared: "The American Negro must remake his past in order to make his future. . . . For him a group tradition must supply compensation for persecution, and pride of race the antidote for prejudice." The volume contained extensive material on black folk culture and African cultural origins. It gave considerable attention to the impact of urbanization and northward migration, which Charles S. Johnson said created "a new type of Negro." James Weldon Johnson described the new cultural life arising out of this urbanization of New York, and E. Franklin Frazier contributed an essay on "Durham: Capital of the black middle class."

This cluster of ideas emphasizing race pride, group solidarity, and self-dependence was growing more prominent for over a generation and in protest organizations, and with the rise of the middle class that exploited the black market and championed economic nationalism. This class, having achieved respectable economic and educational status, felt entitled to the rights that Washington said accrued to a race that had accomplished the aforementioned achievements. Furthermore, we have dealt with the dualism in black thought, the racial consciousness that at once identified blacks with

American society and yet tended toward ethnocentrism. We now examine some of the purely intellectual aspects of the movement—the rising interest in black history, a new interest in black folk culture and in Africa, and the striving for a race literature and cultural life—what might be termed evidence of a *cultural nationalism*. We then examine some of the more extreme ethnocentric sentiments (most notably African emigrationism) and finally, the roots of urbanization and northward migration, which to a large extent underlay the spirit of the 1920s.

The black history movement gained fresh vigor during the age of Washington. Few actually wrote what purported to be "history"—and these few were usually not outstanding in their other fields of endeavor—but R.H. Terrell was undoubtedly representative when he expressed the hope that black children would be taught something about colored heroes. "It is lamentable," he said, "to see the little they know about their own people who have played such an important part in the development of this country." As Kelly Miller put it: "All great people glorify their history, and look back upon their early attainments with a spiritualized vision." George Washington Williams (1849–1891) was one of the early writers of black history. His major historical works were *The History of the Negro Race in America, 1619–1880*, published in 1883; and *A History of the Negro Troops in the War of the Rebellion*, published in 1888. Although Williams' work was generally well received, of his first book the Literary World of Boston commented that it was "the most nearly satisfactory continuous account yet written of the African in America."

Representative of the score of historical works that appeared during the age of Washington were W.H. Councill's *Lamp of Wisdom, Or Race History Illuminated*, 1898; Rev. C.T. Walker's *Appeal to Caesar*, 1900, which employed the facts of Egyptian civilization and its influence and the facts of the black's progress and contributions to America as an argument for citizenship rights; a pamphlet published in 1901, which by 1913 had reached its ninth edition, entitled *Jesus Christ had Negro Blood in His Veins*, by a Brooklyn physician, W.L. Hunter; the Baltimore minister Harvey Johnson's *The Nations From a New Point of View*, 1903, which rehearsed the old materials regarding ancient civilizations; Du Bois' *The Souls of Black Folk*, 1903; Pauline Hopkins' *Primer of Facts Pertaining to the Early Greatness of the African Race*, 1905, which aimed to instill race pride as encouragement for American Negroes to aid the "restoration" of Africa; Joseph E. Hayne's *The Ammonian or Hametic Origin of the Ancient Greeks, Cretans and all the Celtic Races*, 1905, which held that Greek and Cretan civilizations were created by descendants of Ham and that the Celtic British owed their achievements to their Negro ancestry; Booker T. Washington's *Story of the Negro*, 1909; and James Morns Webb's *The Black Man, The Father of Civilization*, 1910. Less ephemeral, because they were based on better scholarship, were *The Aftermath of Slavery*, 1903, by William Sinclair, secretary of the Constitution League, which was notable for its defense of black Reconstruction; Benjamin Brawley's *Short History of the American Negro*, 1913; J.W. Cromwell's *The Negro in American*

History, 1914 (chiefly biographical); and, most important of all, Du Bois' slim volume, *The Negro*, which appeared in 1915. Du Bois, the most widely learned and most discriminating of black scholars and propagandists, brought to bear the latest anthropological theories, including the work of Franz Boas. In addition to criticizing the Aryan myth and describing the ancient cultures of Ethiopia and Egypt, Du Bois devoted five of the book's dozen chapters to a discussion of the history of West and South Africa and the culture of contemporary Africa. Other works had specialized concerns. Several dealt mostly with military history, and R.R. Wright, Jr., pioneered the examination of the role of blacks in the discovery and exploration of the New World.

Frequently, history was held to be of value in instilling race pride, solidarity, and self-help, whether these attributes might be directed toward agitation for political and civil rights, toward economic cooperation, toward an all-black community, or even toward colonization. Yet those who urged the study of black history ranged from amalgamationists to extreme nationalists, and from Booker T. Washington to W.E.B. Du Bois. Interest in race history was most characteristic of those who favored a group economy or other forms of separatism, but even the assimilationist *Gazette* insisted that "Every Afro-American school . . . ought for obvious reasons [to] compel its students to study Williams' *History of the Negro Race.*" Certainly, the interest was widely shared, and about the time of World War I, black history courses appeared in a few of the colleges and universities in America.

Unquestionably, as the lines of race hardened in the opening years of the century there was an increasing tendency to use black history to foster race pride and group solidarity as the basis of advancement by collective action, and as an antidote to prejudice and discrimination. This approach was perhaps best represented—though in a somewhat extreme form—by Meharry Medical School Professor C.V. Roman (1911), who a few years later was to propose a bi-racial society and parallel. To Pennsylvania-born, Canada-reared Roman, past president of the National Medical Association, knowledge of history would foster race pride and solidarity enough "to enable us to spurn as poor relations those unfortunate members of our race" who displayed shame of their ancestry by not wishing to belong to black churches, live in black neighborhoods, send their children to black schools, or patronize black business and professional men. Black children should be taught about the "glorious deeds of black men and women first," before they learned of the deeds of the national heroes of the United States. The diffusion of such knowledge would stimulate race pride and would "furnish an atmosphere of mutual cooperation and helpfulness that will change the winter of our discontent into the glorious summer of racial solidarity, that magic alembic in which most of our racial difficulties will disappear."

The increasingly deep-seated historical interest was evident in the formation of historical societies. In 1897, the American Negro Historical Society of Philadelphia was organized to collect relics and facts pertaining to black American progress and development. More influential were the Negro Society for

Historical Research (1912) and the Association for the Study of Negro Life and History (1915), now called the Association for the Study of African-American Life and History.

The leaders of the former organization were its president, John Edward Bruce (pseudonym Bruce Grit), a free-lance journalist and sometime editor, and its secretary, A.A. Schomburg, a Puerto Rico-born bibliophile. As one member of the society put it, the study of race history would "form an effective breakwater against the ever-increasing and cumulative tide of prejudice and discrimination." Schomburg in a speech at Cheyney Institute urged his listeners to learn Arabic "because much of our life is undoubtedly wrapped up" in Africa's traditions, customs, and history; proposed to stimulate racial patriotism by the study of black books; and called for inclusion of black history in school curriculum, because "it is the season for us to devote our time to kindling the torches that will inspire us to racial integrity." Bruce, born a slave in Maryland, had received only a public school education, but was an editor before he was twenty-five. He displayed an indefatigable zeal in gathering historical materials, and maintained a consistent enthusiasm for race pride and solidarity—opposing intermarriage and mixed schools, and apparently accepting the idea of inherent race differences—but in the protest tradition, and usually while being openly hostile to (and consistently suspected by) Booker T. Washington. A member of the extremist school of Biblical interpreters and a later Garveyite, Bruce, in a characteristic speech, that blacks must fight for their rights by organized resistance; espoused higher education; and called Japan "the logical hope of the darker races in the *inevitable conflict which is to decide the supremacy of nations . . . in the very near future.*" Whites, he said, feared contacts with blacks because, knowing that their own, white history was a "monumental fraud," "a total blank" before 850 B.C., they feared "odious comparisons." For from ancient African civilization, which was in many ways vastly superior to that of modern Europe, the white man derived his religion and "stole his alphabet" and his knowledge of the basic sciences.

Less chauvinistic and far more scholarly has been the work of the Association for the Study of Negro Life and History, founded by Carter G. Woodson, who had worked his way up from the West Virginia coal mines to a Harvard Ph.D. in 1912. Woodson was an anti-Bookerite, though he was not active in radical organizations. According to its constitution, the Association's aim was to collect sociological and historical documents and promote studies bearing on the blacks. Woodson's underlying purpose was succinctly summed up in the objective of preventing the race from becoming "a negligible factor in the thought of the world." Strictly speaking, the work of the Association and its *Journal of Negro History* lies outside the scope of this book, but its philosophy—characterized by the usual ethnic dualism—was rooted in the historical-mindedness of the pre-war generation.

Finally, one must note the compensatory and psychological role the black history movement played—no matter what the larger view of its supporters: whether accommodationist like Washington, assimilationist like Smith, or of the agitation-through-racial-solidarity variety like Bruce. For the movement provided dignity in the face of insults and provided arguments for equality in the face of assertions of inferiority. Yet, even though extreme assimilationists showed interest in it, the movement was chiefly significant as part of the complex of ideas that included self-help, race pride, and solidarity.

The interest in African history was part of a larger identification with Africa shared by the majority of black Americans, however attenuated the feelings might be. Even the anticolonizationist *Christian Recorder* urged the "wide-awake, industrious Negro" to make a fortune out of the economic opportunities in his "fatherland." Yet, despite the widespread pride in the antique African past, generally black Americans accepted white stereotypes as to the primitiveness of the black contemporary culture. Both Du Bois' presentation of the culture of contemporary West Africa and Charles W. Chestnutt's lack of concern about Africa—"except as an interesting foreign country"—were unusual and extreme viewpoints.

Chestnutt was the son of runaway slaves from Fayetteville, N.C. Charles Waddell Chestnutt was born in Cleveland, Ohio in 1858. He died in 1932. He was a writer, author of *The Goophered Grapevine* (1882), *The Conjure Woman*, and *The Wife of His Youth*, both in 1899. Most of his stories and novels, including his final two books, *The Morrow of Tradition* (1901) and *The Colonel's Dream* (1905), were accounts of the American racial dilemma from a black man's point of view. His first novel, *The House Behind the Cedars* (1900) dealt convincingly with a black girl's attempt to "pass" as white.

There had been, it is true, occasional evidence of an intellectual interest in African ethnography since the 1880s. A speaker at the Bethel Literary Association in 1881 stirred up considerable enthusiasm by a paper on the Zulus, who had up to that time held off the British, and scattered articles on specialized phases of African culture appeared from time to time. George Washington Ellis, an official at the American legation in Monrovia, capital of Liberia, made a careful and sympathetic study of the Vai-speaking people of West Africa. Most significant was the work of Du Bois. Not only was he aware of the complexity and sophistication of contemporary African culture, but also—acting more on mystic racial yearnings than on scientific investigation—Du Bois was the precursor of the Africanist Melville J. Herskovits in tracing black American culture and institutions to African origins. The sociologist R.R. Wright, Jr., was one of the few to follow in Du Bois' footsteps.

In addition to the interest in African culture, the 1890s witnessed the beginning of an interest in American black folk culture. In Boston in 1890, some of the leading socialites organized the Society for the Collection of Negro Folk Lore, and Hampton Institute gave the movement considerable propulsion, involving in it people like Fortune and Crummell. Concerning an important aspect of folk culture— the spirituals—there was some difference of opinion. These Jubilee Songs, or "plantation melodies," had been introduced to the public by the Fisk Jubilee Singers during Reconstruction, and on innumerable occasions they were sung at probably all of the black schools. Washington often alluded to them in proud terms. Moton recalled his disappointment at hearing them at Hampton where he hoped to sing "better" things, until Armstrong's constant instruction to the students to respect their race, its history and its traditions, convinced him of their value. At the Hampton Conference in 1899, there was considerable discussion of the matter. Those present agreed that ragtime and "coon songs" should be discouraged, but that "the beautiful plantation melodies should be preserved." Reverend Ernest Lyon of Baltimore, a minister to Liberia (1903–1911), thought blacks should not seek to imitate the work of white men. He said that "the plantation songs are our own . . . ; they were born out of our sufferings, and . . . express deep things. Never let them go." Kelly Miller also thought the plantation melody should be glorified, despite its "lowly origin." The *Horizon* reported a "revolt" of Howard University students against singing plantation melodies for visitors, and held that they were intended strictly for religious use among blacks.

Also developing was a definite interest in stimulating creative and intellectual expression in literature and the arts—an interest that paralleled the rise of literary, musical, and artistic organizations. This striving for literary and intellectual accomplishment was multifaceted. It was symbolic of the desire to assimilate to American middle-class culture; it was directed toward demonstrating that blacks did have intellectual and creative abilities; it expressed a belief that only black writers could express the aspirations of the race; it was intended to correct the stereotypes of black characters in the writings of white authors and to argue the race question from the black point of view; it was an outgrowth of the feeling of race pride; it was connected with the idea that it would be the intellectuals who would, on the basis of racial cooperation, lead the race into achieving higher culture and civilization. Not all of the individuals (to be discussed in later chapters) held all of these ideas. It is sometimes hard to see if they advocated cultural activities as a means of assimilating to American culture, or if they were espousing a sort of cultural nationalism. Undoubtedly, many were unconsciously striving toward both—as Locke and others did consciously during the Harlem Renaissance.

Evidence of the desire to create a racial literature was not entirely new, but the idea began to take hold during the 1890s. In 1893, H.T. Johnson, editor of the *Recorder*, outlined the need for racial authors to express racial aspirations.

Du Bois thus advanced the thesis that, given the American race system, with its segregation and discrimination, it was in the cities that whatever group advancement was possible would take place, and that it would take place on the basis of collective action, on the basis of group solidarity. Here, indeed, was the climax of that development of racial solidarity and self-help—in the cities, where a business and professional class could be supported by the black masses; in the cities of the North, where a compact segregated community could elect men to political office. Chestnutt's Cleveland was already being subjected to strains and would soon disappear as a result of the mass migration that created the extensive ghettos that black businessmen, politicians, and professional men would exploit. And it was in New York where the race-conscious artists and literati—paradoxically the most interracially integrated group in black society (due to their contacts with certain white figures)—produced the proudly race-conscious, race-proud, but largely white-fostered Harlem Renaissance. Of course, black economic development, cultural expression, and political participation would have achieved far more if the American race system had not existed, but the direction blacks took and the achievements they did make rested on a rationalization of the value of self-reliance and group solidarity, which in turn was based upon the rapidly growing urban ghetto.

Here, then, was the New Negro, resourceful, independent, race-proud, economically advancing, and ready to tackle political and cultural ambitions. This New Negro believed in collective economic effort, for the most part denied any interest in social equality, and at the same time denounced the inequities of American racism and insisted upon citizenship rights. This New Negro was interested in the race and its past, becoming more conscious of the Negro relationship with other colored peoples and with Africa—an identification that the lower classes perhaps never really lost. In fact, the Garvey Movement was in many ways the lower-class counterpart of the New Negro Movement; both held to a belief in economic chauvinism, an interest in race history, and an identification with Africa; both emphasized race pride and solidarity—though, of course, the Garvey philosophy lacked the dualistic character of the New Negro outlook. The New Negro regarded the race as a distinct group with a distinct mission, yet remaining part of the United States, owing an equal debt to Howard, Fisk, Lincoln, and Atlanta and to Hampton and Tuskegee; to the Niagara Movement and to the National Negro Business League; to Booker T. Washington and W.E.B. Du Bois.

The Niagara Movement

The Niagara Movement was the first organized Afro-American protest group in the twentieth century. Born at a time when black fortunes were at a low ebb, the Niagara Movement represented a challenge to the prevailing black program of acquiescence and accommodation advocated by Booker T. Washington. Led by W.E.B. Du Bois, the organization was founded by a group of twenty-nine black intellectuals who met in Niagara Falls, Canada, during June 1905.

Formally renouncing Booker T. Washington's "work and wait" philosophy, Du Bois and the others drew up a platform for aggressive action, entitled "The Negro Declaration of Independence." This document called for the restoration of black voting rights; freedom of speech and criticism; the abolition of all distinctions based on race; and the universal recognition of the basic principles of human brotherhood. Following this initial organizational meeting, the Niagara group held national conferences in 1906, 1907, and 1908 at Harpers Ferry (in honor of John Brown), Boston (the former seat of eastern abolitionism), and Oberlin, Ohio (the hotbed of western abolitionism during the nineteenth century). The Harpers Ferry meeting, attended by more than one hundred delegates, was of special significance in that a militantly worded (if not radical, for that day and age) resolution and list of demands was issued. Demanding full and immediate manhood suffrage, the elimination of all Jim Crow practices throughout the United States, and the equal and unbiased enforcement of laws for all citizens, the resolution went on to declare: "we claim for ourselves every single right that belongs to a freeborn American—political, civil, and social; and until we get these rights we will never cease to protest and assail the ears of America. The battle we wage is not for ourselves alone but for all true Americans." Absorbed into the framework of the NAACP in 1909, the Niagara Movement not only signaled an impending change in the pattern of Afro-American leadership, but also showed the seeds of future twentieth-century black protest.

As varied as the black intellectual foundation was, so also was the ideological foundation. Essentially, black ideological foundations can be classified into three categories: (1) the Separatist Ideology; (2) the Integrationist Ideology; and (3) the Accommodationist Ideology. Ironically, all three ideologies share some common goals, thus reaching partial consensus. These goals include freedom, justice, equality, respect for human dignity, an end to racism and oppression of blacks, full citizenship, and participation in and sharing in the American dream. These ideological differences may be diagrammed as follows:

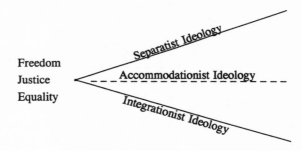

In his analysis of the paradoxes of black leadership, Martin Kilson (1995) suggests three types of black political leadership: (1) pragmatic activist; (2) systemic radical; and (3) ethno-radical.

Pragmatic activist

Kilson refers to this group as the mainstream pattern, pioneered by Du Bois from the Niagara Movement and the founding of the NAACP—which produced a full-fledged, electoral-based black political class. Members of this class accept the basic parameters of the democratic capitalist system, and also accept the broader cultural matrix within which this system is embedded. They insist that

America must purge itself of white supremacy and of the social institutions and cultural identities in which it is reflected.

Systemic radical

This refers to a minor but quite persistent strand of black leadership, whose representatives reject the basic parameters of American capitalism. Their ideological inspiration has largely been Marxist, and in the 1930s and 1940s they came together mostly in the American Communist Party (ACP). Its representatives included James W. Ford (an ACP presidential candidate), Benjamin Davis, Paul Robeson, Richard Wright, and even Ralph Ellison. Du Bois later joined the International Communist Party, at the later part of his life.

Ethno-radical

This group has exhibited what might be called a three-sided schizophrenia in its approach to the democratic capitalist system. First, its representatives endorse the capitalist mechanism for producing and distributing wealth. But, second, they are indifferent or hostile to democratic politics. And, third, they do not accept the underlying cultural matrix. This cultural antipathy is manifest in various ways; depending on personality and organizational style, leaders adopt different postures of rebellion. They indulge in aggressive verbal and symbolic challenges to mainstream culture. They seek some specific black-ethno replacement for standard features of the culture, such as in diet, consumption, personal adornment, and so forth. Or they aim deeper, countering and seeking to displace basic cultural patterns in religion, family, gender, and historical identity. Terms such as *black nationalists*, *black militants*, *Garveyites*, *Black Muslims*, and *Afrocentrists* refer to this group. "The legacy of Malcolm X" makes the same reference. What gives this ethno-radicalism its radical edge is the rejection of the American cultural mainstream and the demand for a black replacement. Kilson's schema may be diagrammed as follows:

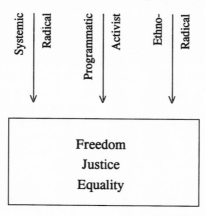

SPIRITUAL, RELIGIOUS, AND MUTUAL BENEFIT SOCIETIES

The institutional organization of the black community is historically rooted in the church and the fraternal (or *mutual benefit*) orders. The origins of both institutions go back to the late eighteenth century.

The independent church movement arose because of racial prejudice in the white-dominated churches. The origins of the African Methodist Episcopal (AME) Church exemplify black response to this treatment. Its leading founder and first consecrated bishop was Richard Allen, a former slave from Maryland who had been converted to Methodism. He later became a Methodist circuit preacher, and—moving to Philadelphia—began attending the predominantly white St. George's Methodist Episcopal Church in 1786. Perceiving that blacks were unable to achieve positions of true leadership at St. George's, Allen urged the creation of a separate place of worship. The response of most black parishioners was cool. But Allen's magnetic personality was drawing ever-larger numbers of colored people to St. George's, much to the annoyance of the trustees, who stopped his prayer service and ordered black communicants to sit in the rear of the gallery. Facing such galling treatment, Allen and his friend Absolom Jones departed from St. George's with their followers. Ultimately, despite opposition from Methodist elders, Allen succeeded in establishing his own church, while Jones founded the first black Episcopal church in America.

One thousand eight hundred and sixteen representatives of African Methodist churches in Pennsylvania, New Jersey, Delaware, and Maryland thus met in Philadelphia and formed a separate Methodist connection, the African Methodist Episcopal (AME) Church. The establishment of the AME Church led the development of the black independent church movement. Thus, the church became a training ground for black Americans. This was particularly true for black leaders in America. Among other things, the black religious movement has helped accomplish three goals: (1) the establishment of a black theology of liberation; (2) the reaffirmation of black faith in America; and (3) the call for national unity.

Mutual Benefit Societies

In their origins, the church and the fraternal or mutual benefit society were closely related. During the late eighteenth century the distinction between the sacred and the secular was not sharply drawn. In a period when there were scarcely any ordained ministers, it was natural for the mutual aid society to perform both religious and secular functions—as did the Free African Society founded by Richard Allen and Absolom Jones a few months before they left St. George's Methodist Church. One of the principal functions of these societies was the quasi-religious providing of a decent burial for deceased members. In Newport, Rhode Island, the mutual benefit societies preceded by many years the creation of the first black church there, which was founded under the auspices of the African Benevolent Society in 1824.

In 1787, there appeared the first mutual benefit societies—the Free African Societies of Philadelphia and Newport—and the first black secret fraternal order, the Masons. They served similar functions: both offered their members companionship, recreation, recognition, and prestige that to some degree compensated for the racial proscriptions facing them. Both offered economic protection in case of sickness or death and sought to encourage thrift, industry, and morality, thus providing a method for upward mobility. The economic functions of these societies would become very clear in the late nineteenth century, when they provided the basis for most of the early black banks and insurance companies. Finally, these societies were an example of race unity and solidarity that offered a feeling of worth and dignity to their members.

THE REVOLUTIONARY PHILOSOPHY AND THE CONSTITUTION

Throughout American history, blacks struggled to demonstrate their faith in the promise of the American Constitution, which embodied the philosophy of the Revolutionary War and the principles of the Declaration of Independence. By endowing all peoples with inalienable rights superior to those of positive law, it was a standing invitation for black freedom—which only a few Americans could accept. For the implications of the Declaration of Independence and the American Constitution, however vague, were that powerful, and so played major roles in the search for freedom by blacks and their acceptance in the American mainstream. It was the American Constitution that gave hope to blacks and later guided their struggle for civil rights. That hope and faith became the cornerstone for black leadership.

THE BLACK PRESS

At first, protest activity among the free people of color was confined to local mass meetings and the irregular publication of pamphlets. Then, at the close of the third decade of the nineteenth century, race protest achieved an institutionalized form with the establishment of the first black newspaper, *Freedom's Journal,* in 1827.

The publishers of colored newspapers viewed their function as advancing the cause of the race. They implicitly, and at times explicitly, called for support from free blacks by appealing for race unity and race solidarity. Colored people, they maintained, must unite behind race newspapers if they were to achieve their rights and overcome oppression. Among others, Frederick Douglass, the most famous and influential black editor during the antebellum period and Reconstruction, articulated this philosophy. Another lucid expression of this viewpoint was by John B. Russwurm and Samuel Cornish, co-editors of the first issue of *Freedom's Journal (Freedom's Journal* Editorial, March 16, 1827). "Too Long Have Others Spoken for Us" was the title of their editorial comment. Among other things, they noted, "We wish to plead our own cause. Too long have others spoken for us. . . . Our vices and degradation are ever arrayed against us, but our virtues are passed by unnoticed" (Russwurm and Cornish, 1827). Black leadership has always depended on its ability to communicate with the American power structure. Black leaders communicated through various means, including the "underground railroad" and the grapevine, but it was the black press that proved most effective. Recent black accessibility to the main press has somewhat diminished the power of the black press.

The foregoing discussion may be summarized in Figure 4.1.

Figure 4.1 Foundations of Black Leadership

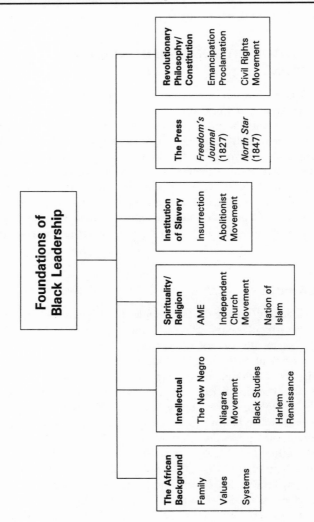

5

The Beginnings of Black Leadership

The beginnings of black leadership in America may be traced to the institution of slavery; specifically, the response blacks to their early experiences in slavery.

Visiting America in the 1830s, Alexis de Tocqueville (1845) observed:

> The prejudice of race appears to be stronger in the states which have abolished slavery than in those where it still exists; and nowhere is it so important as in those states where servitude has never been known.

Recent studies have confirmed the accuracy of Tocqueville's impressions. Anti-black sentiments and legislation marked the nineteenth century. Franklin (1994) observes that the Industrial Revolution in England, the invention of the cotton gin, the persistence of the slave trade into the nineteenth century, all had the effect of establishing slavery and black underclass in the United States on a more permanent basis than ever before. In fact, as the nineteenth century opened, there seemed little prospect that slavery would ever cease to exist in the United States. It took a bloody civil war to confer the status of citizenship on blacks in 1868.

As the issue of human freedom (slavery) dominated the character of American life in the nineteenth century, so did colonization of Africa, Latin America, and Asia, the so-called Third World, dominate the peoples in those regions. Thus, black American leadership did not confront only the plight of black America but the liberation of Africa (the motherland) from the yoke of colonialism as well.

The nineteenth century was characterized by several significant historical movements: abolitionism, expansionism, slavery and sectional strife, "nation building," and the politics of racial inequality. Given the context of the beginning of black leadership, three questions must be addressed: (1) What was the nature of black leadership? (2) Who were some of the leaders? (3) What strides did they make toward social change in America?

MORAL SUASIONIST

The nature of the beginnings of black leadership was *moral suasionist*. This type of leadership, according to Thompson (1993), emerges in society at points of crisis; its actions are often based on assumptions that the rulers of society can be induced or persuaded by reason and argument to modify, change, or abandon policies that seem detrimental to some or all sections of society. Moral suasionists also assert themselves when they contend that society's values have been debased, disregarded, flouted, or left nonexistent. Often, they respond promptly when human beings are found trampled on by the excesses of civil authorities, or when those authorities seem insensitive to or are oblivious of pleas and representations by their victims or the spokespeople for those victims. Their yardstick of evaluating actions is based on and conditioned by, if not purely religious principles, then at least their perception of, individually and collectively, what is right and wrong. Such advocates of a moral purpose are concerned that by deliberate, careless policy or nonchalance, society is called on to pay a heavy price for actions not very well regarded. In North America, as elsewhere, the moralists (some of whom joined the abolition of the slave trade and antislavery crusades) believed that with ongoing efforts to adduce arguments against the entire activity, the trade and the servitude of Africans in the Americas would be brought to an end. In fact, the early abolitionists of the United States were of this mind (Jordan, 1968). This type of leadership also emerged among the African-derived peoples in the Americas. It consisted of a *congeries* of reverend gentlemen or clergy, who provided the early leadership in this category and have continued to be in the forefront of this leadership. In the late eighteenth century and for much of the nineteenth century, they could be identified and named in large numbers, employing the pulpit to good effect to sound their ideas and influence the thoughts and actions of their congregation while attaining local or national reputation and influence in the process. They were not all prelates, yet they were people whose outlooks had been influenced by the Christian religion. From the West Indies, the three most outstanding leaders of thought who conducted their activities in British society—principally, London—were Ottobah Cugoano (christened John Stewart), Olaudah Equiano (christened Gustavus Vassa), and Ignatius Sancho. They were by no means the only leaders, but Cugoano and Equiano made their impact on the British abolition movement with their publications of antislavery books within two years of each other, and with their pleas and arguments for the abolition of the slave trade and slavery (Cugoano, 1787). Their protests came loud and clear as those of authentic Africans rescued from slavery. These leaders were outstanding men. The failure of the Western Indian society under slavery to produce an intellectual leadership—one of quality, with literary merit—from even among the white population has been commented on by the Reverend Caldecott (Caldecott, 1896). Slavery in all its theaters thrived on ignorance, and further perpetuated it. Despite the proclaimed intentions of the Society for the Propagation of the Gospels in Foreign Parts (SPG), that organization's endeavors after receiving the behest of Sir Christopher Coderington's plantations in Barbados showed no desire to rise above what was sanctioned by custom, which was, in fact, nothing (Bennett, 1958). As the plantocracy and slavocracy frowned on the idea of literacy for the African-derived slaves, seeing this inculcation as a dangerous indulgence, literacy could be acquired only through secrecy and by clandestine means. But even the religious prelates of the slave societies failed dismally in their duties by failing to instruct slaves, or even initially admit them into their Christian community. Only when the prelates saw the value of Christianity in conditioning the slave into obedience was it felt necessary to give Christianity to the slaves with all its distortions, accretions, and limitations. But it hardly imparted much literacy in those early days. It most certainly dulled their vision in relation to the nature of their struggles. But Christianity later became a weapon in the armory of the African diasporan struggles, judging from contradictions observed by the thoughts and actions of its proponents.

Both Cugoano and Equiano could rightly be referred to as the first black abolitionists on English soil. Their books complemented each other, as Robert July rightly observed, and arrived on the British scene when the antislavery trade debate was commencing and becoming a parliamentary and extraparliamentary preoccupation (July, 1968). They were, however, more than just black abolitionists. They were among the first of the emergent leaders among the Africans of the diaspora. In their books they endeavored to reconcile their African values with their European experiences. Cugoano's book was published in 1787 using the legal style of his day, and Equiano's book was published in the year of the first French Revolution, 1789. It had several editions. Both Cugoano and Equiano expressed their disapproval of the beastly treatment that robbed Africans of dignity. They appealed for complete abolition of the slave trade, as a prelude to slave emancipation Their works represented the earliest of modern African disquisitions on the consequences of European "civilization" of Africans in general. There was no biblical justification for the enslavement of Africans; Cugoano argued and assailed prelates who held the contrary viewpoint. He insisted that skin color was a mark of environment, not an emblem of slavery. His arguments were an amalgam of the humanitarianism of the times and his Christian convictions.

Equiano's book was a descriptive narration of his experiences from his capture in Africa, but he had a philosophical dimension in his assailing of slavery. Like Cugoano, he highlighted the contradictions and duplicity of European conduct as both enslavers and humanitarians. Both the writers were aware of the economic arguments against the slave trade and the institution of slavery. They saw these occurrences as catastrophically destructive of African development and hoped that abolition would provide the opportunity for meaningful and profitable commerce between Britain and Africa. In keeping with their zeal for change, they were enthusiastic for the Sierra Leone colonizing venture until Equiano, on principle, found himself unable to be associated with the venture, and was thus discharged.

From their writings can be gleaned their moral philosophy and the extent to which it had been bolstered by Christian convictions. They stressed the equality of man and were the first exponents of the concept of an "African personality." Their works deserve to be read in full to appreciate the quality of their minds and their advocacies. They were examples of moral suasionists who with others also agitated the question of equality on antislavery platforms. In that respect, they were activists, and examples of overlapping philosophies among the three categories of leadership. A typical statement by Cugoano read:

Everyman of any sensibility whether he be a Christian or heathen, if he has any discernment at all, must think that for any man, or any class of men to deal with their fellow creatures as with the beast of the field, or to account them as such, however ignorant they may be, and in whatever situation or whatever they find them, and whatever country or complexion they may be of that those great men who are the procurers and holders of slaves, are the greatest villains in the world. (Cugoano, 1787)

This statement by Cugoano was tantamount to saying that those who abused their fellow human beings in such a manner had also abused themselves. As a complement to this Equiano wrote:

Surely this traffic be good, which spreads like pestilence, and taints what it touches! Which violates the first natural right of mankind, equality and independence and gives one man dominion over his fellows which God could never intend! For it raises the owner to a state as far above man as it depressed the slave below it; and, with all the presumption of human pride, sets a distinction between them immeasurable in extent, and endless in duration! Yet how mistaken is the avarice even of the planters. Are slaves more useful by being thus humbled to the conditions of brutes, than they would be if suffered to enjoy the privileges of men? . . . When you make men slaves you deprive them of half their virtue, you set them in rapine and cruelty, and compel them to live with you in a state of war; and yet you complain that they are not honest or faithful! You stupefy them with stripes, and think it necessary to keep them in a state of ignorance; and yet you accept that they are incapable of learning, that their minds are such a barren soil or moor, that culture would be lost on them; and that they come from a climate where nature, though providing of her bounties in a degree unknown to yourselves, has left man alone scant and unfinished, and incapable of enjoying the treasures she has poured out from him! An assertion at once impious and absurd. Why do you use those instruments of torture? Are they fit to be applied by one rational being to another? And are you not struck with shame and mortification, to see the partakers of your nature reduced so low? But above all are there no dangers attending this mode of treatment? Are you not hourly in dread of insurrection?

But by changing your conduct, and treating your slaves as men, every cause of fear would be banished. They would be faithful, honest, intelligent and vigorous; and peace, prosperity and happiness, would attend you. (Equiano, 1967)

Believing as Cugoano and Equiano did that Africans generally were part of the human family while simultaneously desiring "many rules of civilization in Africa," in many respects Cugoano nevertheless argued that "we may boast of some more essential liberties than any of the civilized nations of Europe enjoy; for the poorest amongst us are never in distress for want, unless some general and universal calamity happens to us" (Cugoano, 1787). In both Cugoano and Equiano's calling for the combined efforts of mankind to abolish the slave trade, they typified the abolitionists of the world. As both leaders were to be found in the rank and file of abolitionists and on antislavery platforms in Britain agitating for the abandonment of the slave trade and slavery, they were, at one and the same, moral suasionists and activists.

The other intellectual leader of note in London was Ignatius Sancho, brought to London at the age of two after being rescued from a slave ship bound for Cartegena. The stories concerning Sancho's early years lack consistency, but he was known to have been given to three ladies residing in Greenwich. He became protégé of the Duke of Montagu, who helped him indulge his passion for reading and writing. In time, Sancho became known in literary circles. He was noted for his exquisite letters, still extant (Nichols, 1782). As a moral suasionist, his sentiments on slavery were expressed in sympathy for his brethren. It was, however, a tame affair compared to the poems of George Moses Horton of the United States.

On the North American scene, among moral suasionists were poets like Phillis Wheatley (1753–1784), Jupiter Hammon, and George Moses Horton of Raleigh, North Carolina. Although Phillis Wheatley's poems were inspirational, they do not demonstrate the fervor of the author of *Hope for Liberty,* published in 1829 and reproduced in 1838 as the *Poems of a Slave.* Despite Wheatley's composition of a poem titled "Liberty and Peace," concerned with the American struggle against Britain, not having had personal experience of the harshness of slavery in a consistent way seemed to have allowed Wheatley to demonstrate little awareness of its consequences on the African-derived people. In writing about Africa, she wrote that it was "mercy that brought" her from "her pagan land." Unlike George Moses Horton, she did not articulate her thoughts expressing the abhorrence of slavery in a poignant way. It is therefore not uncharitable for the distinguished historian, John Hope Franklin (1994), to have said of her: "Her writings are, perhaps, a good example of the search for independence through the method of escape, which was to become a favorite device of the Negro of a later century." Her contributions for the liberation of her people had a negative impact, but she seemed to have occupied the intermediate position servitude and freedom. Yet, her contemporaries in slavery had far less opportunities, and were able to demonstrate their preoccupations with liberty and its full implications. By contrast, Horton intensely expressed his preoccupation with liberty in his poems. His poetry was known to the students at the University of North Carolina. His poems brought him close to securing his manumission, but his hopes were later frustrated. Yet his legacy is one of moral suasion. His words re-echo today with much resonance:

Come melting Pity, from afar,
And break this vast enormous bar,
Between wretch and thee;
Purchase a few short days of time,
And bid vassal's sear sublime,
On wings of Liberty. (Horton, 1838)

But the epitome of moral suasion was the Right Reverend Richard Allen. From an assessment of the circumstances of the eighteenth and nineteenth centuries, Allen was a tower of strength among the moral leaders of the African diaspora in the Americas. As indicated earlier, this leadership of religious prelates is persistent, and continues to exist and be vibrant. (Such leadership also arose among descendants of Africa in Canada.) Allen and his associate, Absolom Jones, were the prominent figures of the late eighteenth century. Allen knew slavery firsthand, and after the purchase of his freedom he settled in Philadelphia to harness the gifts that he had for preaching, admonishing, and counseling. It was concern for his people that resulted in one of the first welfare societies for mutual aid among Afro-Americans—the Free African Society (1787)—significantly, established in the year of Cugoano's book. From this society emerged Bethel Church and, later, the African Methodist Episcopal Church.

The preoccupations of this society were self-improvement and help for the needy through contributions of the membership. The society was guided by principles among which were, first, the rejection of drunkenness and disorderly behavior; second, the disqualification from membership if dues were unpaid; third, punctilious attendance at monthly meetings, with fines for nonattendance (unless prevented by illness); and fourth, benefits conferred on widows of deceased members to enable them to educate their children if they were unable to attend "free schools" (Wesley, 1935). But Allen's preoccupations went beyond the welfare society; he sought to build—and eventually did establish—a church to assert the spirit of independence for his people, after they had been discriminated against in worship by white Methodists. But prior to the emergence of the church, Allen stressed and sought to inculcate discipline among his brethren. Some of his views appeared in *Freedom's Journal,* the first Afro-American newspaper in the United States established by John Russwurm, who later left for Liberia and established the now defunct *Liberia Herald.* Two churches emerged out of Allen's and Absolom Jones's preoccupations—St. Thomas African Protestant Episcopal Church (alias, the African Church) under Absolom Jones, and Bethel African Methodist Episcopal Church under Allen in July 1794, the former preceding the latter by 12 days (Frazier, 1962).

Among the principal preoccupations of Allen and the church founders were the apprenticing of children to trades and the teaching of lessons in thrift, sobriety, and industry to the Afro-American population. The church founders rendered assistance to the needy of the society and paved the way for extensive cooperation in the social advancement of a much larger population, and later, fraternal organizations. Among white humanitarians sympathetic to their cause who took the initiative to establish schools for Afro-Americans were Whitfield and the Quaker, Anthony Benezet. The first initiative failed, but not the second. Another Quaker school was established soon after Benezet's. In 1789, a society for the "Free Instruction of Orderly Blacks and People of Color" was founded. Also, a school was begun in St. Thomas under Absolom Jones. These facts do not support the thesis of the Right Reverend Dr. Daniel Payne (a later Bishop of the AME church), who in his history of the church said that neither Jones nor Allen thought about a school and education for black people because "they were ignorant men" (Payne, 1968). There is much evidence in Charles Wesley's research to the contrary.

The school instruction may have been rudimentary both for adults and children, but this was consistent with Allen's vision of the elevation of his people; their need for trained leadership, which he valued; and the development of a leadership rooted in the precepts of Christianity, in accordance with Allen's lights. He saw this leadership as a prerequisite for Afro-American independence, especially in ecclesiastical matters. He seemed aware of the fact that persons of African descent in the United States would continue to suffer discrimination unless they responded by producing their own leadership, articulated through the African-American church, school, and economic organizations, with each involving group action. Throughout this, there was an underlying principle—independence. In seeking this Allen wanted to fortify Afro-Americans against further degradation and the destruction of their spirits. The advocacies of Allen's leadership perspective need urgent revival in this age of *apparent* community. But for Allen, organization was the watchword. The independence of spirit piloted by Allen was to extend beyond the confines of Philadelphia, into other parts of the United States. It contributed to the proliferation of independent African churches, most of them of the Methodist and Baptist varieties. Methodism, which had begun as a religion of the masses, was failing to live up to its proclaimed intentions. This forced the African-derived peoples to hold it to its true protestations of faith by establishing their own churches after Euro-American racism denied them the right to worship in Americans' Methodist churches. They sought to worship without the unpleasantness or constraints of racial bigotry.

In evaluating the moral leadership provided by Richard Allen, we find that his type of leadership was the first and the epitome of its kind among Afro-Americans, and was to recur through the nineteenth and twentieth centuries—a leadership of religious prelates and clergy. Allen was guided by his own understanding of Christianity and religion (which was fundamentalist), and this shaped his perspectives in his admonishments to his brethren. He had no doubt that his approach would help them realize their salvation, both in this world and the next. This position would not have impressed the modern humanist, but seemed appropriate for its age, and Allen was sincere, even if he might be judged "misguided." In seeking the exertions of his people in the spheres of religion, property acquisition and accumulation, and counseling, education, and industry, he kept the goal clear: to realize the unity of his brethren for action through organization. Both the earlier trends through the Free African Society and, later, the AME Church provided a good deal of experience. Allen was certainly one of the earliest of Afro-American philanthropists. Furthermore, his constant petitions for slavery abolition were highlighted in some issues of the *Freedom's Journal*. His appeal to those who kept slaves and approved the practice was a case in point (Allen, 1960). His defense of the role of Afro-Americans during the yellow fever outbreak in Philadelphia in 1791 was another.

In the first case, Allen appealed to slave owners to abandon the enslavement of man. The appeal was naïve and unrealistic, even if firmly believed. It was based on a presumption that flew in the face of the facts—that through mere argument the slave owner would take steps to abolish slavery. For the tenacity of the opposition to abolition was demonstrated by the fact that a civil war was needed in the United States for the institution to collapse. Allen ignored the economic aspect of slavery, with the quick monetary returns its practitioners sought. As a suppliant in a weaker bargaining position, he was spiritually a tower of strength and his advocacies were tantamount to the need for "equality of opportunity"; for Allen (1880) had argued that it was not good enough to subject African slaves to an abject condition and then plead their incapacity. He cited parallels from the Israelite experience in and after bondage; of how they had for a while continued to manifest a slavish mentality. He pleaded for giving Afro-Americans the opportunity for advancement through education and believed Afro-Americans would demonstrate they were neither lacking nor inferior in mental endowment. Believing that the slave mentality was pervasive and took time to shed off, he argued, "And why would you look for better from us? It is in our posterity enjoying the same privileges with your own that you ought to look for better things."

His concern for his brethren in terms of their yearning for freedom and their welfare was unflinching. He addressed messages to them. Among these were his "Address to the People of Color" and "A Short Address to the Friends of Him Who Hath No Helper." But in terms of their emancipation, he admonished them to place their trust in God. He urged those who had secured manumission not to show ingratitude or rancor or "ill-will" to their former masters for past mistreatment, as such rancor was contrary to God's laws. But his enthusiasm for the elevation of his people within the United States led him and members of the AME Church (approximately 3,000 people) to assemble in 1817 to protest against the American Colonization Society's activities and advocacies for removing the freed colored people from the United States (Wesley, 1935). The American Colonization Society was founded in Washington, D.C., in December 1816. Despite the intimidatory tactics that had been employed by some slave-owning members of the Colonization Society to compel freed Afro-Americans to emigrate to Africa with the organization's sponsorship, the protest in Philadelphia was loud and clear. As Afro-Americans were assailed in New York, Pennsylvania, Delaware, Maryland, and other places, they soon saw the need for organizing themselves to confront issues of mob violence, mob law, and laws enacted to abridge the liberties of the *free people of color* in the United States. It was out of these endeavors that there emerged the Convention Movement of Colored People beginning in 1830, in time becoming a celebrated annual event. In this achievement, Allen was again in the forefront. One of the points the convention of 1830 considered was the possibility of "removal" to Africa. But Allen, not an advocate of emigration to Africa, was unequivocal on this matter. He was elected president on that occasion. The convention aimed to seek ways and means to achieve the swift elevation of the colored people to a more exalted status than slavery and slave codes had allowed them. This new movement admonished Afro-Americans to be diligent, to purchase land, work for unity, and seize every opportunity provided by the benevolence of friends of humanity for elevating their conditions and achieving their advancement. A Constitution of the Convention Movement was formulated. Allen died in 1831. His name remains immortalized in the AME Church.

In the context of the early period of dispersion of the African peoples into the Americas, "leadership" hardly existed. Individuals could decide a course of action—say, revolt on board a slave ship—and others might join in, but resistance would not be sustained as the revolts, except in a few cases, were put down with merciless severity. Leadership was a feature that emerged with increasingly greater and better organization, although the voices of leaders were heard before they actually formed organizations. Their voices sometimes *called forth* the organization, and—with the emergence of such organizations—either strengthened or weakened them. The social *milieu* also determined whether leadership could emerge—and the type of that leadership. Within the context of slave societies, the emergence even of a vocal personality was deemed a danger to the system, and so was promptly discouraged. Thus, the kind of leadership that could emerge would emerge among those not in bondage—or among those in bondage who had the capacity to conceal their organization for a while. The first type was represented by the many religious prelates and founders of African churches; the latter belonged to those represented by Denmark Vesey, Tackey, Toussaint, and many others who led slave revolts. Both types lived under threats; their sheer persistence has immortalized their struggles.

In this evolution of leadership (for evolution it was), there were many individualistic expressions of leadership (some copied, but not the majority). Such persons merely demonstrated the revulsion, as well as their own sense of worth, toward a system that sought to stifle and restrain their lives, limbs, and thoughts. Examples of this leadership may be found among people who raised slave revolts on board ships at home before transportation, during the middle passage, and on the plantations. Many among such leaders ran away from the plantations soon after landing, like the Maroon communities, or sometime later. By so doing they let it be implied that others could follow their example. It was leadership after a fashion, but it is not the type that this book considers, although it was important and also had its part in the entire evolution of leadership. Its equivalent today would be successful middle-class leaders who would wish to say: "You see I have done it by my own effort; copy me." But the issue is not as simplistic as that, because paths to elevation are fraught with hazards and frustrations. Leaders who sought to carry some or all their brethren with them (the subject of this book) knew the trials and tribulations of trying to lead a desperate, disarranged, and often confused, downtrodden people. But in their endeavors and in their capacity to inspire, they constituted the real leadership of the people.

Much of this latter kind of leadership belongs to the second half of the eighteenth century—a time when the enslavement of Africans and their transference to the Americas had been more than two centuries old. The leadership became stronger and more articulate in the nineteenth century. What has been termed "early leadership" in this chapter belongs to the period dating from the late eighteenth century to the first sixty years of the nineteenth century. This leadership was diverse in kind and preoccupation, but the essential goal it strived for was the same: the uplifting from degradation. It was, of course, concerned with its destiny in a *milieu* that had hitherto been hostile and forbidding, where manifestations of hostility still abounded. It also showed signs of assimilation of aspects of the broader cultural pattern while struggling to retain aspects of its own. Despite the numerous techniques by which the operators of the slave systems in the Americas tended to divide both peoples of African descent and those peoples resulting from intermixture of persons of many origins (principally African, European, and American Indian, as well as Creole), some legal stipulations—ignoring the divide-and-rule techniques of color differentiations and privileges for some whose colors were lighter—tended to throw people of many hues into one melting pot by defining them all as "Negroid" whether or not they had European or Euro-American roots from one parent. Thus, by the broad definitions of North American society, the mulatto, known to the societies of the Caribbean and South America, was unknown in law and custom; mulattoes were still classified as "Negro," unless having first escaped the net by "passing" for white. Thus, "Negro" slaves and free mulattoes, alias "colored" slave and free, found themselves collectively thrown into the general struggle for their common elevation. Of course, where the color-shade complex had wreaked havoc through prolonged inculcation, custom, and even legal stipulations (as it had done in the Caribbean), these *congeries* of people found cooperation difficult and operated as separate classes— separated not only by color-shade gradations, but also by economics and status, apart from the attitudes that had earlier been induced and fostered until they became the tradition. The tragedy of this manifested itself in the St. Dominque (Haiti) struggle for liberation, as the mulattoes' struggle was conceived as separate from the Negro one until the stark realities dawned on both groups that they could lose the struggle if they continued along the path of color superiority and inferiority. Despite the later cooperation, the "mulatto" or "color" problem remains one of the most lasting, unpleasant legacies of French conduct in St. Dominque and other Caribbean theaters of slavery.

Prince Hall

Prince Hall (c. 1748–1807), fraternal leader, was born at Bridgetown in the British West Indian island of Barbados. His father was an Englishman and his mother a free black of French extraction. His father taught him the trade of a leather worker, but Prince was seeking a broader opportunity. In 1765, he sailed for Boston.

He worked as a leather worker in Boston and educated himself at night, studying the Bible zealously, until he became a minister in a Methodist church in Cambridge. Among the blacks in the city of Boston, Prince Hall was looked upon as a leader. He urged the Committee of Safety to let slaves enlist in the American Revolution in 1775, and, in 1777, petitioned the Massachusetts legislature for emancipation, arguing that slavery was incompatible with the patriot cause.

In 1778, Prince Hall enlisted in Medford for a nine-month term in the army during the American Revolution; but when Washington came to assume command at Cambridge, he barred all black soldiers. It is said that Prince Hall called on Washington with a delegation and explained their grievance. They were reinstated. Lord Dunmore, a British commander aware of difficulty on the American side with regard to the black soldiers, issued a proclamation offering slaves and free Afro-Americans service in the British Army. Washington countered with an offer to accept free Afro-Americans, and wrote Congress about his decision, saying: "It has been presented to me, that the free Negroes, who have served in this army, are very much dissatisfied at being discarded. As it is to be apprehended, that they may seek employ in the ministerial (British) army, I have presumed to depart from the resolution respecting them, and have given license for their being enlisted."

On March 6, 1775, a month before fighting broke out at Lexington, Kentucky, Prince Hall and fourteen other free black men were initiated into masonry in Boston by British Army Lodge No. 441 of the Fifty-eighth Regiment of Irish infantry. Hall and his friends became the first Afro-American Masons. When the British regiment withdrew, African Lodge No. 1, the first organized body of black Masons in America, was established on July 3, 1776.

On January 13, 1777, Prince Hall filed a petition with the General Court of Massachusetts, which in part read:

The petition of a great number of Negroes, who are detained in a state of slavery in the very bowels of a free and Christian country, humbly showing, that your petitioners apprehend that they have, in common with all other men, a natural and inalienable right to that freedom, which the great Parent of the universe hath bestowed equally on all mankind, and which they have never forfeited by any compact or agreement whatever. But they were unjustly dragged by the cruel hand of power from their dearest friends, and some of them even torn from the embraces of their tender parents—from a populous pleasant and plentiful country, and in violation of the laws of nature and of nations, and in defiance of all the tender feelings of humanity, brought hither to be sold like beasts of burden, and like them, condemned to slavery for life—among a people possessing the mild religion of Jesus—a people not insensible of the sweets of national freedom, nor without a spirit to resent the unjust endeavors of others to reduce them to a state of bondage and subjection.

The petitioners cannot but express astonishment that it has never been considered, that every principle from which America has acted, in the course of her unhappy difficulties with Great Britain, bears stronger that a thousand arguments in favor of your humble petitioners. They therefore humbly beseech Your Honors to give their petition its due weight and consideration, and cause an act of legislature to be passed, whereby they may be restored to the enjoyment of that freedom, which is the natural right of all men, and their children (who were born in the land of liberty) may not be held as slaves after they arrive at the age of twenty-one years. So may the inhabitants of this state (no longer chargeable with the inconsistency of acting themselves the part which they condemn and oppose in others) be prospered in their glorious struggles for liberty, and have those blessings secured to them by Heaven, of which benevolent minds cannot wish to deprive their fellow man.

After applying, and being refused a charter from white Provincial Masonic authorities in America, Hall wrote to the British Grand Lodge in 1784, and received a charter on September 29, 1784. Due to a mix-up, though, the charter was not delivered for three years, until May 6, 1787. On this date, African Lodge No. 459 was formally organized with Prince Hall as master, and in 1789, Hall organized lodges in Philadelphia and Providence.

In June, 1791, the African Grand Lodge was formed with Prince Hall as grand master.

Prince Hall spoke about the woes and tribulations of blacks to the African Masonic Lodge on June 24, 1797, at Menotomy (now West Cambridge):

Let us see our friends and brethren; and first let us see them dragged from their native country, by the iron hand of tyranny and oppression, from their friends and connections, with weeping eyes and aching hearts, to a strange land, and among a strange people, whose tender mercies are cruel, and there to bear the iron yoke of slavery and cruelty, till death, as a friend, shall relieve them. And must not the unhappy condition of these, our fellow-men, draw forth our hearty prayers and wishes for their deliverance from those merchants and traders.

Now, my brethren, as we see and experience, that all things here are frail and change-able and nothing here to be depended upon: Let us seek those things which are above, and at the same time let us pray to Almighty God, while we remain in the tabernacle, that he would give us the grace of patience and strength to bear up under all our troubles, which at this day God knows we have our share. Patience, I say, for were we not possessed of a great measure of it, you could not bear up under the daily insults you meet with in the streets of Boston, much more on public days of recreation, how are you shamefully abused, and that at such a degree, that you may truly be said to carry your lives in your hands; and the arrows of death are flying about your heads; helpless old women have their clothes torn off their backs, even to the exposing of their nakedness. (Afro-American Ency-clopedia 1974)

In November 1807, Prince Hall caught pneumonia, and died in December of the same year.

In 1808, at the delegate convention of black Masons, the African Grand Lodge was renamed the Prince Hall Grand Lodge. Mr. Nero Prince was elected grand master succeeding Prince Hall.

There were other individual blacks in the eighteenth century who helped pave the way for black liberation. Among several other prominent black pioneers were Crispus Attucks and Benjamin Banneker. These two men epitomized the character of early black leaders in American history.

Crispus Attucks

Crispus Attucks (d. 1770), martyr for freedom, many historians believe was advertised for in 1750 in Boston as a runaway black slave from Framingham, Massachusetts. When Samuel Adams exhorted the dock workers and seamen in the Boston port to demonstrate against the British troops guarding the customs commissioners, Crispus Attucks responded. He led a group of forty or fifty patriots, who converged on a British garrison in King Street. One of the soldiers in the garrison fired, and Crispus Attucks fell, in what became known as the "Boston Massacre" of 1770. Four other Americans died that fatal night: Samuel Maverick, James Cadwell, Samuel Gray, and Patrick Carr.

Contemporary accounts refer to Attucks as a "mulatto" and, despite periodic attempts to disprove it, there seems little doubt that Crispus Attucks was indeed an Afro-American. (A late-nineteenth century historian, J.B. Fisher, asserted that Attucks was a full-blooded Indian, maintaining that the terms *mulatto* and *Indian* were used interchangeably in colonial New England. A more recent appraisal has been offered by noted historian Benjamin Quarles, who depicts Attucks as "a Negro of obscure origin, with some admixture of Indian blood.") Although the exact story may never be known, most modern historians believe that Attucks was a runaway slave from Framingham, Massachusetts, who had settled in Boston in the early 1750s. (In 1750, his alleged "master," William Brown of Framingham, published a reward advertisement in the *Boston Gazette* for "a mulatto fellow, about 27 years of age, named Crispus, 6 feet 2 inches high, short, curl'd hair, his knees together than common.")

Similar to the question of Attucks' identity, historians have differed in regard to his motivation (and that of other colonists) on the day of the "massacre." Nineteenth-century black historian George Washington Williams (1968), for example, portrayed Attucks as a conscious martyr who poured "out his blood as a precious libation on the altar of a people's rights." On the other hand, modern historian Nathan Huggins has suggested that Attucks "and his white comrades were more motivated to harass the British military than to strike a blow for liberty and independence." Whatever the motivation, in the period immediately preceding the

Revolution, the death of Crispus Attucks did assume the status of martyrdom to thousands of American colonists. His sacrifice (be it deliberate or an accident of folly) has long since been recognized, and his place as an Afro-American "hero" will undoubtedly persevere.

Benjamin Banneker

Benjamin Banneker (1731–1806), inventor and writer, was born on November 9 of a free mother and slave father (who later purchased his own freedom) in Ellicot, Maryland.

Banneker was born free, enabling him to attend an integrated school. In 1761, he constructed the first wooden clock made in America.

In 1789, he predicted the solar eclipse, and within a few years published an almanac containing tide tables, future eclipses, medicinal products, and formulas. It was the first time that an American black had written a scientific book in the United States.

Banneker was later appointed by George Washington to a commission that planned the city of Washington. When Major L'Enfant, chairman of the commission, resigned and took the plans of the city back to France with him, Banneker reproduced the plans, in their entirety, from memory.

When Banneker was fifty years old, there were approximately 757,000 black people in the United States, of which only 59,000 were free. When Thomas Jefferson, then secretary of state under George Washington, doubted the mental capacity of Afro-Americans, Banneker (1792) wrote to Jefferson on August 19, 1791:

This, Sir, was a time when you clearly saw into the injustice of a state of slavery, and in which you had just apprehensions of the horrors of its condition. It was then that your abhorrence thereof was so excited that you publicly held forth this true and invaluable doctrine, which is worthy to be recorded and remembered in all succeeding ages: "We hold these truths to be self-evident, that all men are created equal; that they are endowed by their Creator with certain inalienable rights, and that among these are life, liberty, and the pursuit of happiness."

Jefferson sent Banneker the following reply:

Philadelphia, Aug. 30, 1791

Sir,

I thank you most sincerely, for your letter of the 19th instant, and for the Almanac it contained. Nobody wishes more than I do to see such proofs as you exhibit, that nature has given to our black brethren talents equal to those of the other color of men; and that the appearance of the want of them is owing merely to the degraded condition of their existence, both in Africa and America. I can add with truth that nobody wishes more ardently to see a good system commenced, for raising the condition, both of their body and mind, to what it ought to be, as far as the imbecility of their present existence, and other circumstances, which cannot be neglected, will admit.

I have taken the liberty of sending your Almanac to Monsieur de Condorcet, Secretary of the Academy of Sciences, at Paris, and Member of the Philanthropic Society, because I considered it as a document to which your whole color have a right for their justification against the doubts which have been entertained of them.

> I am, with great esteem, Sir,
> Your most obedient humble servant,
> Tho. Jefferson
> (Banneker, 1792)

In summary, although black Americans are products of two cultures, African and American, the black leadership that emerged in the eighteenth century was deeply rooted in black Americans' reaction to their experiences in slavery. Thus, "the peculiar institution," with its plantation mentality, is the genesis of black leadership in America. The pattern of this leadership has experienced a tradition of reacting, for the most part, to the "American dilemma" (the black problem in American democracy) (Myrdal, 1944).

6

Black Leadership in the Nineteenth Century: Before the War

The list of black leaders in the nineteenth century, especially those leaders who were actively engaged in the antislavery movement, is long. Among the prominent were: Gabriel, Denmark Vesey, Nat Turner, Paul Cuffe, Sojourner Truth, Rev. Henry Highland, Richard Allen, Henry Highland Calls, Daniel Payne, Joseph Cinque, Frederick Douglass, David Walker, Pierra Bonga, Edward Rose, James P. Beckwourth, Harriet Tubman, and Samuel Burris. Only a few of these leaders are highlighted in this chapter, under three categories: the Slave Protest Movement, the Abolitionist Movement, and the Westward Movement.

THE SLAVE PROTEST MOVEMENT

The most dramatic and forceful form of African slave protest and resistance in the antebellum South was the organized slave rebellion. There were approximately 2,000 rebellions and/or conspiracies to rebel in the South prior to 1860. The most significant of these were:

1. Gabriel's Revolt (1800)
2. Denmark Vesey's Conspiracy (1822)
3. Nat Turner's Insurrection (1831)

Gabriel

Gabriel (1775–1800) was a slave of Thomas Prosser of Herico County, Virginia. He and another slave, Jack Bowler, organized an estimated 2,000 slaves for the purpose of seizing Richmond. About 32,000 black slaves versus 8,000 whites lived in the immediate vicinity. It was hoped that if Richmond were seized, the slaves would join forces with Gabriel and then proceed to liberate all of Virginia's 300,000 Africans. All slave owners were to be massacred with swords and bayonets, and other weapons. The revolt was planned for August 30, 1800. The conspiracy, however, was betrayed by two slaves who wanted to spare their masters. Martial law was declared, and 600 armed militiamen hunted down most of the slaves. Thirty-five were arrested and executed. Gabriel was hanged December 7, 1800.

Denmark Vesey

The second major conspiracy of the South was led by Denmark Vesey (1767–1822). A slave for over thirty years, he purchased his freedom with money he won in a lottery in 1800. He later became a Methodist minister, his church as a base of operations for a proposed siege of Charleston, South Carolina. He built weapons and planned for action the second Sunday of July 1822. His goal never materialized, for he was also betrayed by internal informers and spies who alerted Charleston authorities. Nine thousand Africans had been enlisted in the Vesey plot, but only forty-seven and Vesey were executed.

Nat Turner

The most spectacular slave insurrection in American history occurred on August 21, 1831, and was led by a slave preacher in Southampton County, Virginia. Born in 1800, Nat Turner (d. 1831) was a visionary mystic who claimed that God had directed him to strike a divine blow against the institution of slavery. On the appointed day, Turner and six confederates initiated their revolt by killing Turner's master, Joseph Travis, and his family. Within twenty-four hours, Turner killed sixty whites, secured guns and ammunition, and increased his army to sixty men. However, state and federal troops overpowered Turner. In the end, more than 100 slaves were killed, twenty of which, including Turner, were tried and executed.

The Nat Turner Insurrection sent a message throughout the white South. State legislatures were called into special sessions, slave codes were strengthened, and every movement of slaves was carefully watched. Appearing shortly after the publication of the first issue of abolitionist William Lloyd Garrison's *The Liberator* (January 1, 1831), the Turner uprising simply added fuel to the already intense sectional controversy between Northern antislavery and Southern proslavery interests. More significantly the Nat Turner Insurrection provides ample evidence that the slaves were not just happy-go-lucky "Sambos." The Sambo stereotype of African slaves, and by extension of modern African-Americans, is that American blacks are by nature servile, fawning, cringing, docile, irresponsible, lazy, humble, dependent, prone to lying and stealing, grinningly happy, and basically infantile. In other words, the white American conception of Sambo is that of a perpetual child incapable of maturity, merely sitting, grinning, and eating in a watermelon patch.

That some modern blacks as well as some whites possess some or all of these Sambo characteristics cannot be denied. To assume, however, that all black Americans *per se* are Sambos would be an absurd distortion of rarity.

On the other hand, the question of whether Afro-American slaves were Sambos is debatable. One school of thought accepts the Sambo-type personality as being characteristic of most slaves. Historian Stanley Elkins maintains that Africans were transformed into childlike creatures by the harsh process of brainwashing, similar to the Nazi brainwashing techniques in Jewish concentration camps during the 1930s and 1940s. Another school argues that although plantation slaves may have acted as Sambos, they were merely playing a role dictated by the sheer helplessness of their situation. There is no reason to conclude, according to historian John Hope Franklin (1994), "that the personality of the slave was permanently impaired by his engaging in duplicity in the slave–master relationships." He argues that some of the slave actions were for the purpose of misleading the slave owners regarding their true feelings.

THE ABOLITIONIST MOVEMENT

Dred Scott

Dred Scott (1800–1858) was the most famous slave of his time. He was sold to an army surgeon and later taken to free territory in the North, where slavery was prohibited. It was there that Scott brought suit for his freedom. The Supreme Court ruled against him. The Court declared him a slave, and stated further that slaves could not become citizens of the United States.

Dred Scott Case

The Dred Scott case (1857) was decided by the United States Supreme Court on March 6, 1857. The Court held that a black, a slave under the laws of Missouri, had no constitutional right to sue in a federal court in order to obtain his freedom.

The importance of the case is that it concerns issues involving political controversies that were broader than those discussed in the opinion.

The Kansas-Nebraska Act of 1854 repealed provisions of the Missouri Compromise that excluded slavery from the northern portion of the Louisiana Purchase. This repeal and the bloody fighting in Kansas made sectional bitterness about slavery more intense. The South justified the new legislation by contending that Congress had never had the constitutional power to exclude slavery from the territories of the United States. The Northern leaders contended that the Supreme Court had not had an occasion to decide the constitutional question.

At first, the Court arranged to decide the Dred Scott case without any discussion of the power of Congress over slavery in the territory, but two dissenting judges argued that Congress had the power, so the majority of the Court decided to enlarge their discussion and deny the power. Some hoped that the decision of the United States Supreme Court would settle the question, and even save the Union.

The seven majority judges wrote opinions. Chief Justice Taney, it is generally considered, was the opinion of the Court, but on one of the contentions, only two of his associates agreed with him.

Dred Scott claimed his freedom on the grounds that with the consent of his master, he had lived in a territory where slavery was forbidden. Chief Justice Taney (U.S. Supreme Court, 1860) said that "within the meaning of the Constitution, the Negro was not a citizen who had a right to sue in the Federal Court by virtue of his citizenship." His argument was as follows: "When the Constitution was adopted, Negroes were regarded as persons of an inferior order. They were not regarded as citizens, and they were not intended to be included by the Constitutional provision given to citizens of different States the right to sue in Federal courts."

His second argument was that, apart from the question as to whether any black could be a citizen in the Constitutional sense, no slave could be *made* a citizen. Dred Scott had originally been a slave. He had not become free by residence in territory covered by the Missouri Compromise, because Congress had no constitutional power to enact the Missouri Compromise. Unless Dred Scott had some other claim to freedom, he was still a slave, and, therefore, not a citizen entitled to sue in the Federal Court.

The third contention of Chief Justice Taney was that "whatever the temporary effect of Dred Scott's brief residence in the free State of Illinois, his status after his return to Missouri was determined by Missouri law. The Missouri courts had held that he was a slave; therefore, he was not a citizen and, therefore, could not sue in the Federal Court."

On the first point, Chief Justice Taney expressed an opinion that he had long held and that he had submitted officially twenty-five years earlier, when he was attorney general of the United States. Though some of his associates probably agreed privately in the opinion, only two of them concurred that the statement was necessary to the decision of the Dred Scott case. The holding was never repudiated by the Court itself, but it was superseded by that part of the Fourteenth Amendment that declares that "[a]ll persons born or naturalized in the United States and subject to the jurisdiction thereof, are citizens of the United States and of the State wherein they reside."

As to the second point, it went to the heart of the discussion about the extension of slavery. The decision that Congress had no power to exclude slavery from the territories struck a blow to the contention of the antislavery forces. The discussion of the question was logically relevant according to the way Chief Justice Taney wrote it.

The case might have been decided on the third point alone, without commitment as to the other two points. Justices McLean and Curtis, in dissent, renounced the unnecessary breadth of the decision.

The abolitionist press followed with attacks on the Supreme Court, which were very bitter. These inflamed discussions also, however, helped along the situation, but eventually would precipitate the Civil War.

The broad writing of the decision, therefore, had a different effect from what the judges had wanted it to be. Aside from the sectional interest, the case is important; it was the first in more than a half a century in which the Supreme Court held an act of Congress unconstitutional.

Frederick Douglass

We would begin this section with a man whose life and works have been well documented in American history (White, 1985; Franklin, 1985; Factor, 1970; Douglass, 1884; Holland, 1891). Clearly, Frederick Douglass (1817–1895) epitomizes the black response to America. He was a man of several talents and ideals. His activities ranged from the antislavery movement to President Lincoln's consultant on African-American affairs. He interpreted the president and the party to his people, and black people to white leaders. Douglass' influence, contacts, and prestige in the Republican Party enhanced his position of race leadership. At the same time, his growing strength among the black citizenry authenticated his right to speak as their representative to the white community. He always believed that there could be progress for his people, but not without struggle.

Douglass, the abolitionist, was born in slavery on the eastern shore of Maryland. He educated himself and had an inquiring mind and extraordinary gift of oratory. During the Civil War, Douglass used his oratory to condemn slavery, which he knew firsthand. He was over six feet tall with a vast, well-proportioned head and a great shock of kinky hair.

From 1845 to 1895, Frederick Douglass was in the forefront of black leadership as an orator, an abolitionist, an editor, a politician, and a prophet. He was born Frederick Augustus Washington Bailey in February, 1817. It was rumored that his father was his master and that he only saw his mother several times. Under slavery, there was no father or mother.

Over 110 years ago, Douglass staged a sit-in on a Massachusetts railroad, because he wanted integrated schools in Rochester, New York. He said,

The whole story of the progress of human liberty shows that all concessions yet made to her august claims had been borne of earnest struggle. If there is no struggle, there is no progress. Those who profess to favor freedom and yet deprecate agitation are men who want crops without plowing up the ground; they want rain without thunder and lightning. They want the ocean without the awful roar of many waters. . . . This struggle may be a moral one, or it may be a physical one, or it may be both moral and physical, but it must be a struggle. Power concedes nothing without a demand. It never did, and it never will. Men may not get all they pay for in this world, but they must certainly pay for all they get. If we ever get free from the oppressions and wrongs heaped upon us, we must pay for their removal. We must do this by labor, by suffering, by sacrifice, and if needs be, by our lives and the lives of others.

In 1838, at the age of twenty-one, Douglass escaped from slavery. He began to read Garrison's *Liberator,* the mouthpiece of the abolitionist movement, and to attend meetings. By 1841, he was the leader of the black community. Garrison heard Douglass speak and offered him $450 a year to become a lecturer for the Massachusetts Antislavery Society. Douglass accepted, and at age twenty-four was in the fight to free slaves.

He worked for six years with Mr. Garrison, and in 1847, he went out on his own to publish a newspaper in Rochester, New York, called the *North Star.* As superintendent of the Underground Railroad in Rochester, he helped many slaves escape into Canada.

Frederick Douglass was an active sympathizer for women's rights, having participated in the 1848 Seneca Falls Convention, which was the first meeting of the suffragettes. He died in Washington, D.C., on February 20, 1895.

Harriet Tubman

Harriet Ross Tubman (c. 1821–1913) was a daring woman conductor on the Underground Railroad who escaped from slavery and dared to return to her former master's plantation to help others escape to freedom. A tablet commemorating her work was unveiled in Auburn, New York, on June 12, 1914, by the Cayuga County Historical Association.

"The Underground Railroad" was the name given to the method of helping slaves escape from bondage along secret routes on land and on sea to the free states of the North and to eventual freedom and safety in Canada. The "stations" along the "tracks" of the Underground Railroad were homes of dedicated abolitionists in which the fugitives were sheltered, fed, and concealed until nightfall, before being handed over to the next "conductor."

Harriet Tubman always carried a gun or a revolver, which had a twofold purpose; one was to see that any wavering slave of her contingent was given an explanation of why he or she could not turn back and had to continue. She had seen her brothers lose heart and turn back. If one wavered or faltered, then she would take her revolver and say, "You'll be free or die"—and it always followed that they managed to have the strength to go on.

Over the course of ten years, Harriet Tubman made nineteen secret trips below the Mason-Dixon Line and brought to freedom over 300 slaves. She was often called "Moses" because, like Moses in the Bible, she delivered her people from slavery into the promised land of freedom. Slave owners offered a $4,000 reward for her capture.

In 1860, she began to make speeches at both the women's rights meetings and at abolitionist meetings. She also attended private meetings, and her opinions were greatly respected. She died of pneumonia in Auburn in March 1913.

David Walker

It should be noted here that the publication in 1829 of David Walker's (1785–1830) *Approach to the Coloured Citizens of the World* was an expression of David Walker's mission to liberate the black race by whatever means necessary. The appearance of David Walker marked a transition in the liberation movement from the quiet protest of the colonial leaders to the revolutionary posture of the militant abolitionists.

David Walker was born in Wilmington, North Carolina, in 1785. The Revolutionary War phrases of "liberty" and "pursuit of happiness" were still echoing faintly in the air. His mother was free, which entitled him to the status of free-born, but his father, Merel Walker, was a slave. Young David hated slavery. He finally left home and wandered to Boston, where he became a permanent resident, and in 1827 opened a second-hand clothing store.

David Walker was self-taught and read literature on human slavery extensively. He concentrated on the history of resistance to oppression. He became an abolitionist and writer, publishing his first edition of *Appeal* in 1829. He proclaimed to the slaves, ". . . It is no more harm for you to kill the man who is trying to kill you, than it is for you to take of drink of water." Although the *Appeal* was the only work produced by Walker, it was the boldest attack by a black writer against slavery in America at that time.

Martin R. Delany

The nineteenth century was a crucial period for black men, because of the disquieting forces of slavery and the imperialism at work in America and Africa. During the century, black leaders emerged in both Africa and America to challenge white power and prevent the complete subjugation of their race. One of these leaders was Martin Robinson Delany (1812–1885). Although born in the United States, Delany was passionately proud of his African ancestry. His attachment to the motherland became a major factor in the development of his Pan-African ideology. Delany clung to the concept that black men from the New World should join with Africans to build viable nationalities on the continent. Thus, he became one of the most articulate Afro-American precursors of Pan-Africanism in the nineteenth century.

Throughout his long life, Delany worked at various occupations. In Pittsburgh he published a newspaper, and subsequently studied medicine. At the same time, he developed into an avid nationalist and eventually led a movement for emigration to Africa.

Recent scholars have begun to recognize Delany's contributions to Pan-Africanism. Such Africanist historians as Hollis R. Lynch, George Shepperson, and A.H.M. Kirk-Green have alluded to Delany's work, but noted the lack of available research data. (No definitive study had been made of Delany's back-to-Africa movement, its results, or its significance regarding the interaction of Africans and Afro-Americans in the nineteenth century.)

Delany's early experience of white racism, then, became the chief motivation for his nationalism. In his formative years, he had seen the degradation of slavery in the South, and he had witnessed prejudice against free blacks in the North. After observing such outrages, Delany decided to be a spokesman for his people's rights. As he grew older, however, he embraced emigrationism. Although his effort to take some of his countrymen to Africa was unsuccessful, Delany emerged as one of the earliest exponents of Pan-Africanism.

BLACK LEADERSHIP AND THE WESTWARD MOVEMENT

Franklin (1994) provides an excellent summary of black pioneers in the westward movement. In addition, it is important to note other scholarly works in this area. Frontier influences were treated in a series of highly significant essays in Frederick Turner, *The Frontier in American History* (1920); William Katz, *The Black West* (1971), a documentary and pictorial history of African-Americans in the westward movement; Kenneth Porter, *The Negro on the American Frontier* (1971); and W. Sherman Savage, *Blacks in the West* (1976). Black roles in the movement have also been discussed in several essays in the *Journal of Negro History*.

All too frequently, students of history overlook the role of African-Americans in the exploration and settlement of the American West. Whenever white Americans undertook the task of winning the West, black Americans, slave and free, were involved in the process. Thus, when Meriwether Lewis and William Clark set out in 1803 under orders from President Jefferson to explore the Louisiana Territory recently purchased from France, Clark took with him his trusted slave, York. A large and powerful man, York contributed to the success of the expedition by befriending and entertaining the Indians and providing sustenance for the explorers through his considerable skill in hunting and fishing. Upon completion of the expedition, Clark emancipated York; legend has it that York returned to the Western interior, where he became a chief in an Indian tribe.

In the immensely profitable fur trade that followed in the wake of the Lewis and Clark expedition, black trappers quite frequently were the most reliable liaison between white entrepreneurs and the Indians. While their reliability and integrity have often suffered at the hands of many recognized historians of the West, their presence—and indeed their contributions—can hardly be denied. In the 1820s, for example, Edward Rose served as a guide, hunter. and interpreter for the Missouri Fur Company. Despite the fact that Washington Irving was among those who spoke of Rose's bad character and reputation, a contemporary, Col. Henry Leavenworth, wrote in 1823 that Rose had resided among the Indians for several years, "knew their language, and they were much attached to him." Leavenworth and, more recently, Kenneth W. Porter, have spoken of Rose's invaluable services in the fur-trading activities in the West.

In the Minnesota Territory, several blacks became prominent as trappers and traders. Among them was Pierre Bonga, a trusted slave of a Canadian fur trapper for the North West Company. Bonga was a skillful interpreter and did much of the negotiating with the Chippewas for his owner's company. His son, George, became even more proficient, having learned English, French, Chippewa, and several other Indian languages. As an assistant and interpreter for Governor Lewis Cass of the Michigan Territory, George Bonga negotiated treaties with the Indians even while working as a voyager for the American Fur Company. In time he became a free man and a "prominent trader of wealth and consequence." According to William L. Katz (1971), Bonga Township in Cass County, Michigan, is named for Bonga's family.

Easily the most intrepid and remarkable of the black explorers of the American West was James P. Beckwourth. Born in 1798 of racially mixed parentage, Beckwourth served an apprenticeship to a St. Louis blacksmith. Desiring more freedom, he fled westward and secured employment with the Rocky Mountain Fur Company. Soon he became an accomplished wilderness fighter, equally skilled in the use of the gun, bowie knife, and tomahawk. In 1824 he was adopted by the Crow Indians, became their beloved "Morning Star," and married the chief's daughter. He led the Crows in numerous bloody raids and, rising to the position of chief, was known as "Bloody Arm." He had a varied career, serving as a scout in the third Seminole war in Florida and trapping and prospecting for gold in California. In 1850, he discovered the pass in the Sierra Nevada near Reno that still bears his name.

There were others, including John Marsant and John Stewart, who served as missionaries to the Indians. Among still other African-Americans who participated in the westward march were those who had been emancipated by John Randolph of Virginia and who settled in Ohio: those who migrated from Northampton County, North Carolina, and settled in Indiana; and the celebrated sculptress Edmonia Lewis, part Chippewa, who attended Oberlin College before moving on to Boston, where she studied the art for which she later became famous. There were indeed hundreds of others—some obscure and others well known, at least in their time—who left their mark as black contributors in the winning of the West.

The westward movement was accelerated by the War of 1812. Slavery flourished as the soil was exploited, and many land-hungry planters, with their slaves, deserted older regions of the South to push into the fertile lands of the Gulf region. Forces set in motion by the emergence of this new kingdom largely account for the United States' acquisition of Florida and Texas. They also help explain the reason for Southern insistence that the entrance of Missouri into the Union be as a slave state.

7

Black Leadership in the Nineteenth Century: The Civil War and Its Aftermath

The role of blacks in the Civil War, especially the "buffalo soldiers," has been extensively documented (Hargrove, 1985; Billington, 1989, 1991; Arnold, 1990; Knapp, 1992; Schubert, 1993). For a generation following the Civil War, two regiments of black cavalry of the U.S. Army—the Ninth and Tenth—served meritoriously on the western frontier. Concentrated at one time or another in New Mexico, Arizona, Colorado, and the Dakotas, these troops were called "buffalo soldiers" by the American Indians. The traditional account for the origin of this term is that the Indians saw a similarity between the hair of the black soldier and that of the buffalo. The term was not used in a derogatory manner, because the buffalo was considered to be a sacred animal by the Indians. Accordingly, the black troops willingly accepted their designation, even to the point of adopting the buffalo as a part of their regimental insignia. More than 30,000 black soldiers died in the Civil War.

President Lincoln's declaration in August 1861 that his primary objective in the Civil War was "to save the Union" and "not either to save or destroy slavery" affirmed a war aim widely shared by Northern whites. Preservation of the Union, not abolition of slavery, was the stated goal of the Lincoln administration. This attitude, distasteful as it was to black people and abolitionists, gradually gave way to a more humanitarian goal. The freeing of the slaves was a significant result of the war.

When Lincoln called for volunteers after the bombardment of Fort Sumter, blacks were prominent among those who rushed to offer their services. Their offers were rejected, and for the first eighteen months blacks were denied permission to enlist in the armed forces of the Union. Despite continuing opposition of many Northern whites to arm blacks and permit them to wear uniforms, the exclusion policy had to be abandoned. The length of the conflict and the need for more manpower led not only to a change in Union policy but to the active recruit-ment and use of black fighting men.

Slaves and free blacks were pressed into the service of the Confederacy as laborers. This kind of assistance was welcomed, but to arm blacks and ask them to fight was quite another thing. Reverses in the field and manpower shortages combined to produce enough of a change in official thinking, so that by March 1865 the Confederate Congress provided for the recruiting of slaves to be used as soldiers. By this time the war, to all intents and purposes, was over.

Franklin (1994) correctly characterizes federal policy concerning black people at the beginning of the war as "uncertain" and "vacillating." Supporting this description is the lack of uniformity in the matters of relief and employment extended to slaves who poured into Union lines as the federal armies moved into the South. The question of the disposal of fugitive slaves, as a practical matter, was at first handled by the commanding officers in the field. Uniform treatment had to wait until the enactment of the Conscription Act by Congress in August 1861. The lack of a uniform federal policy for relief of freedmen prompted pri-vate agencies to emerge and to render aid. Private organizations also made sig-nificant contributions toward the education of the former slaves.

Despite continued opposition from articulate segments of the Northern white population to the black man's utilization as a soldier, the policy of bypassing him had to be abandoned. The length of the war and the consequent need for more manpower led to the official decision to enlist blacks. Even before the official pol-icy was enunciated, General David Hunter, Commander of the Department of the South, had made an abortive attempt to organize an all-black regiment. Meanwhile, hostile feelings toward blacks (encouraged by the irresponsible jour-nalism of anti-administration newspaper editors), fear of job competition from freed blacks, and resistance to being drafted help explain the New York draft riots of 1863.

Lincoln's views on emancipation included gradual emancipation with finan-cial compensation to owners, and subsequent removal of freedmen from the United States. During the war, laws were passed that liberated slaves in the District of Columbia and abolished slavery in the territories. Another law set free all slaves escaping from disloyal masters into Union-held territory. However, the president was unsuccessful in his efforts to persuade masters of slaves in the loyal border slave states to accept any plan for compensated emancipation.

RECONSTRUCTION AND BLACK LEADERSHIP

The Civil War resolved two important controversies: It ended chattel slavery and permanently established the ultimate supremacy of the national government. On the other hand, the war created problems, not just for the South but for all sec-tions of the nation. Perhaps the greatest effect of the conflict was the stimulation that it gave to industrial growth in the North. Along with this stimulation came the growing power of industrial capitalism and the rise in political importance of the Northern business and financial leaders. Even before the war, the Republican party had allied itself with the Northern industrialists, and this alliance became stronger in the post-war years. The party sponsored protective tariffs, aided railroads, opposed inflation, and aided industrial capitalism. Growing interest in these areas was accompanied by a lessening of concern for the freedmen on the part of Congress and the North. It is necessary to understand this in order to assess properly what went on in the South between 1865 and 1876, as well as to understand the direction taken by the nation after the settling of the disputed presidential election of the latter year.

Thus, Reconstruction was not simply a Southern phenomenon, but an integral part of the nation's history. Most citizens were affected by problems following the war, but it was the freed slave who was the target of much attention, and ultimately the victim of the post-war chaos. In the South, an entirely new political structure had to be erected out of the wreckage left by war, with consideration given to the new rights and duties of the freedmen. Two separate and distinct policies of reconstruction were tried. The first followed the beliefs and ideas of Presidents Lincoln and Johnson. This presidential plan encountered much opposition from Congress and was eventually defeated.

The congressional plan, which replaced that of President Johnson, provided for the active participation of black men in the drawing up of new state constitutions and in the political process of each of the reconstructed Southern states. Erected after black suffrage was instituted, these so-called Radical Republican governments were administered by a coalition of whites and blacks. Despite assertions to the contrary, these governments were at no time ruled by illiterate blacks.

During the years after 1867, black people benefited from the widespread interest in their education and rehabilitation. This interest was transformed into action by private organizations, as well as by the federal government. The adoption of the Fourteenth and Fifteenth Amendments to the United States Constitution represented attempts to write into the supreme law certain safeguards for blacks. It is unfortunate that in succeeding decades the intent of these amendments was either circumvented or ignored.

Among the immediate post-war problems was that of economic rehabilitation. Other pressing problems were the restoration of seceded states to their place in the Union and, extremely important, the role of the black man in this process. In solving these problems, it was essential to try to replace sectional bitterness with a new spirit of conciliation and goodwill.

Black Republican Reconstruction

"Black Republican Reconstruction" is an expression used to describe those years during the Reconstruction era after the Civil War in which former black slaves, with the aid of northern carpetbaggers and southern scalawags, won election to political offices throughout the former Confederacy. The term "Black Republican" itself was an expression of contempt used by white southerners to describe white Radical Republicans who aided freedmen in their quest for public office during the late 1860s and early 1870s. During this period, nearly thirty southern blacks won election to the U.S. Congress, while two southern state legislatures (Louisiana and South Carolina) were for a brief time dominated by black majorities. With but few exceptions, however, these black officeholders were used as pawns by the real "rulers" of "Black Republican" governments, the carpetbaggers and scalawags. Southern freedmen were unscrupulously used by Republican politicians to build a viable party machine in the South, while never sharing in the spoils of office in proportion to their numerical strength.

Freedmen's Bureau

Established by Congress on March 3, 1865, the Freedmen's Bureau was designed to protect the interests of former slaves ("freedmen") and displaced southern whites ("loyal refugees") following the American Civil War. Intended primarily to act as a safeguard for the freedmen against possible attempts at re-enslavement, the bureau was also empowered to provide the former slaves with food, medical and hospital care, educational facilities, and homestead land. In addition, the bureau assisted the freedmen in obtaining employment, settling legal disputes, and finding suitable housing facilities. Functioning the aegis of the War Department, the Freedmen's Bureau was headed by General O.O. Howard. Although the official "life" of the bureau extended until 1872, most of its major objectives were accomplished by 1869.

During late 1865 and early 1866, agents of the Freedmen's Bureau, scattered throughout the South, were primarily concerned with helping the former slave and refugees return home and providing medical services, as well as dressing and feeding approximately 50,000 to 150,000 individuals daily. More significant, perhaps, were the educational projects of the bureau. In addition to building more than one thousand schools for freedmen, the bureau spent nearly $500,000 to establish Afro-American teacher-training institutions.

The humanitarian activities and accomplishments of the Freedmen's Bureau were somewhat offset by the fact that bureau officials in the South, who were invariably Republicans, often interfered in local political affairs. Moreover, the charge that the bureau was an agent of Republican control throughout the South cannot be refuted. Many officials of the agency served as Republican organizers among the former slaves following the passage of the Fifteenth Amendment. "This political activity," according to historian George R. Bentley, "probably hurt the freedmen more than it helped them, for black support of the Republicans increased the race prejudice of white southerners."

The men and women who provided leadership for the black community after the Civil War assumed an enormous burden (Lowe, 1995). The onset of congressional reconstruction in 1867 brought black southerners their first opportunity to hold public office. Those who accepted the challenge generally faced extreme hostility from the majority of whites, and only lukewarm support from their colleagues in the fledgling Republican party. Moreover, many were still adjusting to the responsibilities of earning a living and supporting their families as free men and women. It is difficult to imagine the courage and perseverance required of the first black officeholders across the old Confederacy, especially those who operated exclusively at the local level in rural areas.

For example, in 1868, John Willis Menard (1839–1893) of Louisiana, was the first black elected to the U.S. Congress. He was awarded his full salary, but never seated. The committee on elections ruled that it was too early to admit a black to Congress. He was appointed inspector of customs of the port of New Orleans.

In recent years, historians have given considerable attention to black leaders during Reconstruction, but most of the leaders studied held at least a few state-level positions, usually serving in constitutional conventions or state legislatures. The same is true of the black leaders described in the works of Texas historians. J. Mason Brewer's 1935 pioneering study dealt only with state legislators. Merline Pitre's *Through Many Dangers, Toils and Snares: Black Leadership in Texas, 1868–1900* (1997) documented the struggles of those who served in the constitutional conventions of 1868–1869 and 1875, and in the legislature from Reconstruction to the turn of the century. An 1986 article by Alwyn Barr provided a notable analysis of the fourteen African-Americans who served in the Twelfth Legislature (1870–1871). Thus, in Texas, as across the South, much less attention has been given to blacks who held office only at the local level in rural areas— those who served, for example, on commissioners courts or in lesser positions in county government. Reasons for this neglect are numerous, the most obvious being the difficulty of finding enough material to tell the stories of officeholders who never held office outside a particular county. Therefore, every shred of evidence on the experiences of local black officeholders is valuable.

The officeholders who provided leadership for the southern black community after the Civil War were faced with tremendous responsibilities. In order to secure full participation in the political process for themselves and their followers, they were required to perform herculean labors. They had to join white Unionists and Republicans (whose interests were not always congruent with their own) in creating the machinery for a new political party, a formidable job in itself. They also had to define black Americans' place in the nation's political life, mold opinion among inexperienced black voters (most of whom were illiterate), hold offices never before held by blacks, overcome white hostility, and accomplish all these objectives under the scrutiny of the national white majority, some of whom anticipated their humiliating failure and some of whom expected their instant success.

Partly because of the difficulties they faced and partly because they were the leaders of a completely new class of American citizens, black leaders of the Reconstruction era have interested historians for more than a century. Most early treatments dismissed these leaders as the "dregs of the population," uneducated, propertyless, and generally worthless to society. This negative estimation of black Reconstructionists was first countered by black scholars beginning in the 1910s and 1920s. The Rehabilitation School sought to provide a more balanced, and positive, picture of black leaders by pointing out that many of them were educated, intelligent property holders who "gave a good account of themselves" in Reconstruction politics. In the 1930s and 1940s a few white scholars joined the movement, and three decades later the "revisionist" school of Reconstruction historiography, appearing during the height of the civil rights movement, swept away all before it and included many studies that contributed to the rehabilitation of black leadership during Reconstruction (Rabinowitz, 1982).

More recent scholars have hailed the destruction of the negative stereotypes of black Reconstruction leaders, but they have also called for historians to move on to new approaches, especially collective biographies, in order to develop a deeper understanding of political leadership in the emergent black community of Reconstruction. Since the 1970s, increasing numbers of collective biographies have appeared in print. Most of these, however, have examined black leaders on the state and national levels, rather than on the local level. The very few collective studies of local black leaders have virtually all concentrated on cities—New Orleans, Memphis, Petersburg, Richmond, Lynchburg, and a few others (Franklin and Meier, 1982; Rankin 1974).

The aforementioned pattern of collective biographies of black leaders is beginning to emerge because the sources necessary to study state and national leaders and urban black leadership are much richer and more numerous than those for county and local leaders stationed outside cities. Newspapers followed the activities of state and national officials very closely, and the records of federal, state, and city governments provide valuable information not usually available for black leaders outside urban areas. In fact, in most southern states scholars are not even certain which black men provided leadership at the local level. Only three collective biographies of local non-urban black leaders have been published, and each deals with very small numbers. Martin Abbott (1959) studied eighteen county leaders; Edward Magdol (1974) examined forty-six men in five southern states; and Richard Lowe (1995) examined five local leaders in Virginia: Ordand Brown, Thoma Wood, Tazewell Branch, James Bland, and Charles Hodges.

Congressional Reconstruction

To some in Congress, it was obvious that radical measures were necessary to halt disloyalty in the South. Two abolitionists, Thaddeus Stevens in the House and Charles Sumner in the Senate, led the "Radicals" of Congress to enact new laws. Over the vetoes of President Johnson, Congress passed legislation that provided for military control of the South, gave equal rights to blacks, and canceled the rights of ex-Confederate leaders.

Reconstruction in the South

In the South, "Radical Reconstruction" led to the beginning of a new social order. The former slaves' right to vote was protected by the Fourteenth and

Fifteenth Amendments to the Constitution. In an 1864 letter to General Wadsworth of New York, President Lincoln had said that he felt that black soldiers "have demonstrated in blood their right to the ballot, which is but the human protection of the flag they have so fearlessly defended." Congressman Thaddeus Stevens saw the suffrage of freedmen as absolutely necessary to protect their rights and keep the South loyal. "If it be just," he said, "it should not be denied; if it be necessary, it should be adopted; if it be punishment to traitors, they deserve it." Although the majority of ex-slaves could neither read nor write, neither could many white southern voters or European immigrants who voted in northern cities.

Blacks and poor whites then began rebuilding their state governments. They drew up new constitutions, approved the Fourteenth and Fifteenth Amendments, returned their states to the Union, and elected men to Congress. Although black voters outnumbered whites in several states, they never sought to control any government at any time. Though blacks held offices from local sheriff to state governor, they were always willing to support white candidates. One black, P.B.S. Pinchback (1837–1920), served forty-three days as Governor of Louisiana when the white governor was removed by impeachment.

At South Carolina's Constitutional Convention, blacks played a decisive role— there were 76 of them among the 131 delegates. Among the delegates were such brilliant and educated blacks as Francis Cardoza and Robert B. Elliott, both educated at British universities. But it was another black college graduate and delegate, Reverend Richard Cain, who proclaimed the great purpose of the convention:

I want a constitution that shall do justice to all men. I have no prejudices and feel above making any distinctions. . . . I hope we will take hold high upon the highway of human progress. . . . I want to see internal improvements, the railroads rebuilt, and, in fact, the whole internal resources of the State so developed that she shall be brought back more happy and prosperous than she ever was. (Bennett 1969)

The constitution drawn up by the blacks and whites of South Carolina brought the great reforms of the North to the South. Louis F. Post, who was to serve Woodrow Wilson for eight years as assistant secretary of labor, was present in South Carolina and recalled: "By every truly democratic test, that black-made constitution of South Carolina stands shoulder high above the white man's Constitution which it superseded." The state lowered the taxes on the poor, abolished imprisonment for debt, and granted voting rights to all, regardless of property or race. The state's first public school system was established. Women were granted greater rights than ever before. Presidential electors were chosen directly by the people. Courts, county governments, hospitals, and charitable and penal institutions had to be built or reorganized.

It should also be noted that the South Carolina General Assembly was the first state legislative body with a black majority, when it met on July 8, 1868. There were eighty-seven blacks and forty whites in the lower house. The whites, however, had a majority in the state senate. Francis L. Cardoza (1837–1903) was the first black South Carolina secretary of state, 1872–1876.

Years later, black congressman Joseph Rainey, a former slave who escaped during the Civil War, pointed with pride to the justice of the South Carolina Constitution:

Our convention which met in 1868, and in which Negroes were in a large majority . . . adopted a liberal constitution, securing alike equal rights to all citizens, white and black, male and female, as far as possible. Mark you, we did not discriminate, although we had a majority. Our constitution towers up in its majesty with provisions for the equal protection of all classes of citizens.

In Mississippi, too, "a state government had to be organized from top to bottom" and this "important task was splendidly, creditably, and economically done," reported black leader John R. Lynch, later Mississippi's lone black congressman (Brock, 1981).

Vast political changes were taking place from Virginia to Texas. Touring the South in 1873, Edward King (1875), a northern writer who had many anti-black prejudices, found the black's contributions to government remarkable for a people just released from slavery. In Virginia, he found that black officeholders often had a "ludicrous" manner of speech, "but it was evident that all were acting intelligently." He visited a city council meeting and found it "as well conducted as that of any Eastern city." In Arkansas, he found black officials "of excellent ability." In Florida, he found that the state superintendent of education was a colored "gentleman of considerable culture and capacity."

In Mississippi and South Carolina, King saw large numbers of black officials among the higher- and lower-level officers of the states. He noted them in Natchez, managing city affairs in "a very satisfactory" manner. In South Carolina, King found that "the President of the Senate and the Speaker of the House, both colored, were elegant and accomplished men, highly educated, who would have creditably presided over any commonwealth's legislative assembly." As King stood in the library of the state university, two black Senators were enrolling in the law classes. "I was informed that dozens of members were occupied every spare moment outside of the sessions in faithful study."

A new day had dawned in the South. In Natchez (which had a black mayor), black and white children played together in the streets. Louisiana School Superintendent Thomas Conway described the school integration: "The children were simply kind to each other in the school-room as in the streets and elsewhere!" But 99 percent of the southern schools remained segregated. Black parents knew that school integration would lead to the closing of schools. They accepted education on a segregated level, rather than face this dreaded possibility.

Concluding the 1873–1874 session of the South Carolina legislature, the black Speaker of the House, S.J. Lee, thanked the men of both races who had made it a success. He admitted that the group was little skilled in government, but stated that they sincerely sought to serve the best interests of the state. He pointed out how they had reduced the debt from $20 million to $6 million, and said that they "in a large degree, regained the confidence of the public." Turning to the future, he said: "The first thing necessary for us to do is to secure as much intelligence as we can. Intelligence is *the* power, the controller of a nation's fate, and that we must secure at all hazards." He pointed with great pride to the growing number of schools and the increasing number of "competent, well-trained teachers." New scholarships at the university were established for the poor and "the people are becoming daily more enlightened." "The colored people . . . are progressive and thrifty, and striving to educate themselves, and thereby become worthy and prosperous citizens." He ended by thanking the legislature for electing him Speaker. "I felt my inexperience and the heavy responsibility resting upon me. I have tried, and hope successfully, to be impartial and just. If sometimes I failed," Mr. Lee admitted, "attribute it rather to the head than the heart."

Blacks in Congress

From 1870 to 1901 twenty-two blacks served their states as congressmen. Others who served in the U.S. Congress included Hiram Rhoades Revels (1822–1901), the first black senator, from 1870–1871. Southern blacks sat in every Congress from the Forty-first to the Fifty-sixth, with one exception. Although half of them were former slaves, the group included brilliant men and superb orators. Republican presidential candidate James G. Blaine, who served with many of these men, said of their abilities, "The colored men who took seats in both the Senate and the House did not appear ignorant or helpless. They were as a rule studious, earnest, ambitions men whose public conduct . . . would be honorable to any race" (Franklin, 1994).

None of them, pointed out one former Confederate leader, had ever been touched by the corruption that had reached so many men in the federal government during this era of easy money and low public morality.

Half of the black legislators were college-educated men, and several held college degrees. Robert Smalls, who served five full terms as a South Carolina congressman, was the war hero who had delivered a Confederate gunboat to the Union Navy. All of the men were vitally interested in protecting the new rights of the freedmen and battled long hours for passage of civil rights laws. The interest of black legislators in civil rights often stemmed from their own bitter experiences on trains or in restaurants. Jefferson Long, Georgia's only black congressman, spoke from personal experience against violence during elections. While seven of his supporters were shot in street fighting one Election Day, Long hid in a church belfry. These black legislators also demanded protection for the many whites in the South who faced violent attack for defending equality.

The twenty-two black members of Congress (two were Senators from Mississippi) took an interest in a wide range of issues besides civil rights. As loyal Republicans, they supported higher tariffs to protect American industry. Some favored soldier's pensions, internal improvements, and federal aid to education. "I am true to my own race . . . but at the same time, I would not have anything done which would harm the white race," said one. Another black congressional member lived by this concept, though each faced discrimination. South Carolina Congressman Rapier, "in order to know something of the feelings of a free man—left home and travelled six months in foreign lands" (Brock 1981).

The Violent End of Reconstruction

The downfall of the black–white governments of the South was inevitable, given that blacks had few guns, little land, and less government protection. Organized violence was the main weapon of those who sought to restore the old order.

Masked night riders such as the Ku Klux Klan sprang up everywhere to terrorize black voters and their white supporters. The main Klan targets were black officials, teachers, and successful farmers. When former slaves "made good money and had a good farm, the Ku Klux went to work and burned 'em down," recalled one black. In 1869, a Louisiana agent of the Freedmen's Bureau reported: *"Driving the freedmen from their crop* and seizing it themselves when it is grown, is a complaint against the planters that comes to us from every quarter." Cane Cook of Georgia was beaten senseless by his landlord in 1869 when he tried to argue about his share of the crop. Each year, along with the "generous yield of nature, so welcome, so needed, so widespread, come, too, reports of injustice, outrage, violence, and crime," wrote a United States official.

The 25,000 troops assigned to control the South—and guard the entire Mexican border—were not able to halt the Klan attacks. While some offficers did their best, others made only token efforts. Striking at night, masked, and on fast horses, the Klan picked off the most competent and daring of the black leaders. No courts convicted the Klan leaders. "We are in the hands of murderers," wrote 300 Vicksburg voters in 1875. "They say they will carry this election either by ballot or bullet." Blacks who were ready to fight back often had been stripped of their weapons by white sheriffs, or were too poor to afford guns. Abraham Burriss appealed to Governor Ames of Mississippi: "But give us guns and we will show the scoundrels that colored people *will fight."* After thirty blacks were massacred at Meridian, Mississippi, in 1871, Congress passed a law to end the Ku Klux Klan menace, but other organizations sprang up at once to take the Klan's place.

Blacks reacted to the mounting violence in many ways. Black militia companies were formed, some sponsored by the state governments. Others warned of the consequences of meeting violence with violence. Reverend Charles Ennis of Georgia explained the problem:

We have no protection at all from the laws of Georgia. . . . A great many freedmen have told me that we should be obliged to rise and take arms and protect ourselves, but I have always told them this would not do; that the whole South would then come against us and kill us off, as the Indians have been killed off. I have always told them the best way was for us to apply to the Government for protection, and let them protect us.

Among other prominent black leaders during the Reconstruction were John Mercer Langston (1829–1897), a public official elected in Virginia in 1888;

Blanche Kelso Bruce (1841–1898), born into slavery in Virginia, who served Mississippi as sergeant-at-arms, was elected Senator in the U.S. Senate in 1875 and later was appointed by President Garfield as registrar of the United States Treasury Department; and Joseph Hayne Rainey (1832–1887), born in South Carolina of slave parents, who served as state senator and in 1871 was elected to the U.S. House of Representatives—where he presented ten petitions for a civil rights bill.

POST-RECONSTRUCTION BLACK LEADERSHIP

Deterioration of the status of blacks in the late nineteenth century produced a broad spectrum of nationalist ideologies, ranging from the advocacy of race unity as a prerequisite to effective protest activity, through a stress upon black support of black business, to proposals for colonization abroad. One theme underlying all these various nationalistic ideologies was the exhorting of colored men to have pride in themselves. An illustration of this theme of *race pride*, widely voiced from the 1880s through the 1920s, is Alexander Crummell's speech "We Must Learn to Love Ourselves," reprinted as an editorial in the *A.M.E. Church Review*.

No one was better equipped to articulate the rising tide of nationalist sentiment than Crummell, the noted nineteenth-century intellectual. Also a prominent ante-bellum colonizationist, Crummell had gone to Liberia under the auspices of the American Colonization Society in 1850; twenty-three years later he returned to the United States and became rector of St. Luke's Episcopal Church in Washington. Crummell's views are of special interest not only because of is prominence but also because the close relationship between the ideology of emigration and that of racial solidarity for advancement within the United States is nowhere shown more clearly than in his sermons and addresses.

In an address entitled "The Social Principle," printed in 1882, Crummell presented a well-organized brief for the importance of race unity and solidarity. Delivered in 1875 as a Thanksgiving sermon, it was based on a similar talk advocating support for the Liberian national state established at Monrovia in 1859. In the later version, "What This Race Needs in This Country Is Power," Crummell appeals persuasively for race unity as a prerequisite for the development of the race power necessary to advance the black race in the United States.

Crummell believed that the college-educated elite had a special role in elevating the black race and bringing it to a position of power. It was the responsibility of the intellectuals to "lift up this people of ours." Here was an elitist conception of racial solidarity and self-help, which Crummell, together with W.E.B. Du Bois, was developing in the 1890s and which would in the early twentieth century become famous as Du Bois' theory of the "Talented Tenth." Moses (1989) has documented Crummell's inaugural address as the first president of the American Negro Academy. This club of forty black intellectuals, organized in 1897, aimed to stimulate black cultural development as part of a program of racial cooperation and solidarity.

One aspect of the revived emphasis upon race pride and race solidarity was an advocacy of separate institutions. Not only were separate churches carefully justified (Payne, 1891; Reynolds, 1887), but there was considerable debate in the black community over the relative advantages of separate and integrated schools. For one thing, there was much discussion in the 1880s over whether blacks should fight for the elimination of public school segregation in the northern states. A large body of opinion held that separate public schools were better for colored children than were mixed schools, partly because the elimination of separate schools usually meant a loss of jobs for black teachers; partly because colored youth in black schools would not be subject to the ugly prejudice of their white schoolmates and teachers; and partly because black children would find in black teachers and principals role models who could inspire them to success.

A related matter was the question of control over black colleges, the majority of which were in the hands of white missionary boards. One point of contention was whether because whites financed these colleges, they had a right to control the boards of trustees and administrations. A second point of contention was the charge that there was often discrimination against colored men in the hiring of faculty. Although the number of black professors and administrators was growing in some schools, these charges had some substance, especially in Congregational and Presbyterian institutions. Indeed, a few colleges of these denominations failed to employ black faculty members until the 1920s or even the 1930s, and others were slow to place blacks in influential administrative positions. The third point of contention was the argument that black teachers and administrators could in fact serve as role models for the students. Finally, there was the overriding question of who—whites, blacks, or both—would really control and make the decisions for institutions dedicated to the advancement of the black race. In his speech "Black Teachers for Black Schools," the noted Presbyterian minister and protest leader of Washington, D.C., Francis J. Grimké, persuasively argued for greater black control of these educational institutions. Grimké's address is significant particularly because throughout most of his long career he was a passionate integrationist and assimilationist.

The views discussed here represent what were becoming widely expressed ideas in the 1880s. Bishop Henry M. Turner of the AME church was atypical. Known particularly as a flamboyant colonizationist, he demanded an indemnity, in order "To Go Home to Africa." He also used the pages of his newspaper, *Voice of Missions,* to advocate other controversial ideas. Among these ideas was the assertion that God was black (Turner, 1898). This theme, like Turner's emigrationist ideology, reflected a belief that blacks could achieve racial dignity and pride only by rejecting American society and culture. Not unnaturally, this idea has cropped up several times since among militant separatist philosophies—most notably those of Marcus Garvey, the Black Muslims, and, in the late 1960s, the Detroit minister Albert Cleage, pastor of the Shrine of the Black Madonna.

During the half century that followed the end of Reconstruction, territorial separatism and emigration were recurrent and interrelated themes in African-American life. Their base was among the masses; and except for some of the all-black towns like Mound Bayou, Mississippi, and an occasional advocate of African colonization like Bishop Henry M. Turner, few of the elite spokespersons for the race endorsed proposals along these lines.

During the late 1870s, the growing racism that accompanied the close of Reconstruction combined with economic depression to produce considerable interest among working-class blacks in the possibilities of migrating to a more favorable location. Both the American Midwest, especially Kansas, and Africa were regarded as likely places of refuge (Senate Report, 1880; African Repository, 1877 and 1880). Sentiment for moving to either area, though undoubtedly basically precipitated by stark economic conditions, involved disillusionment with the South and revealed distinct nationalist overtones. Following the exodus of 1879 of approximately 70,000 blacks from Tennessee, Mississippi. Louisiana, Texas, and South Carolina, Benjamin "Pap" Singleton (1809–1892) told a congressional committee, "I started it all; I was the cause of it all."

In 1873, after returning to the South from Canada, Singleton led 300 blacks to Cherokee County, Kansas, to start "Singleton's Colony." This number increased to over 19,000 in twenty months. Other migrations northward were started by Henry Adams of Louisiana and Isaiah Montgomery of Mississippi. These failed somewhat, and many blacks returned to the South. The exodus stopped in 1881, and Ben Singleton died in 1892. Today, however, Nicodemus remains an all-black town in Kansas. Gordon (1993) has documented the impact of "Pap" Singleton's Exodus movement in Kansas history.

Later in the century, both the attempt to create an all-black state in Oklahoma and all-black towns like Mound Bayou, Mississippi on the one hand, and the brilliant rhetoric of Bishop Henry M. Turner on the other, were to offer more dramatic evidence of nationalist feelings. These in turn would be overshadowed in the twentieth century by the Garveyites and the Black Muslims. The desire for a "territory of our own," as Henry Adams put it, "whether within the United States or Africa, was an old and recurring theme" (Senate Report, 1880).

On the fringes of the movement for separation was the plan of an obscure man named Arthur Anderson for the creation of a black nation within the geographical confines of the United States. Like Garvey later, Anderson had been associated with African nationalists abroad, most notably with Duse Mohamed Ali, the Sudanese-Egyptian nationalist and editor of the London *African Times and Orient Review*, whose writings were largely responsible for the striking similarities in the doctrines of Anderson and the more recent Black Muslims. Like the Black Muslims, Anderson asserted that the blacks were the original race of mankind from which the whites, an inferior and diseased race, evolved; and he envisioned a glorious future for the American black race in a separate territory provided by the U.S. government as an indemnity for past oppression.

The post-Reconstruction era did not end well with black America. It was during this period that the doctrine of "separate but equal" became the law of the land, in the case of *Plessy v. Ferguson,* in 1896. Yet, it was during the same period that black America perhaps made its greatest impact on American political leadership.

Plessy v. Ferguson (163 U.S. 537)

A black man who was seven-eighths white was arrested on June 7, 1892, for riding on a Louisiana train in a section reserved for whites only. Homer Plessy was the man, and he came to symbolize a turning point in black American history. Protected on paper by the Fourteenth Amendment, blacks had not long enjoyed their constitutional privileges before new and more subtle means of segregation were found to limit their liberties. This shift in attitudes eventually found its way to the Supreme Court of the United States. In 1896, seven justices (with one not voting) upheld the Louisiana conviction of Plessy and further ruled that segregation could be practiced if the facilities were "separate but equal." Thus, the doctrine of separate but equal became the law of the land for the next sixty-eight years. The lone dissenter, Justice John Marshall Harlan, in a prophetic statement, envisioned the trend that would follow this lawful separation of the races:

It was said in argument that the state of Louisiana does not discriminate against either race, but prescribes a rule applicable alike to white and colored citizens. But this argument does not meet the difficulty. Everyone knows that the statute in question had its origin in the purpose, not so much to exclude white persons from railroad cars occupied by blacks, as to exclude colored people from coaches occupied by or assigned to white persons. Railroad corporations of Louisiana did not make discrimination among whites in the matter of accommodation for travelers. The thing to accomplish was, under the guise of giving equal accommodation for white and blacks, to compel the latter to keep to themselves while traveling in railroad passenger coaches. No one would be so wanting in candor as to assert the contrary. The fundamental objection, therefore, to the statute is that it interfered with the personal freedom of citizens. "Personal liberty," it has been well said, "consists in the power of locomotion, of changing situations, or removing one's person to whatsoever places one's own inclination may direct, without imprisonment or restraint, unless by due course of law." If a white man and a black man choose to occupy the same public conveyance on a public highway, it is their right to do so, and no government, proceeding alone on grounds of race, can prevent it without infringing the personal liberty of each.

The Supreme Court decision in 1896 was in many ways the ultimate nadir in American history at the end of the nineteenth century; it was the triumph of white supremacy. Indeed, it paved the way for the "color line" and the epidemic of race riots that characterized the early part of the twentieth century in American history.

Part Three

Twentieth Century and Contemporary Black Leadership

If there is no struggle, there is no progress. Those who profess to favor freedom, and yet deprecate agitation, are men who want crops without plowing up the ground. They want rain without thunder and lightning. They want the ocean without the awful roar of its many waters. This struggle may be a moral one; or it may be a physical one; or it may be both moral and physical; but it must be a struggle. Power concedes nothing without a demand.

Frederick Douglass

The twentieth century may be characterized as an era of epidemic race conflicts and the pursuit of democracy. The century also witnessed the Great Depression, American dominance in world politics, and the fall of colonialism and communism.

At the turn of the twentieth century, blacks had high hopes for a fair and just America. But William Edward Burghardt Du Bois (1900), one of the most prominent and influential black leaders of the twentieth century, wrote, "The problem of the twentieth century is the problem of the color line, the reaction of the darker to the lighter races of men in Asia and Africa, in America and the islands of the sea." Du Bois' prediction and assessment of race relations in the twentieth century in America was correct. In fact, the same is most likely to be the case in the twenty-first century.

Blacks have been unhappy with their status in America and have been revolting against it ever since they first arrived in the new world. Herbert Aptheker (1945) points to the existence of over 200 black slave revolts. Countless Africans committed suicide during the passage to America. Many slaves chose the individual form of revolt of simply running away. Others chose passive resistance. They gave the slave owner the minimum level of cooperation and compliance they could safely get away with. Some free blacks helped organize and operate the

Underground Railroad. Abolitionists included blacks among their ranks. Blacks fought in the Civil War; they were active participants and leaders in the southern Populist movement at the end of the nineteenth century (Woodward, 1966). By the early twentieth century, they had founded the Niagara Movement, the NAACP, and the Urban League.

Many of the most violent racial riots in American history took place during the first two decades of the twentieth century. Beginning with the New Orleans riot of 1900, racial confrontations followed in Springfield, Ohio (1904 and 1906), Atlanta (1906), Springfield, Illinois (1908) and East St. Louis (1917). The East St. Louis riot was of particular significance in that forty-four blacks were killed, many of whom died when they were blockaded and burned alive in their houses. Property damage was estimated at $500,000, while nearly 6,000 blacks were driven from their houses.

The black American response came in the 1960s. The 1960s was a time of revolution among blacks in the United States. The sit-in movement, the freedom rides, the marches and demonstrations, and the voter registration drives were supported by untold numbers of whites as well as blacks. The road to black revolution was marked with violence: the assassination in 1963 of John F. Kennedy, whom many blacks had come to regard as their friend; the murder of Malcolm X in 1965 and the feeling, shared by many blacks, that the prosecution of his assailants was less than vigorous. In the mid-1960s there was, moreover, the murder of numerous civil rights workers as well as innocent children, and for these crimes no one was convicted or even seriously prosecuted. Finally, on April 4, 1968, Martin Luther King, Jr., was shot down in a motel in Memphis, where he had gone to give support to striking garbage workers. To many blacks, this violent act symbolized the rejection by white America of their vigorous but peaceful pursuit of equality. In more than 100 cities, several days of rioting and burning and looting ensued, a grave response by many blacks to the wanton murder of their young leader and other blacks at the turn of the century. In 1967, the Black Power Conference in Newark, New Jersey, called for "partitioning of the United States into two separate independent nations, one to be a homeland for whites and the other to be a homeland for black Americans." Meanwhile, a group of young California militants led by Huey Newton and Bobby Seale organized the Black Panther Party for Self-Defense, and Eldridge Cleaver, its most articulate spokesperson, declared that the choice before the country was "total liberty for black people or total destruction for America" (Foner, 1970).

For the purpose of clarity, five major areas of leadership have been selected for examination in this Part: (1) social movement and political leadership; (2) educational leadership; (3) corporate leadership; (4) community leadership; and (5) military and international leadership. The focus is on the leaders themselves, their organizational goals, leadership styles, and contributions to American society, and on blacks in particular.

The decision as to what to include in a book of this kind is made difficult by the presence of black rebellion and protest throughout American history. I have decided to limit the book to the inclusion of only those aspects of black activities that clearly fall within the criteria representative of a social movement. For this reason, we must pause and examine the nature of social movements.

8

Social Movements and Black Leadership

Social movements and political dynamics are different from other types of complex organizations, such as educational systems, and communities. Eichler (1977), Wildavsky (1983), and Pye (1983) observe that social movement theory has, so far, not been able to come up with a definition of *social movement* that satisfactorily identifies the time and social boundaries of a movement. In other words, social movement theory lacks a commonly accepted definition that delimits social movements in terms of time, membership, and geographical space.

Social movements are one of the major vehicles for social change and as such have been studied since the beginning of the social sciences. Yet, in spite of a long-standing recognition the importance of social movements, we have not yet satisfactorily answered the most elementary question of all: namely, what is a social movement?

A *social movement* may be defined as a continuing, collective attempt to restructure some basic segment of the social order through means other than institutionalized channels. As such, a social movement encompasses both organized and unorganized elements working toward a common objective. The common objective does not have to be very clearly defined or specific. It may be sufficiently diffuse as to encompass within the same social movement elements that differ sharply from one another. Given agreement on the common goal, there may be considerable disagreement over tactics, as well as over specific and secondary objectives. There may be many core associations within the same social movement. These organizations may range from those attempting to reform existing society to those attempting to restructure it completely; from those preferring the use of respectable pressure tactics to those willing to use violence. Unorganized, individual participants are likely to differ even more than organizations. Sometimes these differences will be so extreme that the various segments of a movement may expend more time and energy in fighting each other than in contending with the larger society.

African suicides and runaway slaves are clearly examples of revolt, but they do not necessarily constitute a part of a social movement, as they represent individualistic revolts rather than collective attempts to change the social order. The slave revolts, on the other hand, were collective actions on the part of small numbers of slaves on widely separated plantations. However, they likewise do not qualify as part of a social movement, because of the relatively small numbers involved in any particular revolt; their lack of continuity over time and space; and the low incidence of their having been aimed at fundamental changes in the social order. In contrast, the Underground Railroad and the abolitionist movement were segments of a continuing social movement. They are not included in the "black revolt" because, although they may have had the interests of blacks in mind and they did include blacks, they were dominated and controlled by whites. The activities organizations such as the NAACP, the Niagara Movement, and the Urban League are included in this examination as they possess sufficient collective behavior characteristics to constitute part of social movements. To a large extent, they were formally organized pressure groups with little in the way of active mass support. The Niagara Movement was a black movement, but it had a very short life span. The NAACP and the Urban League had continuity over time but, prior to 1955, they were white-dominated and had a primarily white membership.

For the aforementioned reasons I have also chosen to include in this Part only selections dealing with the black revolt from the time of the birth of the civil rights movement (around 1955) to the present. During this period, the black revolt clearly constituted a social movement. It was a collective attempt to change the social order; it had both organized and unorganized elements within it; it had both mass participation and continuity over time; and it developed both on behalf of and on the part of blacks.

The earlier, pre-social movement acts of rebellion should not be written off as unimportant. They have great significance in the history and development of black protest in America. These incidents and organizations constitute important bits of evidence that black Americans have always found their circumstances of life in America intolerable and have never passively accepted or been satisfied with them. However, a continuing and fully developed social movement cannot be built upon misery. Despair may produce episodic, rebellious outbursts, but a fully developed revolutionary movement or a continuing reform-oriented social movement requires that dissatisfaction with the present be supplemented by hope and faith. One must have hope in the sense that one must believe that a better world is possible, just as one must have faith, believing that by joining together with others of a similar mind, one may develop sufficient collective power to bring about this better world. Neither hope nor faith is produced in a vacuum. Both are products of social experience. Thus, the discussions that follow in this chapter are reflections of the social experiences of selected African-Americans. They also reflect the organizational leadership of black Americans in their struggle to "make America do the right thing."

W.E.B. Du Bois

William Edward Burghardt Du Bois, (1868–1963), educator, author, and civil rights leader, was born on February 23 in Great Barrington, Massachusetts. He was the son of a wandering mixed-blood father and a mother who helped to support the family by taking in washing and boarders.

Du Bois received his bachelor of arts degree from Fisk University in 1888, graduated *cum laude* from Harvard in 1890, and later earned his Ph.D. from Harvard in 1896. From 1892 to 1894, he did graduate work at the University of Berlin and traveled extensively in Europe.

Du Bois was a professor of Latin and Greek at Wilberforce University in Ohio, and the University of Pennsylvania. From 1896 to 1910, he was professor of economics at Atlanta University. His first important work, *The Suppression of the Slave Trade,* was published in 1896.

In 1899, he published a systematic study of social conditions among the Negroes in Philadelphia, *The Philadelphia Negro.* In 1901, Dr. Du Bois edited a study of Negro problems through *The Atlanta University Studies of the American Race Problems.*

He launched the Niagara Movement in 1905, demanding full citizenship for blacks. The movement was made up of black professional people and was the forerunner of the NAACP. Some months earlier, Du Bois had written a credo reflecting upon his life and his racial attitudes. It follows:

. . . I believe in the Negro Race; in the beauty of its genius, the sweetness of its soul, and its strength in that meekness which shall inherit this turbulent earth.

I believe in pride of race and lineage itself; in pride of self so deep as to scorn injustice to other selves; in pride of lineage so great as to despise no man's father; in pride of race so chivalrous as neither to offer bastardy to the weak nor beg wedlock of the strong, knowing that men may be brothers in Christ, even though they be not brothers-in-law.

I believe in Service—humble reverent service, from the blackening of boots to the whitening of souls; for Work is Heaven, Idleness Hell, and Wages is the 'Well done!' of the Master who summoned all them that labor and are heavy laden, making no distinction between the black sweating cotton-hands of Georgia and the First Families of Virginia, since all distinction not based on deed is devilish and not divine.

I believe in the Devil and his angels, who wantonly work to narrow the opportunity of struggling human beings, especially if they be black; who spit in the faces of the fallen, strike them that cannot strike again, believe the worst and work to prove it, hating the image which their Maker stamped on a brother's soul.

I believe in the Prince of Peace. I believe that War is Murder. I believe that armies and navies are at bottom the tinsel and braggadocio of oppression and wrong; and I believe that the wicked conquest of weaker and darker nations by nations white and stronger but foreshadows the death of that strength.

I believe in Liberty for all men; the space to stretch their arms and their souls; the right to breathe and the right to vote, the freedom to choose their friends, enjoy the sunshine and ride on the railroads, uncurled by color; thinking, dreaming, working as they will in a kingdom of God and love.

I believe in the training of the children black even as white; the leading out of little souls into the green pastures and beside the still waters, not for pelf or peace, but for Life lit by some large vision of beauty and goodness and truth; lest we forget, and the sons of the fathers, like Esau, for mere meat barter their birthright in a mighty nation.

Finally, I believe in Patience—patience with the weakness of the Weak and the strength of the Strong, the prejudice of the Ignorant and the ignorance of the Blind; patience with the tardy triumph of Joy and the mad chastening of Sorrow—patience with God (see Du Bois, 1968).

Dr. Du Bois proposed the idea for a Negro encyclopedia in 1909, but the idea took time to develop. In 1932, the Phelps-Stokes Fund authorized a small appropriation to help finance Dr. Du Bois' venture. Guy B. Johnson of the University of North Carolina was hired as an editor, and the project was incorporated in the District of Columbia with a board of directors and an advisory board. Although the project was never brought to completion, two small preparatory volumes were published under the title *Encyclopedia of the Negro*.

The NAACP was organized in 1909, partially because of the Niagara Movement, and Du Bois served as the director of publications and editor of *Crisis* magazine until 1934. He became the spokesperson for stressing education for the Negro in the liberal arts and humanities, as opposed to the vocational education views of Booker T. Washington.

From 1944 to 1948, Dr. Du Bois was head of the special research department of the NAACP. In 1961, he emigrated to Ghana, West Africa, where he became a member of the Communist party, and began work on a summary of African culture, entitled *Encyclopedia Africana*.

Dr. Du Bois' enormous literary output of more than twenty books and over 100 scholarly articles included: *The Souls of Black Folk* (1903); *John Brown* (1909); *Quest of the Silver Fleece* (1911); *The Negro* (1915); *Dark Water* (1920); *Dark Princess* (1928); *Dusk of Dawn* (1940); *The World and Africa* (1947); and a trilogy, *Black Flame* (1957–1961).

He died on August 27, 1963, in Ghana at the age of ninety-five.

The National Association for the Advancement of Colored People

The NAACP had its beginning on February 12, 1909, on the 100th anniversary of Lincoln's birthday. Three people, William E. Walling, Mary White Ovington, and Dr. Henry Moskowitz, proposed that a conference be called for the discussion of present evils, the voicing of protests, and the renewal of the struggle for civil and political liberty.

The conference lasted from May 30 to June 1, 1909. It was followed by four meetings, and resulted in an increase in membership and the choice of an official name, which was the National Negro Committee. In 1910, the group was renamed the National Association for the Advancement of Colored People and was incorporated in New York State. Merging with the Niagara Movement a year later, the NAACP had established approximately fifty branches throughout the country.

The *Crisis* magazine, edited by W.E.B. Du Bois, became the association's chief instrument for propaganda and an important vehicle for the spreading of educational and social programs.

The objective of the NAACP was, and is, to improve the lot of blacks through "litigation, legislation, and education." The most important judicial victory was won in 1954, when the *Brown vs. Board of Education* case threw out the "separate but equal" doctrine maintained in *Plessy v. Ferguson.* This victory started the elimination of segregation in public education (Hamilton, 1978).

More recently, the NAACP has diversified its program by taking part in "selective buying" campaigns and sit-in tactics. The association is charged with the reputation of representing the middle-class Negro, rather than the Negro masses.

The NAACP has a Washington lobby, which campaigns for new laws designed to help and extend the rights of Negroes. The association's regional offices are in Atlanta, Dallas, and San Francisco, with the main headquarters located in New York City.

Whitney Young, Jr.

Whitney Moore Young, Jr. (1921–1971), civil rights leader, was born on July 31 in Lincoln Ridge, Kentucky. He graduated from Lincoln Institute and received his bachelor of science degree in 1946. After graduation, Young worked for a year as an instructor, a coach, and an assistant principal in Rosenwald High School in Madisonville, Kentucky.

In 1954, Young went into the service and served in the 369th Regiment. During this time, he decided to get into race relations work, and upon his discharge as first sergeant, enrolled in the University of Minnesota, where he received his master's degree in social work in 1947. That same year, Young joined the Urban League as director of Industrial Relations and Vocational Guidance. For the next three years, he was in charge of field work at Atlanta University and at the University of Minnesota.

He became dean of the School of Social Work of Atlanta University, a black institution, in 1954. He served there until he assumed a position with the National Urban League in New York City on August 1, 1961.

The author of many articles published in professional journals and magazines, Young at one time was a columnist for the *World Telegram and Sun* in New York. He was consulted privately by President Kennedy and President Johnson regarding his plans for helping the Negro. He once wrote: "The Negro is in revolt today not to change the fabric of our society or to seek a special plan in it, but to enter into partnership in that society." He also wrote: "We must support the strong, we must give courage to the timid, we must remind the indifferent and we must warn the opposed." Concerning the fact that he was often called an "Uncle Tom," by militant blacks, Young commented, "It isn't a question of moderate and militant, it is a question of responsibility and irresponsibility. I ride through Harlem on my way to work each morning. I think, should I get out at 125th Street and stand cussing out whitey to show I'm tough? Or should I go on downtown and talk to General Motors about 2,000 jobs for unemployed Negroes?" Young chose to go downtown.

In 1971, Whitney Young attended the African-American Dialogues, a conference which met in Lagos, Nigeria. He was one of eight American black delegates. In the afternoon of the second conference day, Whitney went swimming with Ramsey Clark and Tom Wyman. He suffered a cerebral hemorrhage and died almost immediately on March 11, 1971, at the age of 49.

Whitney M. Young, Jr., was the executive director of the National Urban League from 1961 to 1971, the civil rights leader whom contemporaries described as the "inside man" of the black revolution, the man who served as bridge and interpreter between black America and the businesspeople, foundation executives, and public officials who constituted the white power structure.

Whitney Young led no demonstrations and changed no laws. He accomplished much of his best work out of the public eye. His soapbox, the Associated Press said,

was the podium of plush executive suites. When he clenched his fist, it was around the hand of a white executive who had agreed to provide more jobs for Negroes.

If Young marched, he was usually being ushered into the office of a corporation president, and his sit-ins took place around a table with company executives.

Young took on what Jesse Jackson called the toughest job in the black movement: selling civil rights to the nation's most powerful whites. A black man who grew up in a middle-class family in the segregated South, he spent most of his adult life in the white world, transcending barriers of race, wealth, and social standing to build bridges between the black ghetto and the white establishment. He took it on himself to interpret the needs and desires of blacks struggling to make it in American society to those whites who were in a position to help them or to stand in their way. His methods were reason, persuasion, and negotiation; his goal was to gain access for blacks to the basic elements of a decent life—good jobs, education, decent housing, health care, and social services.

With race briefly center stage in American national politics, Young brought the National Urban League into the civil rights movement and made it a force in the major events and debates of the decade. Among his colleagues in the civil rights leadership, he played an important role as strategist and mediator. He understood keenly the value to the movement of creative tension between moderates and militants, and he took good advantage of that understanding to advance his goals. His style and his convictions led contemporaries to call him a moderate, a label he would have preferred to shake off. He insisted that he was just as angry at racial injustice as anyone else; what distinguished him were the means he chose to express that anger and to advance the social and economic welfare of black Americans.

Andrew Young said of Whitney Young that "he was a man who knew the high art of how to get power from the powerful and share it with the powerless" (Weiss, 1989).

The Urban League

The National Urban League was organized in 1911 as the National League on Urban Conditions Among Negroes. The league was a merger of three social agencies: the League for the Protection of Colored Women, the Committee on Urban Conditions Among Negroes, and the Committee for Improving the Industrial Condition of Negroes in New York. The Urban League has been interracial from its inception. It is a voluntary community service agency of civic, professional, business, labor, and religious leaders dedicated to the removal of all forms of segregation and discrimination based on creed or color. Its first executive secretary was Dr. Whitney Young, who formerly was the dean of the Atlanta University School of Social Work. It has a staff of 500 paid professionals among sixty-four affiliated local urban leagues in strategic industrial cities with large Negro populations. In addition, there are 61,000 volunteers. It has a membership of 50,000.

Marcus Garvey

Regarded by some as a self-serving charlatan and by others as a "Black Messiah" or a "Black Moses," Marcus Mosiah Garvey (1887–1940) was a black nationalist during the early twentieth century who single-handedly organized the first black mass protest movement in the history of the United States. In the process and as the result of his emphasis upon black pride, racial separation, and the resurrection of a great black empire in Africa, Garvey unwittingly became the spiritual father of modern black nationalism. In a sense, modern slogans and movements such as "black is beautiful" and "black power" are simply manifestations of a revived form of Garveyism.

Garvey was born in Jamaica on August 17, 1887. During his youth and into his early twenties, he became convinced that the worldwide plight of black people demanded a solution. As a result of independent study, research, and travel, Garvey decided to become a leader of his race in order to unite blacks throughout the world in a nation and government of their own. Toward this end, he established the Universal Negro Improvement Association (UNIA) in Jamaica in 1914. In 1916, he traveled to the United States to organize a New York chapter of the UNIA. Two years later, he founded a newspaper, *The Negro World*, which became the propaganda arm of the UNIA. Coupled with a lengthy speaking tour throughout the United States, Garvey's editorials in *The Negro World* succeeded in attracting thousands of converts to the UNIA. In a matter of months, thirty branches of the organization were established in the United States. By 1920, Garvey claimed that he had 4,000,000 followers and, in 1923, 6,000,000. Although these figures were probably exaggerations, even Garvey's most critical opponents admitted that there were at least 500,000 members in the UNIA at its height.

At the heart of Garvey's ideology was his fervent desire to mobilize the black peoples of Africa, the West Indies, the Americas and elsewhere, for the spiritual, historical, and physical redemption of Africa and Africans, at home and abroad. "If Europe is for Europeans," he declared, "then Africa shall be for the black peoples of the world. The other races have countries of their own and it is time for the 400,000,000 Negroes to claim Africa for themselves." Notwithstanding this pronouncement, one would be mistaken to suppose that Garveyism was just another "Back to Africa" movement. Garvey was realistic enough to appreciate the fact that a mass black exodus to Africa, in the physical sense, was impossible. Although he did believe that black intellectuals and leaders had an obligation to return to their ancestral homeland to assist in its development and liberation, his basic argument revolved around the concept of a *spiritual* return to Africa for the majority of American blacks. He argued that white racism in the United States had created a sense of self-hatred in blacks, and that the only way to purge themselves of this self-hatred and self-contempt was through a spiritual identification with Africa and Africans. By stressing Africa's noble past, Garvey declared that American blacks should be proud of their ancestry and, in particular, proud of their "blackness." Concurrently, American blacks must strive to achieve black community pride, wealth, culture, and independence in the United States by creating and maintaining a nation within a nation. "The fight for African redemption," Garvey stated, "does not mean that we must give up our domestic fight for political justice and industrial rights."

In 1921, Garvey established a provisional government-in-exile for Africa, with himself as president. In addition, he established a black cabinet, a black army (the African Legion) attired in resplendent uniforms, a corps of nurses (the Black Cross Nurses) and even an African Orthodox Church, with a black God and a black Christ. Earlier, Garvey had created a steamship company, the Black Star Line, which acquired several ships for commerce with, and transportation to, Africa. The elaborateness of Garvey's organization coupled with his own charismatic personality had a profound effect upon the black urban masses, who were drawn to him as if he were a magnet.

On the other hand, black intellectuals denounced Garvey as a visionary buffoon and a demagogue. W.E.B. Du Bois, for example, called Garvey's movement "bombastic and impracticable." For his part, Garvey shunned intellectuals like Du Bois as well as the black bourgeois establishment which, in his mind, had betrayed the black race by cooperating with whites. Refusing to accept white donations ("We don't want their money, this is a black man's movement"), Garvey condemned the NAACP as "wanting us all to become white by amalgamation. To be a Negro is no disgrace, but an honor, and we of the UNIA do not want to become white." Garvey's handling of the Black Star Line finally put an end to his meteoric rise. In 1922, he was indicted on mail fraud charges concerning the sale of Black Star stock. Convicted in 1923, he was confined in prison for two years and then, in 1927, deported as an undesirable alien. In his absence, Garveyism (or *Black Zionism*) in the United States lost much of its appeal. Garvey himself subsequently died in London in 1940.

A. Philip Randolph

Why should a Negro worker be penalized for being black?

—A. Philip Randolph, 1935

Asa Philip Randolph (1889–1979), civil rights leader, was born in Crescent City, Florida, on April 15. He completed his high school courses at the Cookman Institute in Jacksonville before moving to the North.

He attended the College of the City of New York, taking courses in economics and political science.

In 1917, Randolph and Chandler Owen launched the publication of *The Messenger.* Its subtitle was "The Only Radical Negro Magazine in the World."

Randolph was arrested in June 1918 by the Department of Justice because of his militant stance against World War I. He was released after a few days.

The ambition to be a leader was an enduring theme in the life of A. Philip Randolph, the man who was to become one of the founding fathers of the modern civil rights movement. "Although I have never had a desire for wealth," he said late in his career, "I have had a passion to create a significant movement which would also benefit others" (Randolph, 1963). The years between 1919 and 1925 served as preparation, during which Randolph honed his public speaking technique and founded the highly respected radical journal, the *Messenger.* Because he espoused socialism, labor unionism, and interracial class solidarity, doctrines foreign to most Afro-Americans, he attracted only a minute number of followers at this stage. Randolph nevertheless clung to these economic ideas and, as a result of experiences in the 1920s, added a virulent anticommunism to his theories. Consequently, much of the rhetoric and many of the strategies he would bring to his later civil rights activity were formulated when he began to organize the Pullman porters in 1925. Thus, before the end of the decade, Randolph had acquired ideological convictions that would remain basically unchanged throughout his career. Not until 1937, however, when he succeeded in gaining recognition for the porters' union, would Randolph be able to overcome the handicap of his economic philosophy to achieve public recognition as a leader.

The Brotherhood of Sleeping Car Porters (BSCP) was formally organized on August 25, 1925, with Randolph at its head. Times were not fortuitous for the new union, however: even established white unions were losing members in the

1920s; Pullman's profits were down; and there were many unemployed blacks from whom the company could draw replacement porters. Pullman propaganda identified the company as a benefactor of the black race, leading many prominent blacks, as well as most of the black press, to oppose the BSCP.

Illness sent him to the Mayo Clinic in April 1968, and that summer he retired as president of the BSCP and vice-president of the AFL-CIO executive council. President Johnson lauded him, stating, "Where monumental civil rights legislation was rising and injustices were falling—there stood Phil Randolph." In a personal letter to Randolph, the president said that he and Mrs. Johnson were "grateful for your long support and treasure your friendship" (Johnson, 1968). The railroad industry's decline paralleled Randolph's, and his beloved union was soon absorbed into the Brotherhood of Railway and Airline Clerks.

A. Philip Randolph died May 16, 1979, on the eve of the twenty-fifth anniversary of the Supreme Court decision outlawing segregation in the public schools. By the time of his death, the prestige of "St. Philip of the Pullman Porters" had so diminished that the head of the NAACP had cause to comment, "It's so sad because there are so many young people today for whom that name means very little." Yet within a dozen years of his death, Randolph would be looked upon as one of the legendary black leaders. In 1989 his likeness would appear on the United States postage stamp for Black Heritage Month, and, in its Centennial Edition, the *Wall Street Journal* would place him in its "Gallery of the Greatest"—the "People Who Made a Difference" in shaping the way Americans did business over the past 100 years (Hooks, 1979).

Drew Ali

Around 1913 in Newark, New Jersey, Noble Drew Ali (Timothy Drew), a forgotten and misunderstood leader, started teaching about the Moorish (North Africa) identity of blacks. Drew was born in Simpsonbuck County, North Carolina, among the Cherokee Indian tribe on January 8, 1886. He traveled extensively in the East and in Africa, and concluded that blacks were not Ethiopians as proclaimed by early black nationalists, but that they were Asiatics; specifically, Moors from Morocco. He believed that the Continental Congress stripped American blacks of their nationality and placed them in the menial role of slave. According to the Moorish movement's historical records, Drew was allegedly taught by Egyptian masters and earned the title "Egyptian Adept," thereby becoming a master in his own right. In Egypt, he had the opportunity to visit the universities and travel through the inner chambers of the pyramids. By being in Egypt, he could see for himself that the black man had laws, sciences, mathematics, art, and Godly esteem. Afterward, according to the movement's accounts, he traveled to Mecca and received his ancient birthright title as "Ali" from Sultan Abdul Aziz Ibn Saud, thus allegedly giving him the authority to teach true Islam to the lost tribes of Israel in North, South, and Central America.

Needless to say, he did not teach pristine Islam (I believe, because he did not know the vastness of Islam, the scriptural purity of the Quran, nor Quranic Arabic. Certainly, one does not need to know Arabic or the Quran to teach Islam, for Islam stands on its own merit. However, in Drew's case, his lack of knowledge in these areas contributed to his mixing Masonry, esotericism, and Garveyism with marginal Islam. My point of contention is, if it is true that he was sanctioned by Ibn Saud, then why did not Saud properly prepare him for his mission? Furthermore, Ali cannot be charged for his misguided errors in Islam—nor can Elijah Muhammad—simply because they lacked complete knowledge of the religion of Islam).

The purpose and goals of the Moorish Movement were enunciated by Drew Ali in the September 14, 1928, edition of *The Moorish Guide*:

1. Dispense charity and provide for the mutual assistance of members in times of distress.
2. Aid in the improvement of health and encourage the ownership of better homes.
3. Find employment for members.
4. Teach those fundamental principles that are desired for our civilization, as obedience to law, loyalty to government, tolerance, and unity.

It has also been said by members of the Moorish communities that Noble Drew Ali traveled extensively in India and perhaps studied among the Ahmadiya. Therefore, it may not be a circumstantial coincidence that after the death of Drew Ali the Ahmadiya were desperately trying to proselytize within the UNIA and the Moorish temples. As I indicated earlier, Drew Ali synthesized esotericism, Sufism, and Christianity, and he accepted and applied some customs and symbols of the Eastern Masonic Lodge. Noble Drew Ali published his so-called Holy Koran of the Moorish Science Temple of America, now known to members of the movement as the Holy Koran of the Moorish Science Temple Circle Seven, and he published a pamphlet and a collection of Moorish Science beliefs, conceived possibly from *The Aquarian Gospel of Jesus Christ,* a book received through the writings of spiritualist Levi Dowling in the 1890s. Ali's alleged Koran consisted of Garvey's teachings, Biblical passages, esoteric or theosophical philosophy, numerology, and Masonic teachings. One point must be stressed here, that Drew Ali's so-called Koran was indeed very similar in verses to *The Aquarian Gospel of Jesus Christ.* Ali seemingly embraced segments of Dowling's teachings because they dealt with aspects of esotericism. One of Ali's perceptions of eastern philosophy was described in terms similar to what Dowling taught his followers. (He taught his followers of "the two-selves"—the higher self and the lower self.)

This dualistic concept bespeaks Zoroastrianism and Manicheanism, which, to a great degree, are eastern precursors to Gnosticism and Christianity.

Returning to the subject of Drew Ali's Koran, I think it is safe to conclude that Ali had very little, if any, knowledge about the true Holy Quran. There were no Holy Qurans in wide circulation during his era. Furthermore, one of the first major English language Qurans was by Maulana Muhammad Ali, and it did not get published until around 1917; additionally, it was not widely disseminated until years later. There were some Orientalist translations in the Library of Congress, but it is doubtful that Ali reviewed them for theological clarity. It is therefore my conjecture that his lack of knowledge of the Quran was somewhat eclipsed by his acquaintance with Masonry and esotericism. Thus, he devised a Koran which, I think, collectivized the best of those philosophies that appealed to him at that time, and that he considered germane for his mission.

Drew Ali's belief in Islam, as limited as it might have been, was never really subordinate to Masonry or esotericism. He presented six principles that are obviously Islamic in nature:

1. Know thyself and thy Father, God Allah.
2. Islam is a very simple faith. It requires man to recognize his duties toward God Allah, his Creator and his fellow creatures.
3. The cardinal doctrine of Islam is the unity of the Father—Allah.
4. To the one who is Supreme, Most Wise, and Beneficent, and to Him Alone, belongs worship, adoration, thanksgiving, and praise.
5. True Wisdom is less presuming than folly. The wise man doubteth often and changeth his mind; the fool is obstinate and doubteth not; he knoweth all things, but his own ignorance.
6. The fallen sons and daughters of the Asiatic nation of North America need to learn to love instead of hate; and to know their higher and lower self.

Elijah Muhammad

Elijah Muhammad (1897–1975), Muslim leader, was born Elijah Poole on October 7 in Sandersville, Georgia. His father was a Baptist preacher, sawmill worker, and tenant farmer. It was necessary to help his large family with his earnings as a field boy and sawmill worker, and when he quit school at the age of sixteen, he had completed only four grades.

Elijah worked for a while in Sandersville and in Macon, as a laborer for the Southern Railroad and a foreman at the Cherokee Buick Company, before moving with his wife and two children to Detroit, where he hoped to find better working conditions.

He worked for the Chevrolet factory in Detroit from 1923 to 1929, but found that the black race was just as oppressed here as in the South. Embittered over the firing of blacks in order to give jobs to whites during the 1930 depression, he turned to the teachings of a new voice, W.D. Fard, or Wallace Fard Muhammad. Saying he was sent from Allah (God) to reclaim his lost people, Fard taught that blacks were members of a superior race, descendants of Muslims of Afro-Asia; thus, the Black Muslim movement was born. It became a militant, disciplined, anti-Christian cult, the Lost Found Nation of Islam.

Elijah Poole became dedicated to Fard and changed his name to Elijah Karriem and, later, Elijah Muhammad, when he was appointed supreme minister of

Detroit's Temple Number One. In 1932, he set up Temple Number Two in Chicago and made a start on Temple Number Three in Milwaukee.

Elijah Muhammad became the leader of the movement after the disappearance of Fard in 1934, and declared himself to be "The Messenger of Allah to the Lost Found Nation of Islam in the Wilderness of North America."

He began to encounter difficulties in 1934, when he was convicted and put on six months' probation for refusing to transfer his children from a Muslim school to a Detroit public school. He fled to Chicago, where threats to his life caused him to move to Washington, D.C., and he set up Temple Number Four. In May 1942, he was arrested on draft resistance and sedition charges. (Muslims objected to military service and refused to bear arms for America in World War II.) Elijah served three-and-a-half years of a five-year sentence in a federal prison in Michigan, and was released in 1946.

Aided by such forceful ministers as Malcolm X, Muhammad began to rebuild his organization, which had declined while he was in prison. By 1960, membership in the organization had probably reached 100,000. Muhammad did not like publicity, but was forced into the spotlight when Malcolm X resigned from the organization in 1963, and was shot to death two years later. Muhammad claimed no involvement in the murder.

The Nation of Islam

Throughout the 1940s and early 1950s, the Nation of Islam, founded in 1930 by W. Fard Muhammad as a breakaway faction of the Moorish Science Temple and led by Elijah Muhammad after 1933, slowly built up its strength among the lower classes and prison inmates. By the end of the 1950s, with the ferment of black protest and the rebirth of Africa, the number and influence of the Muslims was increasing rapidly. The Muslim program, while espousing equal opportunity and equal justice, contrasted radically with the integrationist ideology that dominated this period (Rashad, 1994). Elijah Muhammad stated clearly his desire for "complete separation in a state or territory of our own," and for prohibition of "intermarriage or race mixing." He moved to set up Muslim schools and establish Muslim businesses such as dry cleaning shops, grocery stores, and restaurants, as a first step toward developing black self-sufficiency. These actions in the economic sector carried on Garvey's ideas and foreshadowed the black capitalist ideology of the late 1960s. *Muhammad Speaks,* the Muslim weekly newspaper, published accounts of the activities and struggles of black people throughout the world, in addition to those of the Muslims themselves.

In 1965, Elijah Muhammad published a book about his views, *Message to the Blackman.* The book includes a plea for racial separatism and illustrates the emphasis on self-definition that was a factor in the revival of the "black pride" and "black-is-beautiful" concepts in the mid-1960s.

What Do the Muslims Want?

According to Elijah Muhammad (1962), the Nation of Islam, among other things, demanded complete separation to a state or territory of their own; equality of opportunity; an immediate end to the police brutality and mob attacks against the so-called Negro throughout the United States; and equal education.

What the Muslims Believe

The Muslims claim that they BELIEVE in the One God Whose proper Name is Allah; BELIEVE in the Holy Qura-an and in the Scriptures of all the Prophets of God; BELIEVE in the truth of the Bible, but it must be reinterpreted so that mankind will not be snared by the falsehoods that have been added to it; BELIEVE in Allah's Prophets and the Scriptures they brought to the people; BELIEVE in the resurrection of the dead—not in physical resurrection—but in mental resurrection.

Furthermore, they believe that they are the people of God's choice, that God would choose the rejected and the despised; and BELIEVE that the offer of integration is hypocritical and is made by those who are trying to deceive the black peoples into believing that their 400 year-old openly hostile enemies of freedom, justice, equality are, all of a sudden, their "friends."

Today, while the Nation of Islam continues its tradition, it has also moved in new directions under the leadership of Louis Farrakhan. Professor Henry Louis Gates, Jr. (1996) provides a clear insight to this new direction in his interview of Mr. Farrakhan. As noted by Gates, Farrakhan is passionately concerned about the betterment of black America, addicted to the register of rage—and a host of anti-Semitic conspiracy theories. Minister Farrakhan believes that the Nation of Islam might be understood as a kind of Reformation movement within the black church—a church that had grown all too accommodating to American racism. Perhaps it is this attack on traditional black churches that makes Farrakhan very popular among African-Americans. This populist appeal was demonstrated in the fall of 1995, when Farrakhan organized the Million Man March. That occasion has been widely seen as an illustration both of Farrakhan's strengths and of his weaknesses. Yet, Farrakhan's level of support among black Americans, especially among the black leadership, is vigorously debated. Equally important is the rejection of Farrakhan's leadership role by white America. He was criticized by the white press and Congress for allegedly referring to Jews as "bloodsuckers." He later explained that by "bloodsuckers" he meant all non-black shopkeepers in the inner city, some of whom were of Jewish, Korean, and Arabic descent.

In a recent interview with CNN (1997), Farrakhan intimated his desire to organize a "rainbow" political party. He does not believe that either the Republican party or the Democratic party has the will to lead America. Farrakhan's foreign relationships, especially with Libya's Muammar Qaddafi, puts him even further at odds with the U.S. government. In spite of all these controversies, the Farrakhan phenomenon and the Nation of Islam continue to impact American national discourse on the black American struggle for social equality and the pursuit of happiness.

Congress of Racial Equality

This is the oldest of the nonviolent direct-action protest groups. Known as CORE, it began as a local organization in Chicago, but became a national organization in 1942. Its national director was James Farmer (1920–1999), a former NAACP official. James R. Robertson was executive secretary, and Floyd B. McKissick, an attorney from Durham, North Carolina, was chairperson.

Rooted in the American pacifist movement, CORE's foundations were laid at a time when growing segments of the white public, stimulated by the ideological concerns of the New Deal for America's dispossessed citizens and by the irony of fighting the racist Nazis while tolerating domestic racism, were gradually becoming more sensitive to the black person's plight. Simultaneously, in the black community, as a result of the legal victories achieved by the NAACP during the 1930s, the encouragement of leading New Dealers like Eleanor Roosevelt, and the obvious contradictions between America's democratic war propaganda and its violation of democracy at home, a more militant mood was becoming widely evident.

In the radical vanguard of this slow shift in sentiment among blacks and whites were the founders of CORE. Products of the Christian student movement of the 1930s, with its deep social concerns, they were a small band of dedicated, young pacifists, and members of the Christian-pacifist Fellowship of Reconciliation (FOR). Within the FOR, they belonged to a group that was intensely committed to applying Gandhian techniques of *satyagraha,* or nonviolent direct action, to the resolution of racial and industrial conflict in America. The FOR, established during the first World War, had long been interested in race relations, and numbered several Negroes among its officials. When, in 1940, the radical reformer A.J. Muste became FOR's chief executive, the fellowship moved beyond philosophical opposition to war to experimenting with nonviolent, direct action for social justice in the United States. Among the "peace teams" or "cells" into which the FOR organized its members was one established at the University of Chicago in October 1941; this cell was deeply interested in applying Gandhian principles to racial problems. From the activities of this race relations cell of about a dozen members emerged the first CORE group, the Chicago Committee of Racial Equality (Meier, 1973).

The race relations cell included four of the six individuals who were mainly responsible for founding CORE, while both of the others were FOR staff members who cooperated closely with the cell. James Farmer and George Houser, who started work at the Chicago FOR office in October 1941, had been prominent in Methodist student circles in the 1930s. Farmer, son of a professor at Wiley College in Texas, had received a bachelor of divinity degree from Howard University. There, as a student of Howard Thurman, the noted Negro Methodist pacifist and FOR vice chairman, he had become "deeply versed in Christian pacifist thinking" and had served part-time as an FOR field worker. In the summer of 1941, the twenty-one-year-old Farmer accepted a full-time appointment with the fellowship. Houser, the son of a Methodist minister, was in his third year at Union Theological Seminary when he was sentenced to prison for refusing to register for the draft. After spending a year in Danbury penitentiary he went to the University of Chicago to complete his seminary studies and to work part-time as an FOR field secretary. The prominence of Methodists among early CORE leaders, epitomized by the contribution of these two men, one black and one white, was no accident, for the church was influenced to an unusual extent by the pacifism of the 1930s. As A.J. Muste observed, "The Youth Movement of the Methodist Church . . . is the most progressive of our Protestant Youth Movements" (Meier and Rudwick, 1973).

Two other CORE founders, Bernice Fisher and Homer Jack, both white, were also divinity students at the University of Chicago. Both had been social activists in Rochester when they were in their teens. Jack was studying for the Unitarian ministry; Fisher, an active member of the Baptist Young People's Union, had long been interested in labor and race questions. The remaining two founders were liberal arts students at the University of Chicago. Joe Guinn, a Chicago Negro, who would later be incarcerated as a conscientious objector, was head of the local NAACP Youth Council. James R. Robinson, a graduate student in English, was the only non-Protestant in the group. A white Catholic from upstate New York, his interest in pacifism had been stimulated by reading the *Catholic Worker*, and he had been active in peace circles while an undergraduate at Columbia University. Later, as a conscientious objector, he would serve time in a Civilian Public Service (CPS) camp as an alternative to military service (Wittner, 1969).

The Congress of Racial Equality received student support for one of its most dramatic protest actions: the freedom rides of 1961. Their objective was to test the desegregation of public waiting rooms, restaurants, and interstate bus transportation in the South. A great deal of advance publicity hailed the initial freedom ride, which was scheduled to begin in Washington, D.C., on April 28, 1961, and then proceed southward across Virginia to Carolina, Georgia, Alabama, Mississippi, and New Orleans. In Anniston, Alabama, the riders were set upon by mobs and were badly beaten. A bus was burned, and the Greyhound drivers refused to take the group farther. They went on to New Orleans by way of commercial airline. The cruel treatment became a rallying point for other organizations to form a "freedom riders" coordinating committee, and they sent more than 1,000 volunteers on freedom rides throughout the South.

The Congress of Racial Equality and a coalition of black activists and organizations announced on April 15, 1970, their endorsement of black candidates for state senate and assembly seats from the Harlem district. Roy Innis, CORE director, said the organization would also work nationwide for the election of candidates who would work in the best interests of black people.

Endorsed during a news conference at CORE's Harlem offices were William Chance, a civil rights lawyer seeking the Democratic nomination in the June primary for state senator from the twenty-seventh District, and Wilbur Kirby, a community organizer trying to win the Democratic nomination for assemblyman from the seventy-second District. Two other declared candidates for the assembly seat were George Miller, leader of the John F. Kennedy Independent Democratic Club in Harlem, and Charles Gaskins, a teacher. Mr. Innis said CORE would continue its new policy of selective endorsement of political candidates.

The endorsement by CORE of Mr. Chance and Mr. Kirby came jointly with the backing of the citywide coalition, an amalgamation of groups and individuals, including Eugene Callender, president of the New York Urban Coalition; Hope Stevens, president of the Uptown Chamber of Commerce; and Cora T. Walker, a lawyer heading the Harlem Cooperative Supermarket.

The six persons most responsible for founding CORE were all pacifists; three served terms in jail or CPS camp as conscientious objectors. Four were white, two were black. All had been deeply involved in the 1930s Christian-pacifist student movement, whose members also shared an ideological commitment to interracialism and industrial unionism. Years later, a CORE founder recalled, "the 1930s was the pacifist era and the trend in pacifist-Christian circles was on nonviolence as an alternative to violence. It was natural that this was combined with Gandhism" (Meier and Rudwick, 1973). Unlike the majority of their Christian-pacifist fellow students who changed their views after American entry into World War II, the CORE leaders remained consistent with their earlier ideology. As heirs of the Christian radicalism of the 1930s, not only were they conscientious objectors to war, but they exhibited their social idealism in other ways as well. Half were socialists, and all of them admired the CIO industrial unions and the "direct action" techniques of the sit-down strikers. Farmer wrote in 1942, "similar instrumentalities for racial brotherhood in America must be developed." Indeed, the first CORE sit-ins were called "sit-downs."

From one perspective, CORE in the 1960s had proven a failure. Many of its victories amounted to tokenism, and it consistently met defeat in campaigns against school boards, building trades unions, and police departments. Further frustrations followed the adoption of the "New Directions" program. Finally, CORE all but collapsed in the middle of the decade.

Yet had CORE really failed? In answering this question it is essential to make a distinction between *organizational* success and failure on the one hand and the success and failure of an organization's *goals* on the other. As we have pointed out on a number of occasions, the relationship between CORE's organizational vitality and its successes and failures in various campaigns was a complex one. In the end, CORE, despite numerous achievements, declined largely because of a sense of disillusionment with the pace of social change. On the other hand, while the organization itself became a shadow of its former self, considerable change continued to occur, particularly in the realm of politics and employment, which CORE's earlier activity had done much to initiate.

The contribution of CORE to the black protest movement and to racial advancement had, in fact, been enormous. During the 1940s and 1950s, CORE pioneered the use of direct action techniques, which later swept the country. The Congress of Racial Equality had played a major role in bringing about the desegregation of public accommodations, from its first sit-in at Chicago through its single-handed campaign to segregate public places in a border city like St. Louis and its help for the southern student demonstrators of 1960 to the Freedom Ride of 1961. These activities, followed by the upsurge of southern direct action in 1963, in which CORE took a leading part, culminated in the passage of the Civil Rights Act of 1964. In the North during the early 1960s, CORE was pivotal in the battles for integrated housing, and decent dwellings for the black poor, as well as for making a vital contribution to the attack on *de facto* school segregation and police brutality. Although many of these campaigns got nowhere, CORE was instrumental in helping to break down "whites only" job barriers in dozens of cities. In addition, through its demonstrations CORE sensitized white elites to an awareness of the black people's problems, and thus helped pave the way for the gains that continued to be made even after CORE as an organization had moved to the sidelines. Finally, CORE's participation in the Voter Education Project (VEP) and the Council of Federated Organizations (COFO) experiment contributed to the passage of the Voting Rights Act of 1965 and, more directly, helped set the stage for the new political activism that sent 1,000 individuals to public office in the South alone in 1972, and made the black presence so important a feature of the 1972 Democratic Convention.

Despite discouraging disappointments, and at the cost of enormous sacrifices, CORE, both by itself and with other civil rights organizations, chalked up a significant record—especially in public accommodations, voter registration, and employment. Members of CORE were always deeply aware of how very much more needed to be done before equality was achieved in American society. Yet, CORE helped to set in motion waves of social change that have not yet run their course, and it played a pivotal role in arousing blacks to a greater militancy, which paved the way for the black activism of the 1970s.

Martin Luther King, Jr.

Martin Luther King, Jr. (1929–1968), civil rights leader, was born Michael Luther King in Atlanta, Georgia, on January 15. He later changed his name to Martin Luther King. He came from a long line of Georgia ministers. His maternal grandfather, Reverend Alfred Daniel Williams, founded the Ebenezer Baptist Church in Atlanta in 1895, and was one of the founding members of the Atlanta chapter of the NAACP, which helped organize the first high school in Atlanta for black students. His father, Reverend M.L. King, Sr., was a leader in the struggle for the equalization of salaries for black teachers in Georgia and succeeded Reverend Williams at the Ebenezer Baptist Church in 1932.

Martin Luther King, Jr. attended Booker T. Washington High School in Atlanta, and at age fifteen, entered his father's alma mater, Morehouse College. He planned to be a doctor, but he was so greatly influenced by the college president, Dr. Benjamin Mays, that he decided to study for the ministry. He was ordained by his father in 1947; graduated from Morehouse in 1948; and entered

Drozer Theological Seminary in Chester, Pennsylvania, where he graduated in 1951, with the Plafker Award as the most outstanding student of his class and the Crozer Fellowship for graduate study. King chose to continue his study with two years of philosophy courses at Harvard and earned the doctor of philosophy degree from Boston University in 1955.

During his years at Boston University, Reverend King met and married an Antioch College graduate, Coretta Scott from Marion, Alabama, who was studying voice at the New England Conservatory of Music. On September 1, 1954, Reverend King accepted a call from the Dexter Avenue Baptist Church in Montgomery, Alabama, and he and his wife returned to the south.

On December 1, 1955, Rosa Parks, a seamstress exhausted from a long day's work, refused to surrender her seat on a bus to a white man, as the laws of Alabama required at that time. The black community decided to call a bus boycott and turned to a young twenty-seven-year-old clergyman, Martin Luther King, Jr., for leadership. Within five days, the Montgomery Improvement Association was formed, with King as its president. The boycott lasted 381 days, and King, using nonviolent and passive resistance, despite harassment by whites and the bombing of his home, held his people together; and, thus, a strong black leader emerged. Reverend King and his followers were arrested for "illegally" boycotting the buses. However, the convictions were appealed and overturned, and after a ruling by the Supreme Court that segregated seating was unconstitutional, the city of Montgomery, on December 20, 1956, declared an end to racial segregation on public conveyances.

Dr. King was interested in revolutionizing the status of the southern black, and with that in mind, in 1957, he led a group of Atlanta ministers to form an organization that later became the Southern Christian Leadership Conference (SCLC). In 1959, he moved to Atlanta to serve with his father at the Ebenezer Baptist Church, and continued to work for the SCLC. Dr. King was also involved in organizing the Student Nonviolent Coordinating Committee (SNCC) in 1960, when a sit-in movement was begun by black college students. His crusade for equal rights and first-class citizenship for his people continued with the protests in Birmingham in 1963, which resulted in the major civil rights legislation of 1964 and 1965.

Dr. King attracted broader support from all walks of society than any other black leader. At the peak of his influence was a famous address, "I Have A Dream," at the Lincoln Memorial during the August 28, 1963, March on Washington.

Dr. King received the Nobel Peace Prize in Oslo, Norway, on December 10, 1964, a tremendous recognition for his nonviolent philosophy in the civil rights revolution. He was thirty-five years old, the youngest man to have won the coveted award.

He and his followers made national headlines when they made the famous 1965 Selma march to Montgomery, the state capital, to protest the discrimination in the Negro voter registration in Selma. In July 1966, Dr. King conducted open housing campaigns in Chicago, and later traveled to New York and Cleveland in support of equal rights for his people. On December 4, 1967, he planned for a massive civil disobedience campaign to be staged in Washington in 1968 to apply pressure on the Johnson administration to end poverty by providing jobs for all citizens, regardless of color.

Reverend King's dream as the nonviolent crusader protesting peacefully and suffering brutality in silence came to an abrupt halt on April 4, 1968, in Memphis, Tennessee, where he had gone to help the sanitation workers obtain improved wages and working conditions. He was the victim of an assassin's bullet. The world was shocked at the passing of this great American. James Earl Ray was convicted of Reverend King's murder and sentenced to ninety-nine years in prison.

At the news of King's death, many cities erupted in flames and violence as the American people expressed their rage and frustration. Some 150,000 people attended the Atlanta funeral five days later at his father's church. The mourners from the humble to the mighty came to pay tribute to this man and his dream for a united America.

The money Dr. King earned from his lectures and writings was donated to organizations supporting the civil rights movement. His books included *Stride Toward Freedom: The Montgomery Story* (1958); *Strength to Love* (1963); *Why We Can't Wait* (1964); and *Where Do We Go From Here: Chaos or Community?* (1967).

Dr. King received several hundred awards for his leadership in the civil rights movement. Among them were:

- Selected one of the ten most outstanding personalities of the year by *Time,* 1957.
- Listed in *Who's Who in America,* 1957.
- The Spingarn Medal from the NAACP, 1957.
- The Russwurm Award from the National Newspaper Publishers, 1957.
- The Second Annual Achievement Award from the Guardian Association of the Police Department of New York, 1958.
- Listed by *Link Magazine* of New Delhi, India, as one of the sixteen world leaders who had contributed most to the advancement of freedom during 1959.
- Named "Man of the Year" by *Time,* 1963.
- Named "American of the Decade" by the Laundry, Dry Cleaning, and Die Workers International Union, 1963.
- The John Dewey Award, from the United Federation of Teachers, 1964.
- The John F. Kennedy Award, from the Catholic Interracial Council of Chicago, 1964.
- The Nobel Peace Prize, at age 35, the youngest man, the second American, and the third black man to be so honored, 1964.
- The Marcus Garvey Prize for Human Rights, presented by the Jamaican Government, posthumously, 1968.
- The Rosa L. Parks Award, presented by the Southern Christian Leadership Conference, posthumously, 1968.
- The Aims Field-Wolf Award for his book, *Stride Toward Freedom.*

The awards listed here, along with other awards and numerous citations, are in the Archives of the Martin Luther King, Jr. Center for Nonviolent Social Change, Inc., in Atlanta, Georgia.

THE PHILOSOPHY OF NONVIOLENCE: SIX PRINCIPLES

Because the philosophy of nonviolence played such a positive role in the Montgomery Movement, it may be wise to turn to a brief discussion of some basic aspects of this philosophy.

First, it must be emphasized that nonviolent resistance is not a method for cowards; it does resist. If one uses this method because they are afraid or merely because they lack the instruments of violence, they are not truly nonviolent. This is why Gandhi often said that if cowardice is the only alternative to violence, it is better to fight. He made this statement conscious of the fact that there is always another alternative: no individual or group need submit to any wrong, nor need they use violence to right the wrong; there is the way of nonviolent resistance. This ultimately is the way of the strong man. It is not a method of stagnant passivity. The phrase "passive resistance" often gives the false impression that this is a sort of "do nothing method," in which the resister quietly and passively accepts evil. But nothing is further from the truth. For while the nonviolent resister is passive in the sense of not being physically aggressive to a given opponent, the nonviolent resister's mind and emotions are always active, constantly seeking to persuade that opponent that they are wrong. The method is passive physically, but strongly active spiritually. It is not passive resistance to evil; it is active, nonviolent resistance to evil.

A second basic attribute of nonviolence is that it does not seek to defeat or humiliate the opponent, but to win his friendship and understanding. The nonviolent resister must often express protest through noncooperation or boycotts, but realizes that these are not ends themselves; they are merely means to awaken a sense of moral shame in the opponent. The end is *redemption* and *reconciliation*. The aftermath of nonviolence is the creation of the "Beloved Community," while the aftermath of violence is tragic bitterness.

A third characteristic of this method is that the attack is directed against forces of evil rather than against persons who happen to be doing the evil. It is evil that the nonviolent resister seeks to defeat, not the persons victimized by evil. If opposing racial injustice, the nonviolent resister has the vision to see that the basic tension is not between races. As I like to say to the people in Montgomery: "The tension in this city is not between white people and Negro people. The tension is, at bottom, between justice and injustice, between the forces of light and the forces of darkness. And if there is a victory, it will be not merely for fifty thousand Negroes, but a victory for justice and the forces of light. We are out to defeat injustice and not white persons who may be unjust."

A fourth point that characterizes nonviolent resistance is a willingness to accept suffering without retaliation; to accept blows from the opponent without striking back. "Rivers of blood may have to flow before we gain our freedom, but it must be our blood," Gandhi said to his countrymen. The nonviolent resister is willing to accept violence if necessary, but never to inflict it. The resister does not seek to dodge jail. If going to jail is necessary, the nonviolent resister enters it "as a bridegroom enters the bride's chamber."

One may well ask: "What is the nonviolent resister's justification for this ordeal to which he invites men, for this mass political application of the ancient doctrine of turning the other cheek?" The answer is found in the realization that unearned suffering is redemptive. Suffering, the nonviolent resister realizes, has tremendous educational and transforming possibilities. "Things of fundamental importance to people are not secured by reason alone, but have to be purchased with their suffering," said Gandhi. He continues: "Suffering is infinitely more powerful than the law of the jungle for converting the opponent and opening his ears which are otherwise shut to the voice of reason."

A fifth point concerning nonviolent resistance is that it avoids not only external physical violence but also internal violence of spirit. The nonviolent resister not only refuses to shoot an opponent but also refuses to hate that opponent. At the center of nonviolence stands the principle of *love*. The nonviolent resister would contend that in the struggle for human dignity, the oppressed people of the world must not succumb to the temptation of becoming bitter or indulging in hate campaigns. To retaliate in kind would do nothing but intensify the existence of hate in the universe. Along the way of life, someone must have sense enough and morality enough to cut off the chain of hate. This can be done only by projecting the ethic of love to the center of our lives.

In speaking of love at this point, we are not referring to some sentimental and affectionate emotion. It would be nonsense to urge men and women to love their oppressors in an affectionate sense. Love in this connection means *understanding, redemptive good will*. Here the Greek language comes to our aid. There are three words for love in the Greek New Testament. First, there is *eros*. In platonic philosophy, eros meant the yearning of the soul for the realm of the divine. It has come now to mean a sort of *aesthetic* or *romantic love*. Second is *philia*, which means *intimate affection between personal friends*. Philia denotes a sort of reciprocal love; the person loves because he or she is loved. When we speak of loving those who oppose us, we refer to neither eros nor philia; we speak of a love which is expressed by the Greek word *agape*. Agape means *understanding, redeeming good will for all men*. It is an overflowing love that is purely spontaneous, unmotivated, groundless, and creative. It is not set in motion by any quality or function of its object. It is love of God operating in the human heart.

Agape is disinterested love. It is a love in which the individual seeks not his own good, but the good of his neighbor (I Cor. 10:24). Agape does not begin by discriminating between worthy and unworthy people, or any qualities people possess. It begins by loving others for their own sake. It is an entirely "neighbor-regarding concern for others," which discovers the neighbor in every person it meets. Therefore, agape makes no distinction between friend and enemy; it is directed toward both. If one loves an individual merely on account of their friendliness, one loves that person for the sake of the benefits to be gained from the friendship, rather than for the friend's own sake. Consequently, the best way to assure oneself that love is disinterested is to have love for the enemy–neighbor from whom you can expect no good in return, but only hostility and persecution.

Another basic point about agape is that it springs from the need of the other person—his or her need for belonging to the best in the human family. The Samaritan who helped the Jew on the Jericho Road was "good" because he responded to the human need that he was presented with. God's love is eternal and fails not because men and women need God's love. St. Paul assures us that the loving act of redemption was done "while we were yet sinners"—that is, at the point of our greatest need for love. Because the white people's personalities are greatly distorted by segregation, and their souls are greatly scarred, they need the love of the Negro. The Negro must love the white person, because the white person needs the Negroe's love to remove tensions, insecurities, and fears.

Agape is not a weak, passive love. It is love in action. Agape is love seeking to preserve and create community. It is insistence on community even when one seeks to break it. Agape is willingness to go to any length to restore community. It doesn't stop at the first mile, but goes the second mile to restore community. It is a willingness to forgive, not seven times, but seventy times seven to restore community. For the cross is the eternal expression of the length to which God will go in order to restore broken community. The resurrection is a symbol of God's triumph over all the forces that seek to block community. The Holy Spirit is the continuing community, creating reality that moves through history. Those who work community are working against the whole of creation. Therefore, if I respond to hate with a reciprocal hate, I do nothing but intensify the cleavage in broken community by meeting hate with love. If I meet hate with hate, I become depersonalized, because creation is so designed that my personality can be fulfilled only in the context of community. Booker T. Washington was right: "Let no man pull you so low as to make you hate him." When a person pulls you that low, they bring you to the point of working against community; they drag you to the point of defying creation, thereby becoming depersonalized.

In the final analysis, agape means a recognition of the fact that all life is interrelated. All humanity is involved in a single process, and all men are brothers, all women are sisters. To the degree that I harm my brother, no matter what he is doing to me, to that extent I am harming myself. For example, white persons often refuse to give federal aid to education in order to avoid giving Negroes their rights; but because all men and women are brethren, they cannot deny Negro children without harming themselves. Why is this? Because men are brothers. Women are sisters. If you harm me, you harm yourself. Love, *agape*, is the only cement that can hold this broken community together. When I am commanded to love, I am commanded to restore community, to resist injustice, and to meet the needs of my brethren.

A sixth basic fact about nonviolent resistance is that it is based on the conviction that the universe is on the side of justice. Consequently, the believer in nonviolence has deep faith in the future. This faith is another reason why the nonviolent resister can accept suffering without retaliation. For the resister knows that in their struggle for justice they have cosmic companionship. It is true that there are devout believers in nonviolence who find it difficult to believe in a personal God. But even these persons believe in the existence of some creative force that works for universal wholeness. Whether we call it an unconscious process, an impersonal Braham, or a Personal Being of matchless power and infinite there is a creative force in this universe that works to bang the disconnected aspects of reality into a harmonious whole.

Martin Luther King, Jr., and the Southern Christian Leadership Conference

This is a nonsectarian, coordinated agency of organizations and individuals. Its goals include full citizenship rights and total integration of the Negro into American life. Its motto, "To Redeem the Soul of America," was the theme of its first convention (Fairclough, 1987). Its headquarters are in Atlanta, Georgia, with affiliates in sixteen southern and border states. It was founded in 1957 as an extension of the Montgomery Improvement Association and has a full-time staff of more than sixty people and an annual budget of approximately $1 million dollars. It is interracial. Its board is mostly made up of Negro ministers, and numbers thirty-three in membership. Individuals hold memberships through their affiliated organizations, such as churches, fraternal orders, and civic organizations. The affiliates are restricted to the seventeen southern states and the District of Columbia. Benefits, which feature famous Negro and white entertainers, are important sources of financial support.

Nonviolence has been widely used in Negro protests since the Montgomery bus boycotts of 1955. The late Martin Luther King, Jr., was the chief exponent of this form of protest. As mentioned earlier, Dr. King received his graduate training at the Boston University School of Theology and was a disciple of Mahatma Gandhi's philosophy of nonviolence, *satyagraha*. Its objective is not to defeat or humiliate the opposition, but to overcome it with love and reconciliation.

The issue that set off the boycott in 1955 was the refusal of a Negro woman, Mrs. Rosa Parks, to give up her seat on a public bus to a white man. Specific Jim Crow laws regulated the seating of passengers on public vehicles according to race. The usual requirement was that white passengers would sit in the front while Negro passengers were required to fill all seats from the rear before they could occupy any forward seats. Mrs. Parks' defiance set off a chain of events that led to an organized protest. The local organization that provided the leadership of the bus boycott in

Montgomery, Alabama, was the Montgomery Improvement Association, of which Dr. Martin Luther King, Jr., was elected president. The specific demands that Dr. King set forth—fairer treatment of Negroes as passengers and employment of Negroes as drivers—were presented to the bus company. When the demands were ignored, the Negroes of Montgomery walked, rather than ride the segregated buses. They also utilized a motor pool composed of the automobiles of private citizens. On December 13, 1956, in accordance with a suit brought by the NAACP, the United States Supreme Court ruled that the state law requiring racial segregation on public buses was unconstitutional. Combined with this litigation was "direct action," which resulted in a victory that was important to the cause of the freedom of the Negro. The technique and the spirit inspired by Dr. Martin Luther King, Jr., proved to be successful.

The SCLC excelled during the 1960s in the one activity that mattered the most in the struggle against segregation: the skillful use of nonviolent, direct action. Members of the SCLC out-sang, out-marched, and out-prayed their white oppressors. And, as Adam Fairclough, the author of "To Redeem the Soul of America," a history of the SCLC and its role in bringing about a second Reconstruction in the South, reveals, they also out-thought them.

Three black political leaders must be counted among the most extraordinary American public figures in the twentieth century: Edward William Brooke, Adam Clayton Powell, and Thurgood Marshall.

Edward William Brooke

When he was elected by popular vote to the United States Senate, Edward William Brooke (b. 1919), a Republican from Massachusetts, became the most exciting step forward for American blacks since Lincoln freed the slaves. On the opening day of Congress in 1967, the former attorney general, escorted by his senior colleague, Senator Edward Kennedy, walked down the multicarpeted aisle of the Senate chamber. As the tall and courtly newcomer approached the president of the Senate, Democrats and Republicans, northerners and southerners, liberals and conservatives gave him a standing ovation. After being sworn in by Vice President Hubert Humphrey, Brooke was warmly congratulated by Democratic Senator Harry Byrd of Virginia, whose father had been a segregationist and a bitter foe of civil rights. Moved by the reception, Brooke walked outside, viewing across the Capitol grounds about 1,000 black demonstrators waiting for Adam Clayton Powell, who was in the House of Representatives weeping, "his huge frame bent and his face distorted by the shock of senseless defeat" (Cutler, 1972). He had just been expelled from the House and stripped of the chairmanship of the Education and Labor Committee, the most powerful post held by a black on Capitol Hill. House Speaker John McCormack, shaken, walked out of the caucus predicting to a bystander that every black would walk out of the Democratic Party. The fact is, even up to this date, blacks have refused to walk out of the Democratic Party.

Adam Clayton Powell, Jr.

Adam Clayton Powell, Jr. (1908–1972), public official, was born in New York City. His parents were Mattie Fletcher and Adam Clayton Powell, Sr. Adam, Jr., attended public schools in New York City before attending Colgate University.

During the Depression, Powell began his crusade for reforms, causing several large corporations to drop their unofficial bans on employing blacks (Hickey and Edwin, 1965). In 1930, Mr. Powell organized demonstrations instrumental in making the Harlem Hospital integrate its medical staffs. He also campaigned against the discrimination shown the Negro drivers and mechanics of the city's bus lines.

Adam Clayton Powell, Sr., retired as pastor of the Abyssinian Baptist Church in 1937. His son was named his successor. Within a year, Adam, Jr., was awarded an honorary doctor of divinity degree from Shaw University for the outstanding work he had done.

In 1939, Powell, Jr., was the chairman of the Coordinating Committee on Employment. In this capacity, he helped organize a picket line before the executive offices of the World's Fair in the Empire State Building. This act helped hundreds of Negroes get employment from the fair. In 1941, Powell succeeded in winning a seat on the New York City Council. The following year, he published and edited the weekly, *Peoples Voice,* which was thought to be "the largest Negro tabloid in the world."

Powell went to Washington, D.C., in 1945, as the congressional representative of over 300,000 people, mostly black. While in Washington, he underwent many discriminatory experiences, ranging from not being authorized to use the communal facilities within Congress, to being turned away from a movie in which his first wife, Hazel Scott, was the star. He became identified as "Mr. Civil Rights" and increased his fight against discrimination.

He also was responsible for the Powell Amendment, which denied federal funds to any project in which discrimination existed. This amendment also became part of the Flanagan School Lunch Bill, making Adam Clayton Powell, Jr., the first Negro congressman since Reconstruction to sponsor legislation passed by both houses.

Powell sponsored legislation advocating federal aid to education; fought discriminatory practices on Capitol Hill; demanded that a Negro journalist be allowed to sit in the Senate and House galleries; introduced the first anti-Jim Crow transportation legislation; introduced the first bill to end segregation in the Armed Forces; and forced Congress to recognize the existence of discrimination in such organizations as the Daughters of the American Revolution (DAR).

In 1960, Powell became the senior member and chairman of the House Committee on Education and Labor. While in this capacity, he helped in the development and passage of the Minimum Wage Bill of 1961, the Manpower Development and Training Act, the National Defense Education Act, and the Vocational Education Act. Under Powell's leadership, his committee helped pass forty-eight laws totalling $14 billion in expenditures.

Adam Clayton Powell, Jr., was one of the most controversial blacks in politics, and few would concede that he wasn't the most powerful political figure in Harlem and in the nation during his last years. In one of his speeches in Congress, entitled "My Black Position Paper," Powell presented an outline for living, and a call to action, for America's black people. The speech contained seventeen points; for example, blacks must give their children a sense of pride; black organizations must be black-led; blacks must seek economic self-sufficiency and political power.

Adam Clayton Powell must be counted among the most extraordinary public figures of our times. He has been praised as an agitator for Negro rights ever since the early 1930s. He was an abrasive force for the Negro masses before such names as Martin Luther King, James Farmer, or Malcolm X ever gained national currency. He has been denounced as a charlatan, demagogue, playboy, woman-chaser, opportunist, hypocrite, rabble-rouser, maverick, and master of the "grandstand play"; nonetheless, he has been elected every two years since 1944 to the United States Congress (often with hardly a campaign speech), and is chairperson of the influential House Committee on Education and Labor. He is, in addition, pastor of a church having one of the largest Protestant congregations in the United States, Harlem's Abyssinian Baptist. In the words of one Harlemite, "How in hell you going to beat him? He has a parish with ten thousand people in it and every one is a potential campaign worker."

Many of Powell's detractors claim he is less a "doer" than an irritant—a symbol of the Negro struggle for equality in the United States. Joseph A. Bailey, one of the vanquished opponents for Congress, called him "the greatest Negro orator in the world today—a man who doesn't do anything practical about achieving civil rights, but he expresses our people's outcry against injustice—and they respond gratefully." Roy Wilkins, executive secretary of the NAACP, once wrote that "Powell is a master of all the tricks of rousing what he calls 'the masses.'"

Powell persistently defies the white man, and for that he has the admiration, the gratitude—and even the adoration—of great numbers of Negroes. He enjoys "showing the flat" in such expensive New York restaurants as Sardi's and "21." His performance at such times is a study: word pervades the room that "Adam Powell is here" and at once heads turn and necks crane. He moves from table to table, appearing to know everyone, bestowing his luminous smile and warm handshake in several directions.

At home, Powell is a man of easygoing charm, a pipe smoker who customarily indulges an unerring taste for luxury. "I go to the Salzburg Festival every year," he once told a *New York Times* interviewer, "and I never miss an opening night on Broadway if I can help it. All the producers save tickets for me." His manner of living and his obvious pleasure in moving freely in the white man's world contrast sharply with the slum life of the average Negro, especially those in Harlem. He has plumbed deeper than any other Negro leader the vicarious sense of many lower-class Negroes. "When my people see a picture of me in '21,'" says Powell, "or some other downtown nightclub, they like it. They know I can pass for white, but that I'm as black in my thinking as the blackest of them."

This last remark suggests what is perhaps the greatest irony in the career of this most paradoxical of leaders: no one—not even Powell himself—is absolutely certain how much of his ancestry is Negro. In his book *Marching Blacks*, published in 1945, Powell claimed that his earliest awareness of Negro–white differences occurred when, as a child, he stood on a chair and traced with his finger the letter "P" branded on his slave grandfather's back. Easier to establish is his Choctaw Indian, French, and German blood. It appears that, at least during one brief period of his life, he attempted to pass as white, but was found out. He told Ernest Dunbar, a senior editor of *Look* Magazine: "If I have all white blood and I'm doing what I am for the Negro, I deserve all the more credit."

Whether Negro or not, Powell is undeniably a product of the ghetto, with all that this implies—and it implies a great deal. Like the Reverend Dr. Martin Luther King Jr., he is the son of a patriarchal and strong-minded Baptist minister father. Adam Clayton Powell, Sr. fought his way to Yale University and built Harlem's Abyssinian Baptist Church into the social and political fortress it has been for the last thirty years. Today, Powell and King speak to different regions of the Negro mind, a divergence which is historical, and which symbolizes some new directions in the yearnings of the great mass of Negroes in the United States. Powell is closer in his roots to Marcus Garvey—the "Black Moses" of the 1920s—who came to New York from Jamaica preaching a doctrine of black worthiness; whose explosive oratory made him the most sought-after Negro speaker of his day; and whose Universal Negro Improvement Association labored to inflate the suspicion in the American Negro's mind that being black was not all bad; that it should, in fact, be a source of pride. Adam Clayton Powell, Jr., is in that line of descent. Martin Luther King Jr., on the other hand, is the archetype of the Negro leadership that was forged out of the events of the 1950s and early 1960s beginning with the Montgomery, Alabama, bus boycott of 1955. That eruption presaged a black revolution, the dimensions of which were foreseen by only a perceptive few. There followed "freedom rides," sit-ins, enrollment assaults on all-white southern universities, and hundreds of street demonstrations.

For the first time in their 340-year tenure in the United States, large sections of the Negro masses were participating directly in efforts to improve their condition. The American Negro suddenly was an uncommon form on the world scene: one of the few groups still using nonviolent methods to obtain social and political reforms from a hostile environment.

Remarkably, many blacks discovered they were no longer afraid to stand up for their rights. Although few people recognized it at the time, a new Negro faith was being born. Louis Lomax (1962), in his book, *The Negro Revolt,* said, "This faith was the culmination of a hundred years of folk suffering . . . it was a hodgepodge, as every faith is, of every ethical principle absorbed by my people from other cultures. And so the best of Confucius, Moses, Jesus, Gandhi, and Thoreau was extracted, then mixed with the peculiar experience of the Negro in America."

At the forefront of these activities was a loosely connected cadre of Negroes, who came to be called "The Big Six." They were:

- The Reverend Dr. Martin Luther King, Jr., president of the Southern Christian Leadership Conference (an organization that was born out of the Montgomery bus boycott).
- A. Philip Randolph, international president of the Brotherhood of Sleeping Car Porters, the only Negro vice president of the AFL-CIO, and founder of the Negro American Labor Council.
- Roy Wilkins, executive secretary of the NAACP.
- Whitney Young, executive director of the National Urban League.
- James Farmer, national director of the Congress of Racial Equality.
- John Lewis, the youthful chairman of the Student Non-Violent Coordinating Committee (SNCC).

These men were of differing temperaments, different generations, and sometimes colliding ambitions; but together they succeeded in the task of laying down a strategy for the black revolt, and of holding that revolt on a properly militant and nonviolent track.

Roy Wilkins

Roy Wilkins (1901–), NAACP executive secretary and social welfare executive, was born in St. Louis, Missouri, on August 30. He received a bachelor of arts degree in sociology and journalism from the University of Minnesota in 1923. After graduation, he joined the staff of the *Call* in Kansas City. Having joined the NAACP in college, he became more active in the civil rights organization. Leaving his position with the *Call* in 1931, Wilkins became assistant executive secretary of the NAACP.

Joining a march in 1934 in Washington, D.C., to protest the failure of the attorney general to categorize lynching as a crime for a national study, was the cause for Wilkins' first arrest. In the same year, he became editor of *Crisis* magazine, a post he held for fifteen years.

When Walter White took a leave of absence from the NAACP, Wilkins was named interim executive secretary, and in 1955, upon the death of White, he assumed the position permanently.

While executive director, Wilkins testified before congressional hearings, conferred with the president, and wrote extensively for many publications. His main objective is that of helping Negroes achieve the rights of full citizenship within the bounds of democracy. He is chief spokesperson for the civil rights group's 388,715 members. He also directs the spending of a multimillion dollar annual gross income and the activities of 1,700 branches.

Wilkins is also the chairperson of the Leadership Conference of Civil Rights and trustee of the Eleanor Roosevelt Foundation and the Kennedy Memorial Library Foundation. He is a member of the John La Farge Institute and the Stockbridge School.

He has received many awards, including the Outstanding Alumni Achievement Award of the University of Minnesota, the Omega Phi Psi fraternity's Outstanding Citizen Award, and the Boy Scouts' Scout of the Year Award. In January 1969, he was one of twenty persons awarded the nation's Medal of Freedom, the country's highest civil honor. At age sixty-seven, he was awarded the Freedom Award by Freedom House.

Wilkins was a consultant to the U.S. State Department in San Francisco during the charter organization of the United Nations. As a lecturer representing the United States in Berlin, London, and Paris, he pointed out the values of our democratic heritage and expressed faith in the pluralistic system to solve racial problems.

Thurgood Marshall

Thurgood Marshall (1908–1993), Supreme Court Justice, was born in Baltimore, Maryland, on July 2. He received his bachelor of arts degree from Lincoln University in 1930, and graduated as the top student in his class from Howard University, where he received his law degree in 1933. Marshall worked his way through college as a grocery clerk, dining car waiter, and bellhop, taking time out for the debating team. By nature, Marshall became known for his meticulous research, prodigious memory, and brilliant mind.

During the 1930s and 1940s, Mr. Marshall was a leading lawyer for the Supreme Court cases involving educational equality for the NAACP. He served in Maryland and New York, making several trips to southern communities, where his life was often threatened. In 1950, he was named director counsel of the NAACP's eleven-year-old Legal Defense and Educational Fund.

Marshall played a big role in the 1954 Supreme Court decision involving school desegregation, as well as being a key figure in *Sweatt v. Plainter* (requiring the admission of a qualified black student to the law school of Texas University). He figured in *Smith v. Allwright* (establishing the right of Texas blacks to vote in the Democratic primaries).

Mr. Marshall served as a federal circuit judge for the second circuit in 1961. He was appointed to be the solicitor general of the United States in July 1965, assuming the task of acting as the federal government's chief legal spokesperson in cases brought before the Supreme Court. In 1967, Marshall was appointed to the Supreme Court of the United States. He was nominated by President Johnson, and was the first black man in history to become a justice. He held one of the most prestigious positions ever held by a black man in the history of the United States (Rowan, 1993).

Judge Marshall holds numerous honorary degrees from Virginia State College, Morgan State College, Grinnell College, Syracuse University, and the University of Liberia. In 1946, he received the coveted Spingarn Medal for his outstanding achievements in the field of law.

THE CONGRESSIONAL BLACK CAUCUS

Although the Congressional Black Caucus (CBC) was not formally organized until 1971, the notion of joint action by black members of the U.S. House of Representatives has a longer history.

In 1954, Representative Diggs' election marked the beginning of an effort to promote communication between himself and the other black House members. As black congressional representation increased with the elections of Representative Robert Nix in 1957, Representative Augustus Hawkins in 1962, and Representative John Conyers in 1964, informal discussions developed among the members. When Representatives William Clay, Shirley Chisholm, and Louis Stokes were elected in 1968, the need to institutionalize ties among the black congressional representatives became apparent. Then, in January 1969, the three newly elected African-American representatives joined the six incumbent African-American representatives to forte the Democratic Select Committee. The Democratic Select Committee was reorganized as the Congressional Black Caucus in 1971, after the election of Reps. George W. Collins, Ronald V. Dellums, Ralph H. Metcalfe, Parren Mitchell, Charles Rangel, and Del. Walter Fauntroy. The founding members believed that collectively they could influence the course of events that were pertinent to the African-American community and other similarly situated people (Clay, 1992).

One of the first official acts of the organization was to request a meeting with President Nixon. After the CBC members boycotted the president's State of the Union speech he finally consented to the meeting, fourteen months after the initial request. The CBC met with President Richard M. Nixon on March 25, 1971, and presented him with sixty-one recommendations for action in the areas of economic security and development, community and urban development, justice and civil rights, and foreign policy. The issues and concerns of the Caucus were bipartisan and beyond the scope of individual constituencies. The results of the meeting were disappointing, but it marked the first time the organization received national attention. The CBC was established as a legitimate representative of blacks and other minorities. Presently, it continues to meet with the president, at the White House, when critical issues arise.

Throughout its history, the CBC has worked to find effective ways to influence U.S. domestic and foreign policy. The Caucus has been active in all stages of development of legislation. The scope of the legislation has ranged from nonbinding resolutions to comprehensive legislation providing for specific and concrete action. In addition, the CBC has: advanced the CBC Alternative Budget; developed and endorsed recommendations for policy initiatives; coordinated and disseminated information among various levels of government, outside organizations, and the public; sponsored workshops and conferences on policy areas and issues; organized or participated a number of demonstrations and boycotts; and promoted letter-writing campaigns and clemency appeals for political prisoners and their families.

Currently, there are forty African-American Members of the CBC—thirty-nine in the House of Representatives and one in the Senate—eleven women and twenty-nine men. They represent a variety of districts—urban and rural, northern and southern, expanding from coast to coast. Members, past and present, have been advocates for many constituent interests, national and international. They continue working to develop an expanded legislative agenda while simultane-ously providing service to various congressional districts.

The vision of the founding members (Clay, 1992) ". . . to promote the public welfare through legislation designed to meet the needs of millions of neglected citizens," continues to be woven throughout the legislative and political activities of the CBC. The CBC promises to continue to be the conscience of Congress. It should also be noted that the CBC has been more of a political posturing organi-zation than an outcome-based organization on behalf of black Americans. The CBC's effectiveness will ultimately be measured by the extent to which it can uplift black America.

9

Black Leadership in Education

American leadership in educational institutions has been widely criticized for its ineffectiveness in adjusting to changing times. Black educational leadership is no exception. Education continues to be held up by American society as the institution that makes possible upward mobility. Without a doubt, education is the key to social, economic, and political mobility. It is an essential prerequisite to self-fulfillment, employment, and full participation in today's changing society. Yet blacks' encounters with it have resulted too often in destroyed aspirations and failure (Glasgow, 1980). Over the past decade, studies have projected new economic and social realities for America. Among these new realities are major shifts in the nation's demographic makeup as it moves toward the twenty-first century. These shifts demand transformational leadership and constructive institutional changes.

In addressing the problems of black education, Smith and Chunn (1991) observed that many institutions that once worked well, no longer do so. Many ambitious social programs and policies that originally promised much have been abandoned, have failed, or just faded away. Pivotal to these times and changes as characterized by Smith and Chunn, is the question of the extent to which the American educational system has been, or still is, capable of being responsive to incorporating and even instigating equity and excellence for black Americans.

The following pages examine the black men and women whom we have selected as champions of the cause of black education in this century. These selections were designed to show the varied responses of black Americans to black educational leadership. These men and women were confronted with two major issues: (1) the struggle for educational opportunities within the broader society, and (2) the ideological differences about black education among black Americans. A classic example of the division among black educational leaders was the controversy between Booker T. Washington and W.E.B. Du Bois. Both men were leaders of many talents, and yet they never commanded a mass following among blacks as compared, for example, to Marcus Garvey or Martin Luther King, Jr.

Booker T. Washington

Booker Taliaferro Washington (c. 1856–1915) was born a slave and grew up in the foothills of the Appalachian Mountains in Virginia. Of his nativity, there are scanty records. His father was said to have been a white plantation worker; the child was born sometime in the late 1950s. As a youngster, he ran about in a single garment, a rough and scratching flaxen shirt, and answered to the single name of "Booker." At school one day, when a second name was called for from all students, he blurted out "Washington," and that became his surname.

Former slaves at this time were getting into the habit of using middle initials, letters which often stood for no name, but as Washington said, were simply a part of what the free Negro proudly called his "entitles." When he found that his mother had thought of calling him Taliaferro, he added that name to his and used the "T" as a middle initial.

After a little local schooling, he heard one day of Hampton Institute, and he started out to find it, trudging along on his bare feet toward the seacoast, working his way and picking up rides where he could. He finally arrived at Hampton, and later was met by one of the teachers. She gave him no pencil, no paper, but a broom and a dust cloth to clean up the room. This was his test. Three times he swept the room, and then with his dust cloth, he poked into every corner again and again. He was admitted to Hampton.

Washington completed the curriculum in June 1875. He gave credit to Hampton for his training and for the ideas to which his whole career was devoted. General Armstrong, the founder and the head of the school, was his inspiration and ideal. After teaching for a few years in schools near his own home, Washington was called back to Hampton to take charge of a group of Indians and to serve as a night school teacher.

Then came the call to take charge of a school in the "black belt" of Alabama. Washington went, and soon Tuskegee became the most talked of institution of the race and of the whole South. The first class that gathered around Washington at Tuskegee were older, mostly illiterate, and poorly dressed. Washington announced the first day of class would be spent cleaning up. The class complained, but the next day they appeared, and began to clean. The first lesson was neatness; the next was work. New buildings were needed. Washington helped teach the students brick laying. He had lumber and he set up a sawmill. The buildings needed planning. He had the boys learn to draw, and even to make blueprints. He got an old plow horse and mule and ran the first furrows in what later grew into a thriving farm. He taught neatness and cleanliness. His recognition its peak with an invitation to speak at the Cotton States Exposition in Atlanta, Georgia, in 1895. In his speech, Washington urged the South, both white and black, to stop where they were and to go forward: "Put down your buckets where you are; forget for the moment abstract questions of rights and privileges, and work out practical means for the progress of all." The dramatic highlight of the speech came when he said, "In all things that are purely social, we can be as separate as the fingers of the hand, yet one as the hand in all things essential to mutual progress."

This speech transformed southern sentiment. Tuskegee flourished. Washington's influence set a tide toward cooperation in schools, and in black welfare generally.

On July 4, 1881, soon after his arrival at Tuskegee, Booker T. Washington wrote the following description of the school and the conditions he found in the rural South:

I arrived here four weeks ago. Instead of finding my work in a low marshy country as I expected, I find Tuskegee a beautiful little town, with a high and healthy location. It is a town such as one rarely sees in the South. Its quiet shady streets and tasteful and rich dwellings remind one of a New England village. After my arrival I had one week in which to prepare for the opening of the Normal School. I utilized this time in seeing the teachers and others who wished to enter the school, and in getting a general idea of my work and the people. Sunday I spoke in both churches to the people about the school, and told all who wished to enter to come and see me at my boarding place during the week. About thirty persons called and had their names enrolled, others called whose names for various reasons, I could not enroll. With the young people many of their parents came. I was particularly impressed with the desire of the parents to educate their children, whatever might be the sacrifice.

From 1895 until his death in 1915, Booker T. Washington's influence, power, and determination made him a force to be reckoned with. On September 18, 1895, at the opening of the Cotton States and International Exposition in Atlanta, Georgia, Washington delivered his famous address, "The Atlanta Compromise." The speech was designed to "cement the friendship of the races (black and white) and bring about hearty cooperation between them."

Turning to blacks in the audience, Booker T. declared:

Our greatest danger is that in the great leap from slavery to freedom we may overlook the fact that the masses of us are to live by the productions of our hands, and fail to keep in mind that we shall prosper in proportion as we learn to dignify and glorify common labor. No race can prosper till it learns that there is as much dignity in tilling a field as in writing a poem. No race that has anything to contribute to the markets of the world is long in any degree ostracized. It is important and right that all the privileges of the law be ours, but it is vastly more important that we be prepared for the exercise of these vast privileges. The opportunity to earn a dollar in a factory just now is worth infinitely more than the opportunity to spend a dollar in an opera house.

The address caused a sensation and drew a number of criticisms from black leaders. White southerners, however, loved the speech. The speech reflected Washington's rise to fame. In the last twenty years of his life, Washington had a dual role as a black educator and a race leader. His critics noted that Washington's ideas in the position of white-sanctioned race leader and his passion for technical education as an educator were not acceptable.

The most searching and influential critic of Washington's policies was W.E.B. Du Bois (1961). In his chapter, "Of Mr. Booker T. Washington and Others" in *The Souls of Black Folk* (1903), Du Bois was especially critical of Washington's position on black education. Du Bois was an advocate of liberal education vis-à-vis Washington's interest in vocational/technical education. It should be noted, however, that although Du Bois commented that "[e]asily the most striking thing in the history of the American Negro since 1876 is the ascendancy of Mr. Booker T. Washington," he charged that Washington's leadership would result in black disfranchisement, the creation of an inferior civil status for blacks, and the withdrawal of funds from institutions for the higher learning of blacks. He went on to suggest that Washington faced a "triple paradox":

1. He is striving to make Negro artisans businessmen and property owners; but it is utterly impossible under modern competitive methods, for workingmen and property owners to defend their rights and exist without the right of suffrage.

2. He insists on thrift and self-respect, but at the same time counsels a silent submission to civic inferiority such as is bound to sap the manhood of any race in the long run.

3. He advocates common school and industrial training, and deprecates institutions of higher learning; but neither the Negro common schools, nor Tuskegee itself, could remain open a day were it not for teachers trained in Negro colleges, or trained by their graduates. (Du Bois, 1903)

In retrospect, as educational leaders both Washington and Du Bois were right in that blacks needed and still need vocational/technical education and liberal arts education. It was not a matter of *either* and *or*: In a sense, therefore, they were both prophets. What they both saw then is indeed true today.

Another selection of leaders among black educators is a black woman, Mary McLeod Bethune. (Incidentally, at the time of writing of this book there were more than twenty black women college or university presidents in the United States.)

Mary Bethune

Mary Mcleod Bethune (1875–1955), educator, was born in Mayesville, South Carolina, on July 10, to Patsy and Sam McLeod. She was one of seventeen children, but the first to be born free.

The early life on her parents' farm taught her the importance of having faith in what you do, and praying. "Nothing comes without faith and prayer and nothing in my life has ever come without sweat, too."

Mrs. Bethune is often compared to Frederick Douglass; both had to overcome tremendous obstacles during their rise to prominence. Douglass, a former slave, was a famous speaker, writer, and fighter for human rights and equality. Mary, once a farmhand on her parents' farm, became the president of a college, as well as a Spingarn Medal winner.

Mary McLeod's education was no simple matter. School in South Carolina lasted only three months a year; but short as it was, Mary walked the five miles to school every day and devoted many hours to studying her lessons. Her schooling started when she was eleven years old.

The thing that impressed her most was hearing her schoolmates call the black teacher in charge, Miss Emma Wilson, by her last name. She had never heard a black person addressed by anything other than his or her first name. This, to Mary, was a badge of self-respect.

After graduating from this school, Mary McLeod received a scholarship offered by Mary Chrisman, a white seamstress from Colorado, who wanted her money used to educate a black girl. Mary McLeod was sent to Scotia Seminary in Concord, North Carolina, for a period of seven years. She applied to the Moody Bible Institute in Illinois, and was accepted. When she arrived at the school, though, she discovered that she was the only black student there.

Upon graduation from the Institute, she traveled to New York to ask the Presbyterian Board of Missions for a position in Africa, but was turned down because the board felt that she was too young and there was no opening for a Negro in Africa at that time. The refusal of the board to accept her as a missionary was a great disappointment to her. "It was the greatest disappointment of my life, those were cruel days" (Smith, 2000).

She accepted a position teaching at the Haines Normal Institute in Augusta, Georgia, where she worked closely with Lucy Laney, its founder. She organized a Sunday school for the black children in Augusta, Georgia, before accepting a teaching assignment at Kendel Institute, a church-supported school for blacks. She remained in this teaching capacity for two years.

At this time in her life, Mary McLeod met Mr. Albertus Bethune, a young man who was working in a local dry goods store helping his brother through college. They were married the following year.

Mrs. Bethune, not satisfied with the role of being a housewife, decided that her life's work was to help black children receive adequate education. "My people need literacy; they need even more, to learn simple rules of farming, making decent homes, of health and plain cleanliness" (Smith, 2000). She felt that these were the basic needs for her newly liberated race. She accepted a teaching position in Palatka, Florida, only nine months after she bore a son. Four years later, she set out for Daytona Beach, Florida, after finding out that the Florida East Coast Railroad was being extended as far south as Miami, and its black laborers were living under terrible conditions near the site of the construction.

Being the first woman educator to emphasize the importance of industrial training for black youths, she focused the education she gave to the children of the laborers on farming, cooking, sewing, food skills, and health skills. Her school opened on an old dumping ground, after her first five pupils (girls aged eight to twelve) helped to clear away the debris. She traveled by bicycle to solicit funds from various organizations and individuals. She also trained her young students to sing well enough to entertain at meetings, in order to help raise money for the school.

On October 3, 1904, the Daytona Educational and Industrial School for Negro Girls was opened, with Mary McLeod Bethune as its founder–principal. John D. Rockefeller heard Mary's group sing at the Ormand Hotel, and was so attracted by the display and dedication of the children and Mrs. Bethune in regard to raising enough money to run the school, that he became a devoted friend and supporter of the school until his death.

Mary Bethune struggled to raise the scholastic level of her school, to enlarge the school, and to get more funds for its support. In addition to running her own school, she was responsible for a chain of mission schools, Tomoka Missions. The McLeod Hospital came next. It started in 1911 with two beds. A few years later, there were twenty beds, with both Negro and white physicians and Mrs. Bethune's own student nurses. Her school ran the hospital for twenty years—until Daytona Beach provided a hospital for blacks.

There were many demands on her time for many causes, but Mary Bethune's first loyalty was to her school. By 1914, it offered a full high school course, and turned out graduates trained in cooking, nursing, homemaking, and teaching. Following the idea of using singing groups to raise money (an idea which had been started by the Fisk University Jubilee Singers), Mary took her girls north, where their songs made benefactors out of listeners.

During World War I, Mary Bethune took a leave of absence to raise funds for the American Red Cross. Immediately upon the conclusion of the war, she was back in Daytona Beach, Florida, devoting herself to her school and to the community. "Be a David, take a vow of courage, but let the weapons of determination be coupled with the armor of justice and forgiveness" (Smith and McCuskey, 2000).

At the first meeting of the Southern Conference for Human Welfare, an organization established by whites and Negroes to raise the general level of underprivileged groups in the South, a resolution for better schools was proposed by Mrs. Bethune, the delegate from Florida. The chairperson, a white woman, recorded her approval. The chairwoman had never called a black person by any name other than his or her first name, and when Mary completed her amendment, the chairwoman acknowledged her by calling for "the adoption by the conference of Mary's amendment." The motion was made and carried. Mrs. Bethune rose, and said as humbly as she could, "I do not care what anyone calls me as an individual, but as a delegate from Florida, I must insist on respect of that sovereign, and since there are probably dozens of Marys at this conference, I ask that it be entered on the record that the resolutions were presented by Mrs. Mary Bethune" (Smith and McCuskey, 2000).

In 1923, Cookman Institute, a men's college in Jacksonville, Florida, and the Daytona Normal and Industrial Institute, as it had been called since 1921, were merged and deeded over to the Methodist Episcopal Church. The new coeducational school was called Daytona-Cookman Collegiate Institute. A few years later, the name of the school was changed, when the trustees decided that Mary McLeod Bethune's name should be memorialized. With her consent, the school became known as Bethune-Cookman College. After the merger, with a larger administrative staff, Mrs. Bethune gave more time to outside activities. In 1924, she went abroad, and was entertained by the Lord Mayor and his Lady in London, and by the Lord Provost in Edinburgh. She was also received by the Pope in Rome.

Mrs. Bethune became known and recognized as an educator. She was a popular lecturer and availed herself of every opportunity to plead for interracial goodwill and brotherhood, repeating over and over again, the quotation: "There was no superior and there was no inferior race." After World War I, she was elected to the Executive Board of the National Urban League and became a vice president of the NAACP. In November 1930, she was invited by President Herbert Hoover to the General Session of the White House Conference on Child Health Protection. The following year, she was invited to the President's Conference on Home Building and Home Ownership.

After Franklin D. Roosevelt's election to the presidency, Roosevelt honored Mrs. Bethune by asking her to serve on the Advisory Committee on Youth Administration, which was in the process of being formed. When the president set up an office on Minority Affairs of National Youth Administration (NYA), he appointed Mrs. Bethune as its administrator. This was the first such post ever held by a black woman in the United States. Mary Bethune felt that she could not accept it, because of her college duties, but she did feel that it would pave the way for another black woman.

Mrs. Bethune received many awards during her distinguished career. In 1935, she received the Spingarn Award, an award that is presented each year by the NAACP for the highest and noblest achievement by an American black during the preceding year or years. In her stirring acceptance speech, "Breaking the Bars to Brotherhood," Mrs. Bethune appealed to her audience to be prepared against social and political injustices, and make way for a larger brotherhood through cooperation. In 1936, she received the Francis A. Drexel Award for distinguished service to her race, and received a medal from the National Association of Negro Musicians; she later also received the Thomas Jefferson medal from the Southern Conference for Human Welfare, in 1942.

Mrs. Mary Bethune and Mrs. Eleanor Roosevelt became close friends. On one occasion, Mrs. Bethune began to cough. The two women were on the lecture program and were sitting on the same platform. Mrs. Roosevelt poured a glass of water, brought it to Mrs. Bethune and stood over her while she drank it.

While Mrs. Bethune was working with the NYA, she became concerned with the future of the Negro woman, and formed the National Council of Negro Women. The membership was to represent all communities, and to strive for better working conditions, higher standards of living, equal educational opportunities, and civil rights. The Council grew into a powerful organization. A $10,000 donation, obtained from Marshall Field, III, made possible the purchase of a house for the National Council of Negro Women in Washington, D.C.

In 1937, at the Twenty-second Annual Meeting of the Association for the Study of Negro Life and History, of which she had been president, Mary Bethune said: "Our people cry out all around us, like children lost in the wilderness, hemmed in by a careless will, we are losing our homes and our farms and our jobs. If our people are to fight their way up out of bondage, we must arm them with the sword and the shield, the buckle of pride and belief in themselves."

Mary McLeod Bethune's philosophy might be epitomized in a phrase she often used in her lectures to black audiences: "This is our day."

Prior to her death in 1955, she wrote her "Last Will and Testament," which was published posthumously in *Ebony* magazine. Among other things, she noted in her "Will":

Sometimes I ask myself if I have any other legacy to leave. Truly, my worldly possessions are few. Yet, my experiences have been rich. From them, I have distilled principles and policies in which I believe firmly, for they represent the meaning of my life's work. They are the product of much sweat and sorrow. Perhaps in them there is something of value. So, as my life draws to a close, I will pass them on to Negroes everywhere in the hope that an old woman's philosophy may give them inspiration. Here, then, is my legacy.

I leave you love. Love builds. It is positive and helpful. It is more beneficial than hate. Injuries quickly forgotten quickly pass away. Personally and racially, our enemies must be forgiven. Our aim must be to create a world of fellowship and justice where no man's skin, color, or religion is held against him. 'Love thy neighbor' is a precept which could transform the world if it were universally practiced. It connotes brotherhood and, to me, brotherhood of man is the noblest concept in all human relations. Loving your neighbor means being interracial, interreligious, and international.

I leave you hope. I leave you the challenge of developing confidence in one another. I leave you a thirst for education. I leave you a respect for the uses of power. I leave you faith. Faith is the first factor in a life devoted to service. I leave you racial dignity. I leave you a desire to live harmoniously with your fellow men. I leave you a responsibility to our young people.

I pray that we will learn to live harmoniously with the white race.

BROWN V. BOARD OF EDUCATION

Fifty-eight years after the Supreme Court of the United States promulgated the doctrine of "separate but equal" facilities for black citizens, it moved to reverse itself in the education cases that came before the Court in 1954. Argued effectively by the NAACP legal counsel, Thurgood Marshall, the defense was able to show the devastating effects of segregated education on Negro children. In a unanimous decision, written by Chief Justice Earl Warren, the Court drew heavily on psychological studies showing the wholly unequal results of this type of education. The 1954 decision in *Brown v. Board of Education of Topeka* (347 U.S. 483) granted a one-year delay of the court's ruling for the purpose of further argument. Thus, May 17, 1955 became the landmark date on which the Court ordered desegregation of schools "with all deliberate speed."

The education cases resulting in this landmark decision came from the states of Kansas, South Carolina, Virginia, and Delaware. They were premised on different facts and different local conditions, but a common legal question justified their consideration together for this consolidated opinion. In each of the cases, minors of the Negro race, through their legal representatives, sought the aid of the courts in obtaining admission to the public schools of their community on a non-segregated basis. In each instance, they had been denied admission to schools attended by white children under laws requiring or permitting segregation according to race. This segregation was alleged to deprive the plaintiffs of the equal protection of the laws under the Fourteenth Amendment. The unanimous 1954 Supreme Court decision in *Brown v. Board of Education of Topeka* climaxed years of pressure and litigation by the NAACP and other concerned groups and individuals over the question of the legal status of American blacks in regard to public education. Harbinger of a new era in the legal struggle for black equality in the United States, the Supreme Court declared that racial discrimination in state-supported public schools was unconstitutional under the equal protection clause of the Fourteenth Amendment.

This decision, of course, ran contrary to the 1896 decision of the Supreme Court in *Plessy v. Ferguson* (163 U.S. 537), which sanctioned the so called "separate but equal" doctrine. This doctrine maintained that equality of treatment is satisfied when blacks and whites are provided equal facilities, even though these facilities may be separate. Therefore, although the *Brown* decision's primary thrust was directed against segregated public education, it also struck out at all Jim Crow laws that were based on the "separate but equal" doctrine.

In delivering the opinion of the Court, Chief Justice Earl Warren declared that state-imposed racial segregation of public school facilities was detrimental to the psychological well-being of black children. "To separate them from others of similar age and qualifications solely because of their race," Warren stated,

generates a feeling of inferiority as to their status in the community that may affect their hearts and minds in a way unlikely ever to be undone. Whatever may have been the extent of psychological knowledge at the time of *Plessy v Ferguson,* this finding is amply supported by modern authority. Any language in *Plessy v. Ferguson* contrary to this finding is rejected. We conclude that in the field of public education the doctrine of 'separate but equal' has no place. Separate educational facilities are inherently unequal.

Prior to the *Brown* decision, racial segregation of public school facilities was *required by law* in seventeen states and in the District of Columbia. Within this area, approximately eight million white children were attending approximately 35,000 white schools, while nearly three million Afro-American children were enrolled in 15,000 black schools. These figures prompted the *New York Times* (May 18, 1954) to assert that "probably no decision in the history of the Court has directly concerned so many individuals."

The *Brown* decision of 1954 established the constitutional principle, but did not supply the necessary enforcement decree. One year later, therefore, the

Supreme Court mandated that desegregation of public school facilities should begin "with all deliberate speed" toward "full compliance with our May 17, 1954, ruling." However, many states and individual school districts adopted a snail's interpretation of the Court's "with all deliberate speed" ruling. Fifteen years after the initial *Brown* decision, approximately 80 percent of southern black children continued to attend segregated schools. In response, the Supreme Court in 1969 revised its previous stand by declaring in *Alexander v. Holmes County Board of Education* (396 U.S. 19) that the standard of "all deliberate speed" was no longer "constitutionally permissible" and ordered desegregation "at once." Although this order did prod many states and school districts into action, complete desegregation of the nation's schools (both southern and northern) has not yet become a reality.

Four individual black intellectuals/educators have been included in this section of the book for their significant contributions to American education and intellectual leadership. The first is Alain Locke, the first black Rhodes Scholar and the author of *The New Negro* (1925). The second is Carter G. Woodson, the second black to receive a Ph.D. in history from Harvard University and the father of Negro History Week, now known as Black History Month, The third is Benjamin Mays, the late president of Morehouse College, the only all-black, male institution of higher education in America. He also served as school superintendent in Atlanta. The fourth and final selection is Weldon Johnson, a Jacksonville, Florida, educator who authored the Negro National Anthem, now known as the Black National Anthem.

Carter G. Woodson

Carter G. Woodson (1875–1950), historian, was born in New Canton, Virginia, where he attended elementary school. He later worked as a coal miner in Huntington, West Virginia. He studied, and after three years of self-tuition, he passed high school examinations. He continued his education at the University of Chicago, where he received his bachelor's and master's degrees, and his doctor of philosophy degree at Harvard. Later, he attended the Sorbonne.

In 1903, he went to the Philippines as a teacher, and five months later became supervisor of education. Later, he was principal of Armstrong High School of Washington, D.C., then dean of the Liberal Arts College of Howard University and the dean of West Virginia Collegiate Institute.

Woodson's greatest contribution was the *Journal of Negro History*, which he launched in January 1916. He also founded the Association for the Study of Negro Life and History, and was largely responsible for the creation of Negro History Week. Dr. Woodson wrote many articles and published the following books: *A Century of Negro Education*; *History of the Negro Church*; *The Rural Negro*; *Mis-Education of the Negro*; *African Backgrounds Outlined*; and *The Negro in Our History*.

Dr. Woodson once wrote: "We spend millions yearly to straighten our hair and bleach our skin and some of us go so far as to have our noses lifted in the hope of looking like a white man. Monkeys too have straight hair and thin lips."

He also said: "I advocate a more realistic and practical approach to education. It took me over thirty years to get over my Harvard education" (Woodson, 1933).

THE ASSOCIATION FOR THE STUDY OF NEGRO LIFE AND HISTORY (currently known as the Association for the Study of African-American Life and History)

Beginnings

The Association for the Study of Negro Life and History was organized by Carter G. Woodson in Chicago, on September 9, 1915, with George Cleveland Hall, W.B. Hartgrove, J.E. Stamps, and Alexander L. Jackson—four of the many invited by the founder to participate in this organization. The Association was incorporated under the laws of the District of Columbia, October 2, 1915, with Carter G. Woodson, J.E. Moorland, and J.A. Bigham as trustees. The first number of the *Journal of Negro History* was published on January 1, 1916, and since that date the Association has published this scientific magazine every quarter. Complete volumes are available in bound or unbound form.

Purposes

The Association for the Study of Negro Life and History was organized with four major purposes: to promote historical research, to publish books on Negro life and history, to promote the study of the Negro through clubs and schools, and to bring about harmony between the races by interpreting the one to the other.

Promoters

The Association was promoted by a number of well-known gentlemen, including Harold H. Swift, C.B. Powell, Arthur W. Mitchell, Oswald Garrison Villard, Elmer A. Henderson, and F.D. Patterson. Distinguished scholars such as Roland G. Usher, Frederick L. Hoffman, Evarts B. Greene, Charles M. Andrews, H.N. Sherwood, Ambrose Caliver, Benjamin E. Mays, Charles H. Wesley, Henry J. Cadbury, F.J. Klingberg, and J.R. Angell also promoted the work of the Association.

Achievements

The Association can boast of a number of significant achievements since its inception. It has directed the attention of investigations to the neglected field of black American life and history. It has extended the circulation of the *Journal of Negro History* into South America, Europe, Asia, and Africa, and published twenty-five volumes of articles and documents giving facts that are generally unknown. Twenty-seven monographs on Negro life and history have been produced. It has organized and stimulated the studies of local clubs and classes, which have done much to change the attitude of communities toward the Negro. Thousands of valuable manuscripts on the Negro have been collected and made accessible to the public in the Library of Congress. And last, but not least, the Association has had thirteen young men and women trained for research in the social sciences and for instruction in colleges and universities.

The Development of the Ideas

Directing attention to the study of black America as a neglected field, the Association could soon report important results. It led people to see the unreasonableness of the claim made for superiority of race and encouraged them to arrive at their conclusions by scientific investigation. Giving such a stimulus to the reconstruction of thought, then, the Association has changed the attitude of many persons toward blacks and other races. Black persons themselves, too, have been stimulated to higher endeavor by learning from their significant record that they are not the most despised of people.

In 1922 the Association was enabled by a grant to undertake systematic research. Prior to that time its investigation had been purely voluntary. That year, the Department of Research was established and a number of investigators were employed to undertake definite tasks. These researches have resulted in the publication of twenty-seven monographs embracing almost every aspect of black life and history. The Department of Research has recently undertaken the special task of investigating the social and economic conditions of black America since the Civil War, and it has given some attention to black folklore and African anthropology.

In 1926, the Association began the celebration of Negro History Week. This was made an occasion for public exercises, inviting special attention to the achievements of black America. With the cooperation of ministers, teachers, professionals, and businesspeople throughout the country, the celebration proved to be an unusual success. Negro History Week has become "Negro History Year," given that schools are now taking up the study of the Negro as a required course. Students are now learning to think of civilization as the heritage of the centuries to which all races have made some contribution.

Owing to the demand for greater dissemination of information than its facilities then afforded, the Association established in 1927 an Extension Division to embrace the imparting of information by public lectures and the study of Negro life and history by mail. This department, therefore, offered—and still offers—instruction given by the Association staff under the administrative supervision and control of the Association. Such an opportunity for self-improvement is widely sought by literary societies, study clubs, and other institutions for persons who have no other chance to receive this kind of instruction.

Why Black History?

If a race has no history, if it has no worthwhile tradition, it becomes a negligible factor in the thought of the world, and it stands in danger of being exterminated. The American Indians left no continuous record. They did not know the value of history; and where is the American Indian today? The Hebrews keenly appreciated the worth of tradition, as is attested by the Bible itself. In spite of worldwide persecution, therefore, Hebrews are still a great factor in the universe.

The predicament of the Negro may be stated concretely. For example, a man writes a book on the "New Freedom." Someone inquires as to how the author can harmonize his anti-black policy with his progressive doctrine. The author replies that he was not thinking of the black when he wrote that book. An order is given for the training of all young men for military service. A black applies to equip himself for this duty, but is told that the principles involved in the war concern only white people, and that blacks will be encouraged to serve only in subordinate positions. A black supports the successful party in a campaign and then asks for the accustomed recognition of being among the personnel of the new administration, but is told that public opinion is such that the black cannot be safely elevated to positions of trust in the government. A bond issue is passed to improve the facilities of education, but the black school is denied its share, or it is permitted to receive what the white system abandons as "antiquated" and "inadequate." A black is passed on the street and is shoved off into the mud; he complains or strikes back, and is lynched as a *desperado* who attacked a gentleman.

And what if the black is handicapped, segregated, or lynched? According to our education and practice, if you kill one of the group, the world goes on just as well or better; for the black is nothing, has never been anything and never will be anything but a menace to civilization. The black therefore has no respect for him or herself, and others have the utmost contempt for the black.

We call this *race prejudice*, and it may be thus properly named; but it is not something inherent to human nature. It is merely the logical result of tradition, the inevitable outcome of thorough instruction to the effect that the black has never contributed anything to the progress of mankind. The doctrine has been thoroughly drilled into the whites, and the blacks have learned well the lesson themselves; for many of them look upon other races as superior and accept the status of recognized inferiority.

All Races Make Contributions

The fact is, however, that one race has not accomplished any more good than any other race, for it would be contrary to the laws of nature to have one race inferior to the other. But if you leave it to the one to set forth its special virtues while disparaging those of others, it will not require many generations before all credit for human achievements will be ascribed to one particular stock. Such is the history taught the youth today.

James Weldon Johnson

James Weldon Johnson (1871–1938), poet and lyricist, was born in Jacksonville, Florida. Johnson had a varied career as a teacher, author, and publicist. He was admitted to the Florida bar in 1897, while living in Jacksonville. During this year, while serving as a principal of a high school, he began writing songs with his brother, J. Rosamond Johnson, a musician. In 1900, they composed "Lift Ev'ry Voice and Sing," now widely known as the Negro National Anthem. They moved to New York and continued to write songs.

In 1906, James Weldon Johnson accepted the post of consul to Puerto Cabello in Venezuela. He remained there until his transfer to Corinto, Nicaragua, in 1909. He returned home in 1912, after a notable period of service. That same year he became field secretary and, later, secretary of the NAACP He went to Haiti in 1920 to investigate conditions under the American occupation.

In 1930, Johnson became professor of creative literature at Fisk University. He died in a tragic automobile accident at a railroad crossing in Maine in 1938.

Among the most important of Johnson's publications were *Fifty Years and Other Poems* (1917); and *The Book of American Negro Poetry* (1922); he edited and wrote the introduction to *God's Trombones Seven Negro Sermons in Verse* (1927); *Black Manhattan* (1930); and *Along This Way* (1933).

> James Weldon Johnson:
> "Sing a Song Full of the Faith That the Dark Past Has Taught Us" (Lift Ev'ry Voice and Sing)
>
> Lift ev'ry voice and sing,
> Till earth and heaven ring,
> Ring with the harmonics of liberty;
> Let our rejoicing rise,
> High as the list'ning skies,
> Let it resound loud as the rolling sea.
> Sing a song full of the faith that the dark past has taught us,
> Sing a song full of the hope that the present has brought us,
> Facing the rising sun,
> Of our new day begun,
> Let us march on till victory is won.
>
> Stony the road we trod,
> Bitter the chast'ning rod,
> Felt in the days when hope unborn had died;
> Yet with a steady beat,
> Have not our weary feet
> Came to the place for which our fathers sighed?
> We have come over a way that with tears has been watered,
> We have come, treading our path thro' the blood of the slaughtered,

Out from the gloomy past,
Till now we stand at last
Where the white gleam of our bright star is cast.

God of our weary years,
God of our silent tears,
Thou who has brought us thus far on the way;
Thou who has by thy might
Led us into the light,
Keep us forever the path, we pray.
Lest our feet stray from the places our God where we met Thee,
Lest our hearts, drunk with the wine of the world, we forget Thee:
Shadowed beneath Thy hand,
May we forever stand,
True to our God,
True to our native land.
(Johnson and Johnson, 1980)

Alain Locke

Alain Leroy Locke (1886–1954), educator and historian, was born in Philadelphia, on September 3. He attended Central High School in Philadelphia, the Philadelphia School of Pedagogy, and Harvard University, where he was elected to Phi Beta Kappa. After receiving his bachelor of arts degree in 1907, he won the coveted Rhodes Scholarship, an award for two years of study at Oxford University in England. In doing so, he became the first of his race to receive such an award.

After returning to America in 1912, Locke became assistant professor of English and philosophy at Howard University in Washington, D.C. Continuing his study at Harvard in 1916–1917, he received his Ph.D. in 1918. Dr. Locke became head of the department of philosophy at Howard University. Except for leaves as exchange professor, Dr. Locke remained at Howard until he retired in 1953.

His first book, *Race Contacts and Inter-Racial Relations,* was published in 1916. His doctoral dissertation was titled *The Problem of Classification in the Theory of Value* (1918). He was best known for his writings concerning the cultural contributions of his people. He explained the Harlem Renaissance to America in his book, *The New Negro: An Interpretation* (1925). He co-edited *Plays of Negro Life* and edited *Four Negro Poets,* both in 1927.

In 1934, Locke founded The Associates in Negro Folk Education and edited its series of eight Bronze Booklets. He wrote three of them: *Negro Art: Past and Present*; *The Negro and His Music*; and *The Negro in Art: A Pictoral Record of the Negro Artist and of the Negro Theme in Art,* all in 1940.

Locke became ill while working on his "magnum opus," which was to incorporate all black cultural contributions. He had collected the material and had partially outlined his work. He died before he could complete his efforts, but a colleague, Margaret Just Butcher, completed the work and published it in 1956 under the title, *The Negro in American Culture: Based on Materials Left by Alain Locke.*

Since Locke died, several publications have concentrated on his life and works, documenting his impact on American life and thought. Two of these publications were authored by Johnny Washington. The first, entitled *Alain Locke and Philosophy: A Quest for Cultural Pluralism,* was published in 1986; the second, *A Journey Into the Philosophy of Alain Locke,* was published in 1994. (Both were published in Greenwood Press's series on contributions in Afro-American and African studies.) Three other publications are worthy of note: Harris (1989), *The Philosophy of Alain Locke: Harlem Renaissance and Beyond*; Linnemann (1982), *Alain Locke: Reflections on a Modern Renaissance Man*; and in his recent publication, *Color and Culture: Black Writers and the Making of the Modern Intellectual,* Posnock (1998) devoted a major portion to Alain Locke and W.E.B. Du Bois. Other subjects included Afro-American intellectual life in the United States, intellectual life in the twentieth century, American Literature—Afro-American authors, and history and criticism.

Benjamin Mays

Benjamin E. Mays (1895–1984), educator and author, was born on August 1 in Epworth, South Carolina. He grew up the last of seven children of ex-slaves and semiliterate farmers. He attended elementary and high school in South Carolina, and later Bates College in Maine, graduating in 1920. He earned his master of arts degree in 1925, and a Ph.D. degree in 1935, both from the University of Chicago.

He joined Howard University in 1934 as dean of its School of Religion, and in 1940 was named president of Morehouse College. He retired from the presidency in 1967, after placing Morehouse on a sound financial footing, upgrading the faculty (one-half held Ph.D. degrees), and expanding the school's physical facilities during his term as the president of the university.

His published works include *The Negro's Church* (co-author), New York (1933, and republished in 1969); *The Negro's God* (1938, and republished in 1969); *Seeking to Be Christian in Race Relations* (1957); *A Gospel for the Social Awakening* (Selections from the writings of Walter Rauschenbusch) (1950); "The Christian in Race Relations," pamphlet; *Disturbed About Man* (Selected Sermons) (1969); and *Born to Rebel* (1971). Mr. Mays has written many articles in *The Crisis*; *Christian Century*; *Journal of Negro Education*; *Missions*; and the *Negro Digest.*

He has received many honors, including being named vice president, Federal Council of Churches of Christ in America, 1944–1946; placed on the Schomberg Honor Roll of Race Relations, 1944; recipient of *Letter Award* for promoting racial friendship, 1945; Alumnus of the Year, Divinity School, University of Chicago, 1949; Recipient Second Annual State Fair Negro Achievement Award, Texas, 1950; President, United Negro College Fund, Inc., from 1958 to 1961; appointed to the Advisory Council of the United States Committee for the United

Nations, 1959; and appointed member of the National Advisory Council of the Peace Corps Organization initiated under President John Kennedy, 1961.

In recognition of his educational and civic leadership, in 1981 the Atlanta School Board named Benjamin E. Mays High School in his honor. Two major publications about this accomplished educator further illustrate his contributions to American education, particularly to black educational attainment. The first was his autobiography, entitled *Born to Rebel: An Autobiography* (Mays, 1971). The other was a scholarly piece edited by Lawrence Edward Carter, Sr. (1998), *Walking Integrity: Benjamin Elijah Mays, Mentor to Martin Luther King, Jr.*, about his impact as a mentor to the civil rights leader, Dr. King, Jr., while he was an undergraduate at Morehouse College in Atlanta. The book first appeared in 1994 as a *Festschrift* to celebrate the centennial of Benjamin E. Mays' birth.

The foregoing discussion suggests that black Americans have made significant progress in education, presumably because of the efforts of black leaders and well-intentioned white supporters. The current state of black education in America leaves much to be desired, especially if compared to its white counterpart. In practically every field of profession, blacks are lagging behind; they are underrepresented in every field including engineering, medicine, law, teaching, nursing, liberal arts, the biological sciences, and many other professional areas like architecture, and so forth. The dropout rate of blacks in the public schools often doubles that of whites. If progress is to be made in the new millennium, black leadership in education must adopt new strategies. Such strategies may require new leadership styles.

10

Black Leadership in Corporate America

One of the most neglected research areas of black life, especially in the past three decades, concerns black life in corporate America. This chapter is an attempt to examine the most hidden effects on the lives of black Americans, who in ever-increasing numbers are trying to "make it" in the mainstream. It is also our attempt to examine black businesses that *have* made it in corporate America.

Davis and Watson (1982) have documented the human side of the story of black men and women operating in "foreign" social space (corporate America) with unfamiliar protocol, with habits, manners, values, and styles of thinking that until recently were very new to them. Their study used interviews taken from more than 160 managers and experts, along with both scholarly and popular writing in the field. Among other things Watson examined meritocracy as a corporate value and its application to blacks in corporate America; to managerial life; as the new American dream; to the integration of black managerial middle class; and to power relationships in corporate America. Although many black managers have success stories, racism and sexism continue to be major barriers that have created "glass" and "cement" ceilings for black men and women in corporate America. But the problem is more complicated than that. Black managers in corporate America have dual jeopardies: (1) they face glass and cement ceilings, and (2) they are often rejected and labeled as "Uncle Toms" by their fellow blacks, who expect more than they can deliver.

THE "GLASS CEILING"

Notwithstanding all the debate over affirmative action, white males represent 97 percent of the corporate board room. In 1987, the Department of Labor published a report—*Workforce 2000*—that brought dramatic attention to changes taking place in our economy and in the composition of our workforce. Significant among these changes was the increased importance of minorities—people of color and women—to the competitive status of the American economy. The Department of Labor has defined the term "glass ceiling" as "those artificial barriers based on attitudinal or organizational bias that prevent qualified individuals from advancing upward in their organization into management level positions" (U.S. Department of Labor, 1991).

Since the publication of *Workforce 2000*, ample evidence has been gathered to show that people of color and women have made significant gains in entering the workforce. But there is also significant evidence from research conducted by universities, nonprofit organizations, executive recruiters, and the Department of Labor that documents a dearth of people of color and women at management levels—the so-called "glass ceiling." The symptoms of this problem are manifest. Qualified people of color and women are all too often on the outside, looking into the executive suite. Thus, the Department of Labor set out to investigate the glass ceiling in corporate America to see if there was a problem, and if there was a problem, what were the causes, and then how the problem could be fixed. The report of this study, entitled "A Report on the Glass Ceiling Initiative," was published in 1991. The following is an excerpt of the executive summary of the report.

The Initiative

The goals of the glass ceiling initiative were: To promote a quality, inclusive, and diverse workforce capable of meeting the challenge of global competition; to promote good corporate conduct through an emphasis on corrective and cooperative problem solving; to promote equal opportunity, not mandated results; and, to establish a blueprint of procedures to guide the Department in conducting future reviews of all management levels of the corporate workforce. These goals speak to not only what is right and just in our society, but what makes good economic sense as the private and public sectors seek to work together to achieve an ever-improving quality of life for all Americans.

The initiative was a four-pronged effort: 1) An internal educational effort within the Department of Labor; 2) A pilot study looking at nine individual companies; 3) An effort to increase public awareness of the issue and encourage voluntary efforts; and 4) An effort to recognize and reward publicly those companies that are independently removing their own glass ceiling.

The Pilot Study

Nine Fortune 500 establishments were selected randomly for review. The companies represented a broad range of products and services and were located in five of the Department's ten regions. The reviews were conducted by senior officials from the national and regional offices of the Department. After numerous meetings with various organizations, along with an extensive research effort, a blueprint for the evaluation process was developed. The organizations included business, trade and professional associations, human resources officials, and leaders and representatives from organizations representing minorities and women.

The process was designed to produce three basic results: 1) Identification of systemic barriers to the career advancement of minorities and women; 2) Elimination of these barriers through corrective and cooperative problem solving; and 3) Furtherance of the Department's and the employer community's understanding of how to identify and eliminate discriminatory barriers.

In accordance with the legal requirements Federal contractors are required to follow, companies were reviewed to ensure that they did discriminate on the basis of race, sex, color, religion, national origin, disability, or veteran status; that they took affirmative action to actively recruit qualified workers from all segments of the labor force; and that they provided training and advancement opportunities for all employees.

The Findings

It should be pointed out that none of the nine companies in the pilot study were cited for discrimination at the upper levels of their workforces. That's the good news. Yet a number of the pilot companies did not live up to the good faith efforts to meet all affirmative action requirements. This said, the Department of Labor recognizes that the results of nine pilot reviews do not present a scientific sample that can describe, with any confidence, the practices and policies of corporations beyond those examined in the pilot study. The Labor Department believes that attitudinal and organizational barriers, as identified, are an indication that the progress of minorities and women in corporate America is affected by more than qualifications and career choices.

The pilot project also revealed several general findings that applied to all nine companies, despite the vast differences that existed between them in terms of organizational structure, corporate culture, business sector, and personnel policies.

- In some companies, if there is not a glass ceiling, there certainly is a point beyond which minorities and men have not advanced.
- Minorities have plateaued at lower levels of the workforce than nonminority women.
- Monitoring for equal access and opportunity, especially as managers move up the corporate ladder to senior management levels where important decisions are made, was almost never considered a corporate responsibility or part of the planning for developmental programs and policies.
- Appraisal and total compensation systems that determine salary, bonuses, incentives, and perquisites for employees were not monitored.
- Placement patterns were consistent with research data.
- There was a general lack of adequate records.

Among the attitudinal and organizational barriers identified were:

- Recruitment practices involving reliance on word-of-mouth and employee referral networking; the use of executive search and referral firms, in which affirmative action/ Equal Employment Opportunity (EEO) requirements were not made known.
- Developmental practices and credential-building experiences, including advanced education, as well as career-enhancing assignments such as to corporate committees, task forces, and special projects—which are traditional precursors to advancement—were often not as available to minorities and women as they were to nonminorities and men.
- Accountability for disregarding Equal Employment Opportunity responsibilities did not reach to senior-level executives and corporate decision-makers.

BLACK ENTREPRENEURSHIP

Black American entrepreneurial interest can be traced to the eighteenth century, when slaves and free blacks became aware of the American dream. In a very modest sense, even those blacks who were sharecroppers dreamed of managerial life as a part of the American dream—the aspiration level of many Americans. The historical overview provided here is based heavily on the incisive works of two scholars, John Sibley Butler (1991) and Michael D. Woodard (1997). This provides the context within which black-owned businesses developed over time. Admittedly, this is not intended to be an exhaustive history.

About 60,000 free blacks accumulated capital that they used to initiate and sustain business activities. They developed enterprises in almost every business arena, including merchandising, real estate, manufacturing, construction trades, transportation, and mining industries. Their accomplishments were considerable.

As early as 1736, emancipated slave Emanuel Bernoon established an oyster house in Providence, Rhode Island. Anthony Johnson accumulated substantial property in Jamestown, Virginia. John Baptiste DeSable, a wholesaler and merchant, settled in Chicago in 1770. That same year, a free black man was assessed for property taxes on eight acres and a horse in Lancaster, Pennsylvania.

A notable black businessman, Paul Cuffe, born in New Bedford, Massachusetts, in 1759, became a sailor aboard a whaling ship at age sixteen. By 1806, Cuffe was a successful shipbuilder, sailor, and landowner. He established business ties with European and African markets and furnished ships and supplies to blacks who wanted to return to Africa (Marable, 1983).

Around 1800, Richard Allen established a boot and shoe store in Philadelphia, and William Alexander Leidesdorff owned import–export and ranching operations in California (Marable, 1983). In Philadelphia, blacks established a beneficial insurance society in 1789 and a life insurance society in 1810. By 1840, African-Americans in New York City owned two dry goods stores, two excellent restaurants in the financial district, four pleasure gardens, six boarding-houses, one confectionery, two coal yards, and a cleaning establishment. In Detroit, the tailoring and clothing firm owned by James Garrett and Almer Frances boasted annual gross revenues of $60,000 (Marable, 1983).

In the early 1800s, Cincinnati, Ohio, was the center of black economic activities in the Midwest. In 1835, about half of Cincinnati's black population of approximately 2,500 had once been slaves. (Cincinnati was the first point north of slavery where fugitive blacks felt reasonably safe from being apprehended and returned "down South.")

Entrepreneurs in Cincinnati were particularly successful. They included Robert Harlan, a horseman; W.A. Thompson, a tailor; J. Presley and Thomas Ball, contractors; Samuel T. Wilcot, a merchant; and Robert Gord, owner of a coal yard (Marable 1983). In 1850, J. Wilcox, an Ohio River board steward, owned a wholesale grocery store in the downtown business district. He quickly became the largest provisions dealer in the city and established trade links with New Orleans and New York. By the mid-1850s, his gross revenues reached an estimated $140,000.

Two African-American businessmen who joined forces in 1851 procured a $10,000 contract to plaster all public buildings in Hamilton County, Ohio. Henry Body, a former slave artisan, established a furniture store in Cincinnati in the late 1830s. By 1850, he regularly employed twenty to fifty black and white cabinet makers and was worth approximately $26,000 (Marable 1983). This litany of pre-Civil War black entrepreneurs—many of whom catered to white patrons—illustrates that during a time of slavery, free African-Americans somehow established and maintained a wide range of business and accumulated substantial property and wealth. Entrepreneurship for free people of African descent was difficult, but possible, even in the South.

A second group of black business people in the pre-Civil War era were slaves. Only those slaves with determination and a paternalistic master could engage in business activities. The constraints of slavery were such that even highly skilled slaves were barred from becoming entrepreneurs in the true sense of the word. They did, however, during their limited free time, sell their labor and handmade products to earn money to buy freedom for their relatives and themselves.

Frank McWorter was a classic example. Free Frank, as he was called, was born into slavery in 1777 in the northwestern South Carolina Piedmont. Before the turn of the century, he was taken to the western Kentucky Pennyroyal area, where he labored for fifteen years to develop his owner's farm homestead. By 1810, Free Frank hired out his own time and established a saltpeter manufactory during the War of 1812. After paying his owner for allowing him to work during his own time, Free Frank saved enough to purchase his wife's freedom in 1817, and then his own in 1819.

As a free man, Free Frank expanded his entrepreneurial activities on the Kentucky frontier. He continued to manufacture saltpeter, as well as to engage in land speculation commercial farming. In 1830, he moved to Illinois, where he established a homestead in the sparsely populated Mississippi River Valley area of Pike County. There, Free Frank continued land speculation activities and broadened his commercial farming enterprise to include raising stock. During the U.S. expansion period of the 1830s, Free Frank founded the town of New Philadelphia, Illinois, the only documented case of a town founded by a black man during the antebellum period (Walker 1983). In 1837, he legally changed his name to Frank McWorter. Mr. McWorter promoted the development of New Philadelphia until his death in 1854 at the age of seventy-five.

Free Frank's life story reflects the multiple responses of African-Americans under slavery. It also bears testimony to an entrepreneurial spirit and the dogged determination of a people for economic development, even under the most extreme circumstances.

As illustrated in Table 10.1, service businesses remained the cornerstone of the black business community.

Table 10.1
Independent Black Businesses

Type of Business	Number
Draymen, hackmen, and teamsters	43,963
Bankers	17,480
Merchants	7,181
Hucksters and peddlers	2,516
Restaurant keepers	2,157
Salesman and women	1,166
Packers and shippers	567
Hotel keepers	420
Livery stable keepers	390
Undertakers	231

Source: U.S. Bureau of the Census, 1890–1915.

Madame C.J. Walker, the *grande dame* of personal hair-care service, stands out as an example of success despite the odds. Because black hair care was largely ignored by white businesses, Madame Walker took advantage of the opportunity to develop an entire line of hair-care and cosmetic products. In 1905, she developed a hair-care system that transformed dry, kinky hair into soft natural-looking hair. In the process, she transformed herself from Sarah Breedlove, a poor laundry worker, daughter of slaves and orphaned at age six, into Madame Walker, the hair-care tycoon.

Madame Walker's products delighted millions—mostly black women—throughout the country. She also understood the importance of community development to the future of her people. Before her death in 1919, Walker built an endowed school for girls in West Africa.

Madame C.J. Walker (1867–1919)

Sarah Breedlove was born to sharecropper parents in Delta, Louisiana. She was orphaned at the age of six and raised by her married sister. She married Mr. McWilliams at age fourteen and bore a daughter, Lelia. At age 20 she was a widow.

Sarah and Lelia moved to St. Louis in 1887. For the next eighteen years she was employed as a washerwoman, earning $1.50 a day. She struggled to educate not only her daughter but herself as well by attending public night schools. With a carefully saved capital investment of $1.50, she began developing a hair tonic in her kitchen. After much experimentation, she hit upon a unique combination of soaps, ointments, and hair-dressing techniques that became popularized as the "Walker Method."

The popularity of her product spread rapidly. She moved to Denver and began selling her product door-to-door. In 1906, she married newspaperman Charles Joseph Walker, and was known ever after as Madame C.J. Walker. After a year, she was able to establish her office and manufacturing headquarters in Denver. She traveled for two years by herself through the South and East, promoting her preparation. So successful were her efforts that her mail-order business soon required her to open a second office in Pittsburgh in 1908. Putting her daughter in charge of this office, she resumed her traveling.

By 1919, The Madame C.J. Walker Manufacturing Company covered an entire city block in downtown Indianapolis and came to employ over 3,000 people.

As a businesswoman, Madame C.J. Walker was extremely innovative. She developed sales techniques that remain in wide usage today. Her agents were organized into "clubs" for business, social, and philanthropic purposes. Every year, she brought club delegates together for conventions, to share their success stories and to learn new beauty techniques. For many black women, Madame Walker provided the first opportunity for a lucrative, independent business.

She was one of the most generous benefactors to the black community. She was an early admirer and support of educator Mary McLeod Bethune. She made significant contributions to Mrs. Bethune's college. Madame Walker was also an active supporter of the National Conference on Lynching and a friend of the great anti-lynching champion, Ida B. Wells.

She moved to New York City and built a thirty-room mansion facing the Palisades on the Hudson River. The $250,000 home was a showplace and named Villa Lewaro by the noted Italian tenor Enrico Caruso. (He used the first syllables of A'Lelia Walker Robinson's name.) The features of the home were ancient tapestries, a valuable art collection, and an $8,000 organ. Upon Madame Walker's death, the estate was bequeathed to the NAACP. When people asked why she built Villa Lewaro, she replied, "It is not for me. It is for my people so they can see what can be accomplished no matter what their background is."

Madame Walker was a strong, forceful woman, yet she retained a great simplicity and kindness of character throughout her life. In only a dozen years, she went from concocting hair tonic in her kitchen to heading an international business that opened up business careers for thousands of black women. Madame Walker ran her enterprise with a firm hand. When her agents protested the selling of her products in drug stores, Madame Walker remained firm and overcame protests at a national convention of her beauty agents. She was adamant that none of her products be given away. She gave freely of her time and money, but was never known to give away any of her cosmetics.

When Madame C.J. Walker died at age fifty-two, she left an estate of over $1 million dollars, a handsome country villa at Irvington-on-Hudson, New York, and a successful cosmetics company that still bears her name. She died in 1919, the first self-made black female millionaire in America.

BLACK PRESIDENTS IN FORTUNE 500 COMPANIES

A select group of men and women head subsidiaries, divisions, and units of major U.S. corporations. In the last decade, blacks have made modest gains in corporate America. Although some progress has been made, blacks still have a long way to go. A few talented and savvy blacks have joined the corporate elite in the paneled boardrooms and executive suites. It should be noted, however, that there is only one black chairperson/CEO of a Fortune 500 company: Richard D. Parsons of Dime Savings Bank of New York, which has $8.8 billion in assets. According to *Ebony Magazine* (1994), the list of black presidents in Fortune 500 companies comprises twenty companies. The *Ebony Magazine* study also includes several blacks who hold the title of chairperson and chief executive officer or CEO/president at the 500 top industrial and 500 top service corporations (ranked according to sales).

It should also be noted that there are a number of corporate vice presidents at various major companies who out-rank division presidents. Among them is A. Barry Rand, executive vice president of operations at the Xerox Corporation, who is heralded as being in direct line for the presidency of the $18 billion company. In addition, there are numerous corporate executives, including African-Americans, who head units or divisions, but do not hold the title "president." This particular *Ebony* article, however, is limited to including only black executives who hold the title of president or chief executive officer.

And make no mistake: the men and women featured on the following pages are by no means "tokens." Rather, these individuals have worked hard and proven themselves repeatedly. They have demonstrated that they can make prudent decisions, motivate employees, formulate strategies and policies, and, most importantly, turn profits.

Carl Ware travels extensively to oversee Coca-Cola's operations in sub-Saharan Africa, which covers forty-six countries with a combined population of more than 500 million potential consumers. So does Dennis F. Hightower, president of Disney Consumer Products, Europe/Middle East, who cut significantly the time he spends on airplanes by moving to Paris. Hightower says three principles have guided him during his twenty-year career in corporate America: preparation, performance, and perseverance. "They have been a continuing source of inspiration for me," he says. "The one caveat, however, is that the three only work hand-in-hand" (Ebony, 1992).

Echoing that sentiment is Lloyd Ward, president of Frito-Lay's Central Division, which has sales topping $1 billion and employs 8,500 people. He adds that "thinking big" and having aspirations are key to excelling in the business world. In addition, he says his love of adversity has helped him succeed. "We as a people are faced with a lot of adversity," says Ward. "And that builds character. I've found that to be true in corporate America as well. The same conviction and dedication to overcoming adversity in life helps us succeed in business. It builds character, builds strength" (Ebony, 1994).

Twenty-six of the African-Americans listed on the following pages are among those who, with strength of character, have climbed to the prestigious rank of chief executive officer or president at major corporations. The list is not inclusive, for there are numerous other outstanding men and women in the business world. But those featured here are representative of black executives who have defied the odds to rise to the top in corporate America.

Moreover, according to a recent survey of corporate boards by Ebony (1997) and Directorship, a corporate research firm (1996), there has been a significant increase in the number of black Americans who sit on prestigious public Fortune 1000 company boards. The report reveals that since 1994, the number of black Americans on corporate boards has increased from 148 to a total of 179 in 1996. In 1987, there were 80 black directors. On top of the list is the powerful Washington, D.C., attorney Vernon Jordan and his wife, Ann Dibble Jordan, who sit on the boards of a total of eleven major corporations. The following list includes the nation's top black corporate directors of three or more Fortune companies:

Clifford L. Alexander, president, Alexander & Associates, Washington, D.C.: American Home Products Corp., Dun & Bradstreet Corp., MCI Communications, and TLC Beatrice international Holdings Inc.

H. Jesse Arnell, senior partner, Arnelle, Hastie, McGee, Willis & Greene law firm, San Francisco: Armstrong World Industries Inc., Eastman Chemical Co., FPL Group Inc., Textron Inc., WMX Technologies Inc., and Wells Fargo & Co.

Andrew F. Brimmer, president, Brimmer & Co., Washington, D.C.: Airborne Freight Corp., BankAmerica Corp., College Retirement Equities Fund, E.I. du Pont de Nemours and Co., Gannett Co. Inc., Navistar International Crop., and PHH Corp.

Robert J. Brown: Duke Power Co., First Union Corp., and Sonoco Products.

Herman Cain, chairman, Godfather's Pizza Inc., Omaha, Neb.: Supervalu Inc., UtiliCorp United Inc., and Whirlpool Corporation.

James I. Cash, Jr., professor, Harvard University Graduate School of Business Administration, Boston: Chubb Corp., Knight-Ridder Inc., State Street Boston Corp., and Tandy Corp.

Reatha Clark King, president and executive director, General Mills Foundation, and vice president, General Mills Inc., Minneapolis: H.B. Fuller Co., Minnesota Mutual Life Insurance Co., and Norwest Corp.

Johnetta B. Cole, former president, Spelman College: Coca-Cola Enterprises, Home Depot Inc., and Merck & Co. Inc.

Erroll B. Davis, president and CEO, Wisconsin Power & Light Co.: Amoco Corp., PPG Industries Inc., and Merck & Co. Inc.

Willie D. Davis, owner, All Pro Broadcasting, Los Angeles: Dow Chemical Co., Johnson Controls Inc., Kmart Corp., and Sara Lee Corp.

Wayne R. Embry: Centerior Energy Corp., M.A. Hanna Co., and Ohio Casualty Corp.

Ann Dibble Jordan, Washington, D.C., consultant: Automatic Data Processing Inc., Hechinger Co., Johnson & Johnson, Laboratory Corp. of America, and Travelers Group Inc.

Lois Dickson Rice, guest scholar, Brookings Institution, Washington, D.C.: Fleet Financial Group Inc., International Multifoods Corp., McGraw-Hill Companies Inc., and UNUM Corp.

James H. Gilliam, executive vice president and general counsel, Beneficial Corporation, Wilmington, Del.: Bell Atlantic Corp., Beneficial Corp., and Delmarva Power & Light Co.

Bonnie Guiton Hill, dean, McIntire School of Commerce, University of Virginia, Charlottesville: AK Steel Holding Corp., Crestar Financial Corp., Hershey Foods, Louisiana-Pacific Corp., Federated Department Stores, and Rohm and Haas Co.

Earl G. Graves, publisher, *Black Enterprise* magazine, New York: AMR Corp., Aetna Inc., Chrysler Corp., Federated Department Stores, and Rohm and Haas Co.

William H. Gray, III, president and CEO, United Negro College Fund, Fairfax, Va.: Chase Manhattan Corp., Prudential Insurance Co. of America, Rockwell International Corp., Union Pacific Corp., Warner-Lambert Co., and Westinghouse Electric Corp.

Karen Hastie Williams, Washington, D.C., attorney: Continental-Airlines Inc., Crestar Financial Corp., Federal National Mortgage Association, and Sun-America Inc.

Mannie L. Jackson, chairman and owner, Harlem Globe Trotters, Phoenix: Ashland Inc., Reebok International Ltd., and Stanley Works.

John E. Jacob, executive vice president, Anheuser-Busch Companies, St. Louis: Anheuser-Busch Companies, Coca-Cola Enterprises Inc., and LTV Corp.

Linda Johnson Rice, president and chief operating officer, Johnson Publishing Co., Chicago: Bausch & Lomb Inc., Kimberly-Clark Corp., and Viad Corp.

Vernon E. Jordan, Washington, D.C., attorney: American Express Co., Bankers Trust New York Corp., Dow Jones & Co. Inc., J.C. Penney Co. Inc., Ryder System Inc., and Sara Lee Corp.

James G. Kaiser: Mead Corp., Stanley Works, and Sun Company, Inc.

David Baker Lewis: Conrail Inc., LG&E Energy Corp., and TRO Inc.

Delano E. Lewis, president and CEO, National Public Radio: Apple Computer Inc., Colgate-Palmolive Co., GEICO Corp., and Halliburton Co.

Donald F. McHenry, president, IRC Group and professor at Georgetown Univ.: AT&T Corp., BankBoston Corp., Coca-Cola Co., and International Paper Co.

Claudine B. Malone, president, Financial & Management Consulting Inc., McLean, Va.: Dell Computer Corp., Hanaford Bros. Co., Hasbro Inc., Limited Inc., Lowe's Companies Inc., Mallinckrodt Group Inc., Penn Mutual Life Ins. Co., and Science Applications International Corp.

Walter E. Massey, president, Morehouse College, Atlanta: Amoco Corp., BankAmerica Corp., and Motorola Inc.

Steven A. Minter, executive director, Cleveland Foundation: Consolidated Natural Gas Co., Goodyear Tire & Rubber Co., KeyCorp., and Rubbermaid Inc.

Sybil C. Mobley, dean, School of Business and Industry, Florida A&M University, Tallahassee: Anheuser-Busch Companies, Champion-International Corp., and Dean Witter, Discover & Co.

Richard D. Parsons, president, Time-Warner Inc., New York: Citicorp, Federal National Mortgage Association, Philip Morris Companies Inc., and Time-Warner Inc.

Benjamin F. Payton, president, Tuskegee (Ala.) Institute: AmSouth Bancorporation, ITT Corp., Praxair Inc., Ruby Tuesday Inc., and Sonat Inc.

Aulana L. Peters, Los Angeles attorney: Merrill Lynch & Co., Minnesota Mining and Manufacturing Co., Mobil Corp., and Northrop Grumman.

A. Barry Rand, executive vice president, Xerox Corporation, Stamford, Conn.: Abbott Laboratories, Ameritech Corp., and Honeywell Inc.

Dr. Frank S. Royal, Richmond, Va.: CSX Corp., Chesapeake Corp., Columbia/HCA Healthcare Corp., Crestar Financial Corp., and Dominion Resources Inc.

Barbara Scott Preiskel, New York City attorney: American Stores, General Electric, Massachusetts Mutual Life Insurance Co., Textron Inc., and Washington Post Co.

John Brooks Slaughter, president, Occidental College, Los Angeles: Atlantic Richfield Co., Avery Dennison, IBM, Monsanto, and Northrop Grumman.

Joshua I. Smith, chairman and CEO, Maxima Corp., Lanham, Md.: Caterpillar Inc., Federal Express Corp., and Inland Steel Industries.

Robert D. Storey, Cleveland attorney: GTE Corp. May Department Stores Co., and Procter & Gamble Co.

Dr. Louis W. Sullivan, president, Morehouse School of Medicine: Bristol-Myers Squibb Co., CIGNA Corp., Equifax Inc., General Motors Corp., Georgia-Pacific Corp., Household International, Minnesota Mining and Manufacturing.

Franklin A. Thomas: Aluminum Co. of America, Citicorp, Cummins Engine Co., and PepsiCo.

Ronald L. Thompson: Illinova Corp., McDonnell Douglas Corp., and Teachers Insurance & Annuity Assn.

Clifton R. Wharton: Ford Motor Co., Harcourt General Inc., and Tenneco Inc.

The list of black leaders in corporate America appears impressive, considering the obstacles that faced and continue to face them. It should be noted, however, that the apparent absence of transformational black corporate leadership has reduced the economic power of black America. In fact, the development of collective black wealth in America appears impossible. Poverty among black Americans remains a national challenge.

11

Black Leadership in the Community

Over the past century, the nature and structure of American communities has substantially changed. American engineering "know-how" has provided the world with breakthroughs in aerospace, computers, medical, and consumer technologies. The twentieth century may be dubbed "the American Century." In fact, American engineering has improved the quality of life worldwide and has given us many products we use to make our everyday lives more enjoyable and convenient. Certain fundamental changes in American society include shifts in demographics, increased specialization and division of labor, new forms of organization, and new means of communication and transportation. In Warren's (1972) judgment, the diminished role of communities is generated in part by the mobility of residents:

The constant moving back and forth across the country in search of the better job or as a result of the company's planned policy of personnel rotation, or for whatever reason, puts a premium on the tree which can survive with shallow roots. . . . There is increasing association of people on the basis of common occupational or other interests rather than on the basis of locality alone. . . . The individual is oriented toward specialized, vertical systems as the important reference groups in relation to which he forms his self-image.

This implies that communities are less likely than before to provide the focus of interest for the most able leaders, who are often more concerned with a "community of interest" related to professions or specialized organizations than with the geographic community. The remaining community "leaders" often fail to recognize the changed community circumstance, or may be ill equipped to deal with new leadership requirements.

Community leaders may not be conscious of the inability of many existing community institutions to meet public needs; their perspectives and experience may be too limited to solve the most pressing problems. If community concerns are to attract the interest and time of capable people, and if a new kind of more adequate "community" is to emerge, local leadership must learn how to use outside resources in solving problems and in capitalizing on opportunities.

Nix summarizes and interprets studies of community leadership that relate the nature of leadership to type of community. He emphasizes the importance of studies that go beyond mere description of organizational interest groups, associations, and leadership roles, arguing that it is essential to understand the relationships among leaders and subunits of the community. He identifies *exchange* and *coordination* as two important types of relationship. Central concepts required to understand community leadership are noted: *social power, hierarchies, functional classifications of leadership, general or specialized leadership*, and *task* or *social leaders*. He concludes that community structure tends to be (a) focused or unitary; (b) split or bifactional; (c) multifactional; or (d) amorphous. Finally, Nix suggests that the core leadership patterns are the cross-community linkage groups and the degree of competition or collaboration between them.

Lassey and Sashkin focus on requirements for improving community leadership performance, with specific attention to increasing pluralism and broadening participation. They discuss areas in which knowledge is needed and the characteristics of an effective community leadership structure.

External consultants often are important contributors to new initiatives within communities when the local leadership base is inadequate. Lassey and Sashkin also discuss some of the useful roles that consultants can play in helping community leaders organize effective development programs. The leadership behaviors used by effective consultants are also noted, as are characteristics of the consultation process. Finally, six general principles are presented as basic considerations for both consultants and local leaders.

In this chapter we examine a number of questions: What is a community? What is the nature of the black community? How is "social power" shared in the black community? What is the role of professionals in black community development? Who are some of the major black community leaders?

As to the first question, Nix (1983) has defined *community* as a social system whose function is to manage the competition and conflict that arise out of the necessity to exchange goods and services, which, in turn, arise out of (1) the division of labor in society, and (2) the scarcity of goods and services. *Community* may also be defined as a group of people residing in the same locality and under the same government. While both definitions may apply to the black community, another definition that is operationally ideological is worth considering. From this perspective, a *community* may be defined as a group or class of people having common interest; for example, the faith community, the academic community, the black community, or the Jewish community. This definition looks beyond geographical and governmental boundaries. Thus, a community may mean two different things to blacks, as regards the geo-political and ideological perspectives.

Historically, the primary source for black community leadership has been the black church. The institutional organization of the black community is historically rooted in the church, the origin of which goes back to the late eighteenth century. Today, the church continues to be the foundation of the black community, and from all indications it promises to remain the most viable black institution of the future. It is therefore imperative that services directed toward the improvement of the black community involve the black church. This involvement is particularly important for the effective delivery of services by social service agencies, such as health departments and the elderly-care network. One primary purpose of such an endeavor is to provide increased access to black churches for more effective delivery of social services.

The birth of the independent black church movement and the teaching of the free black preachers arose because of racial prejudice in the white-dominated churches. These developments show clearly that Christianity and earthly freedom were inseparable for black Americans. Unlike the white church, the black church was born in protest; its reality stemmed from the eschatological recognition that freedom, equality, and fairness are at the essence of humanity.

Parallel developments were occurring elsewhere. Finally, in 1816, representatives of African Methodist churches in Pennsylvania, New Jersey, Delaware, and Maryland met in Philadelphia and formed a separate Methodist connection, the African Methodist Episcopal Church. The origins of the AME Church exemplify black response to the inhuman treatment of black Americans. As indicated in chapter 4, its leading founder and the first consecrated bishop was Richard Allen, a former slave from Maryland who had been converted to Methodism. Between the period of the Civil War and Reconstruction, hundreds more black churches were developed. Today, according to the National Council of Churches, there are more than 70,000 black churches in America (Gordon, 1985). Thus, the church continues to be the black community's leadership training ground. It should be noted, however, that although most black Americans are labeled as Christian, the impact of the church on black youth has steadily declined since the 1970s. Secular civil rights organizations, such as the Black Panthers and the gang movements that emerged in the 1960s, have attracted many black youth.

Black Panthers

This organization was founded in Oakland, California, in October 1966, by Huey P. Newton and Bobby Seale, two young black activists. The name of the organization was inspired by the example of the Lowndes County (Alabama) Freedom Organization, which had adopted the black panther as its symbol. "An appropriate emblem," Seale explained, "for the black people in America. It is not in the Panther's nature to attack anyone first, but when he is attacked and backed into a corner, he will respond viciously and wipe out the aggressor" (Seale, 1991).

Newton and Seale first met in Oakland in 1961; subsequently, Seale affiliated with the Revolutionary Action movement, a militant black nationalist group founded in 1964. By the end of 1965, however, Seale had disassociated himself from the Revolutionary Action movement, and in 1966 he and Newton conceived the idea of establishing the Black Panther Party for Self-Defense. Eldridge Cleaver, the third member of the Panther "triumvirate," joined the organization early in 1967 (Rout, 1991).

Nora Sayre, writing in *The Progressive,* has said that the Panthers' motto was the famous quotation from Mao: "We are advocates of the abolition of war; we do not want war; but war can only be abolished through war; and in order to get rid of the gun it is necessary to pick up the gun." Cleaver (1992) wrote as one who has often seen the wrong end of a gun: "I don't dig violence. Guns are ugly . . . but there are two forms of violence: violence directed at you to keep you in your place and violence to defend yourself against that suppression and to win your freedom."

It has been argued that "the Panthers provide the first nationwide black political movement—as distinguished from the religious or political groups of the past." For the Panthers, the revolutionary violence is a tool toward "socialist" revolution: "The 'arch-enemy' is capitalism, which [the Panthers] see as intertwined with racism: 'You cannot have a democracy with capitalism. And we don't. . . . '" (Foner, 1990). Eventually, the Black Panthers wish for the establishment of some form of socialist state—and a total redistribution of wealth.

The Panthers' Revolutionary Posture

The Panthers first attained a measure of national attention when, in May of 1967, armed with rifles, shotguns, pistols, and cartridge belts around their waists, they "invaded" the California legislature in Sacramento. They wore the attire that has become the Panther trademark: leather jackets, boots, and tight-fitting trousers. "The Panthers came to Sacramento," explains a former editor of *Ramparts* magazine, "not to 'invade' or 'take over' the Legislature, but simply to exercise their right to attend a session of the Legislature and to state their opposition to a pending bill . . . intended to impose severe restriction on the carrying of loaded weapons in public" (Cleaver, 1992).

Since the Sacramento incident, the Panthers have gained fame (or notoriety) as a paramilitary organization, some of whose members have boasted of storing arms in hidden caches and have frequently made statements (including threats of violence against police) that may be characterized as "revolutionary." Such utterances, in conjunction with numerous highly publicized and hotly debated violent encounters with police, have earned a controversial reputation for the Panthers, which includes the sympathy and support of some elements, and the condemnation of others.

The closest thing to a Black Panther "creed" is a ten-point program of "black liberation," or "social revolution" (Foner, 1970):

1. We want freedom. We want power to determine the destiny of our Black Community.
2. We want full employment for our people.

3. We want an end to the robbery by the Capitalists in our Black Community.

4. We want decent housing, fit for shelter of human beings.

5. We want education for our people that exposes the true nature of this decadent American society. We want education that teaches us our true history and our role in the present day society.

6. We want all black men to be exempt from military service.

7. We want an immediate end to police brutality and murder of black people.

8. We want freedom for all black men held in federal, state, county, and city prisons and jails.

9. We want all black people when brought to trial to be tried in court by a jury of their peer group or people from their black communities, as defined by the Constitution of the United States.

10. We want land, bread, housing, education, clothing, justice, and peace. And as our major political objective, a United Nations supervised plebiscite to be held through the black colony in which only black colonial subjects will be allowed to participate, for the purpose of determining the will of black people as to their natural destiny.

The explanation of the Panthers' aims and goals is perhaps best summarized by Huey Newton (1995):

As far as blacks are concerned, we are not hung up on attempting to actualize or express our individual souls because we're oppressed not as individuals but as a whole group of people. Our evolution, or our liberation, is based first on freeing our group. . . .

A people who have suffered so much for so long at the hands of a racist society must draw the line somewhere. We believe that the black communities of America must draw the line somewhere. We believe that the black communities of America must rise up as one man to halt the progression of a trend that leads inevitably to their total destruction. . . .

The Black Panther Party is a vanguard group leading the revolutionary struggle, playing a part in it, because this is world revolution—all colonized people are now resisting. To work as one of the administrators of this revolutionary action, you have to view yourself as an oxen to be ridden by the people. This is what the Black Panther Party teaches—that we should all carry the weight, and those who have extreme abilities will have to carry extremely heavy loads.

Publicity was initially accorded the Panthers largely because of two factors, the skill of Panther leaders in creating a flamboyant public image and the direct appeal exercised by the Panthers to the needs of the people for whom they claimed to speak. Thus, as the *Wall Street Journal* has observed: "Much of the support for the party [came] from younger people apparently attracted to the Panthers by their panache—their distinctive uniforms of black berets and black reamer jackets, their ostentatious display of guns, their avowed determination to overturn the American 'system,' their refusal to back down under intense police pressure" (1968). Or, as *Newsweek* explained:

[The Panthers] are Media-Age revolutionaries, gifted with words, good at sloganeering . . . , irresistibly photogenic, scary on television, masterful at poster art from their first effort—

that high-camp classic of Newton scowling out of a peacock chair with a gun in one hand and a spear in the other. They put 'pig,' for policeman, into the radical vocabulary. They made berets and black leather de rigueur for splinter groups of Latin, Indian, Chinese, and even Appalachian white dissidents. Ghetto kids walk the Panther walk and talk the Panther talk. White student radicals are entranced by Panther machismo (1968).

More important, perhaps, is the Panthers'

technique for filling the desperate need of the young, undereducated black man to achieve a sense of pride and purpose. At the same time they have created a villain—the police, the 'establishment,' the 'system'—against which he can vent his hostility and hatred. The psychological emasculation which many young black men suffer—or are told they suffer—is being appealed to by the aggressive, super-male image that the Panthers project. In the process of exploiting this feeling, the Panthers have developed a tremendous potential for a black revolutionary party.

Panther Activities and Programs

In addition to Panther problems with the police and the U.S. judiciary, a number of Panther activities have received widespread publicity. Among the more prominent is the so called "Conference Against Fascism," held in Berkeley, California, in July of 1969, in which Panther leaders decried "this business of racial discrimination, whatever its form." The primary purpose of the conference was to organize a national campaign for community control of local police. Bobby Seale explained that the campaign would work to change city charters, in order to permit city neighborhoods to organize and control their own police forces. Seale thus rejected the concept of "black capitalism" in favor of a national drive for neighborhood autonomy.

Perhaps most notorious among Panther activities was the publication in 1968 of a Panther "coloring book," which pictorially advocates the killing of police, depicted as pigs. Responsibility for the book was denied by Panther leaders, who asserted that the book had been withdrawn from publication soon after its release.

Perhaps the most favorably received of Panther activities have been the Panthers' "free breakfast program" for black ghetto children, a free medical care program, and a war on narcotics use among black youth. These programs have developed, according to one source, because "stricter gun laws and frequent arrests have forced the Panthers to stop the regular displays of armed force that first attracted attention to them. In the past several months, they have developed other programs designed to convince ghetto residents that capitalism is incapable of meeting their needs and that socialist forms of organization can do so" (Carson 1982).

The breakfast program is financed, for the most part, by voluntary contributions from local stores. Some merchants have made the claim that the contributions are sometimes the result of pressure; however, "They didn't threaten, but they asked us in a way that we knew we might be opening the door for bad publicity if we didn't give," explains one businessman. "We run a lot of routes all over this area, and we don't want to make any enemies."

Similarly, the Black Panthers' free medical care program depended upon contributions from outside the Panther organization. According to the *Wall Street Journal*:

a growing number of young doctors across the country . . . have volunteered to help the Panthers attack poor health in the ghetto. Many of the volunteers were just out of medical school, and some were serving two-year hitches with the Public Health Service in place of military service. Most were members of the Medical Committee for Human Rights, an organization of about 7,000 doctors and other health professionals, most of them whites, formed in 1965 to fight for better health care for the poor and admission of more blacks to university medical schools.

In San Francisco and other cities across the country, Panthers were to be trained to instruct residents on nutrition, parasite prevention, and oral hygiene on regular home visits, according to the party's medical program. Doctors in several cities already have donated or promised to donate drugs, microscopes, and other equipment to the program and have agreed to train Panther volunteers (1969).

In regard to the breakfast program, the *New York Times* has noted that "while the Panthers say that the program was initiated to feed hungry children, they make no effort to mask its political side." Thus, while the Panthers "feed breakfast to (an estimated) total of 10,000 children a day in cities like New York, Chicago, and Los Angeles, some Panther branches in New York and other cities keep children after breakfast for morning 'liberation' classes at which they are taught the party platform and anti-police songs."

Or, as the Panthers themselves point out, the free breakfast program is designed "to expose a capitalist system that sends satellites to the moon but doesn't solve the problems of hunger. . . . The one thing our system can't stand is exposure. And that is what we are doing by our examples."

The breakfast, medical, and drug programs bring to the Panthers a considerable degree of moderate Negro support. The general question of the Panthers' integrity, however, has been the subject of considerable public debate. Columnists Rowland Evans and Richard Novak reported in January of 1970, for example, that "the full extent of Panther involvement in extortion, robbery, and burglary" was unknown. Evans and Novak pointed to the "extensive evidence of Panther criminal records" and observed that the arrest of more than 350 Panthers on criminal charges in 1969 alone barely scratched the surface of suspected participation in unsolved and undetected crime. "Extortion from white merchants in the ghetto, much of it unreported to authorities, is a regular source of funding in Panther grant strategy. Moreover, there is hard information from former Panthers that bank robberies to obtain funds for the party—in the old Bolshevik tradition of 'expropriation'—were planned and executed in 1968 and perhaps into early 1969 (although recently Panther leaders have discouraged such activity)."

As to the purported financial influence the Communist Party, U.S.A., wields over the Black Panthers, the *New York Review of Books* reports that "while the Communist Party is happy to ride the Panthers' tail, it by no means calls the shots" (1969). Lt. William L. Olsen of the Chicago Police Department in testimony before the Permanent Subcommittee on Investigations of the Senate Government Operations Committee (June 26 and 30, 1969) seems to echo this statement:

The party was financed by a variety of means, ranging from speakers' fees to income received for the sale of *The Black Panther,* the organization's newspaper, published in California. Sympathetic white organizations, like the Chicago Peace Council and the Chicago Legal Defense Committee, have contributed sums of money to the Black Panther party. The Chicago Peace Council is Communist infiltrated and administratively controlled by identified members of the Communist Party. . . . The Communist Party, U.S.A., pays $5 yearly membership dues regularly.

Evans and Novak maintain, however, that "more than any other black revolutionary organization, the Panthers maintain close ties with overseas Communist parties. Whether or not they have been the beneficiary of Communist contributions from abroad is a matter of debate, but there is at least suspicion of financial aid from countries that receive regular and unremitting praise in the weekly newspaper, *The Black Panther.*"

Sit-In Movement

The so-called sit-in movement began on February 1, 1960, when four black students (Franklin McCain, David Richmond, Joseph McNeil, and Ezell Blair, Jr.) from North Carolina Agricultural and Technical College in Greensboro refused to relinquish their seats at a local dime-store lunch counter after being refused service (Williams, 1987). During the next three months, thousands of black students, encouraged by the Southern Christian Leadership Conference (SCLC), were "trained" in the technique of "sitting-in," the general rule being "sit tight, and refuse to fight." These students formed the core of a new civil rights organization, the Student Nonviolent Coordinating Committee (SNCC), which encouraged sit-ins, wade-ins, and kneel-ins throughout the South in restaurants, swimming pools, churches, and other places of public accommodation that practiced racial segregation. Notwithstanding the inevitable heckling, harassment, beatings, and arrests that ensued, the students patiently and nonviolently stood their ground. By the end of the year, these tactics were beginning to bear fruit. Slowly but surely, restaurants, hotels, supermarkets, movie theaters, and a host of similar establishments in the South began lowering their barriers against servicing Afro-Americans.

Student Nonviolent Coordinating Committee

Founded on April 15, 1960, as an interracial "direct action" civil rights organization, the Student Nonviolent Coordinating Committee (SNCC or SNICK) was especially active in the South during the 1960s. Utilizing the tactics of sit-ins and jail-ins (refusal to pay fines in order to serve consequent jail terms), SNCC was instrumental in the desegregation of many public facilities throughout the South.

Following the election of Stokely Carmichael as chairman of SNCC in 1966, the organization became increasingly militant and dedicated to black liberation and black nationalism, as opposed to mere integration. Carmichael himself resigned his office in 1967 to join forces with the emerging Black Panther Party. Following the assassination of Martin Luther King, Jr., in 1968, H. Rap Brown, who succeeded Carmichael as head of SNCC, changed the name of the organization to Student *National* Coordinating Committee. The name change, however, was merely a token gesture, given that the SNCC had already lost much of its momentum and membership as the result of defections to the Black Power and Black Panther movements. Although the organization still technically exists, its influence and activities have been relatively limited since the mysterious disappearance of Brown in 1970.

The legacy of black community leadership is almost nonexistent. The issues that created a strong sense of the black community seem to have disappeared with integration and information technologies. The inner cities are no longer the sole residence for blacks; many blacks who could afford it have moved to the suburbs. Other racial groups, such as Hispanics, poor whites, and the new immigrants, especially Asian-Americans, now share the ownership of the inner cities with blacks. Blacks seem to view national politics, especially presidential elections, as more important than local politics. They seem to have neglected the old saying that "all politics are local." The values that used to solidify the black community are now at risk. If this trend continues, black community leadership will be a thing of the past.

12

Black Leadership in the Global Arena

Black Americans have been inextricably involved in foreign service. In fact, black Americans pioneered the struggle for African independence and made significant contributions to international politics. This chapter examines the role of black Americans in providing leadership in the international arena.

The role of black Americans in U.S. foreign policy toward Africa has been well documented by many scholars. Jake Miller's (1978) *The Black Presence in American Foreign Affairs* examines both the historical and the contemporary contributions of black Americans to U.S. foreign policy. His analysis of individual and organizational contributions to U.S. foreign policy brings together a useful body of knowledge. "The Influence of Black Americans on U.S. Foreign Policy Toward Africa," by Herschell Challenor, documents the persistence of African-American interest in African nations. The paper suggests reasons for the escalation of interest in African affairs since 1960, and examines the constraints and opportunities of a black impact on U.S. foreign policy. Challenor suggests three principal reasons why black Americans have not significantly influenced policy toward their ancestral continent: (1) the historical absence of black political power as a result of disenfranchisement in the South and the neutralization of the black vote in the North; (2) the low esteem accorded to blacks and to Africa; (3) official attempts to discourage close, effective links between Africans and African-Americans (Challenor, 1981).

John Davis, professor of political science and editor of *African Forum: A Quarterly Journal of Contemporary Affairs,* has addressed the subject from a different perspective. In his essay "Black Americans and United States Policy Toward Africa," he discusses the involvement of black Americans in U.S. foreign policy as early as 1788, when African-Americans in Newport, Rhode Island, wrote to the Free African Society in Philadelphia, proposing a plan of emigration to Africa. Davis's hope for black American impact on U.S. foreign policy on Africa is based on two factors: (1) African-content education for black youth, and (2) the rise of black urban politicians who will inherit the black nationalist movement in the United States (Davis, 1969).

Other scholarly works include Milton Morris's (1972) essay, "Black Americans and the Foreign Policy Process: The Case of Africa"; "The African-American Manifesto on Southern Africa," a ten-point document adopted at a conference of organization leaders convened by the Congressional Black Caucus in 1976; "The Afro-American Response to the Occupation of Haiti: 1915–34," by Brenda Plummer (1982); "American Negroes and U.S. Foreign Policy: 1937–1967," by Alfred Hero (1969); and numerous essays written by W.E.B. Du Bois, beginning with his publication of "The Suppression of the African Slave Trade in the United States of America, 1638–1870," in 1896. The list includes the unpublished works of Locksley Edmondson and the publications of the Joint Center for Political Studies in Washington, D.C. (Edmondson, 1971). A few U.S. black diplomats, especially Donald McHenry, have documented the black American role in U.S. foreign policy. These works have dispelled the notion that African-Americans have shown no interest and have not been involved in U.S. foreign policy, especially in the Third World (McHenry, 1974).

Many urban black politicians have attempted to make Davis's dream come true. Perhaps the most outspoken individual in this endeavor is former Representative Charles C. Diggs, Jr. The record shows that this Michigan congressman has led the fight to get a fair shake for black Africa. He argues that the destinies of African-Americans in the United States and of Africans in Africa are inextricably linked. Diggs sees two major areas of policy toward Africa: (1) ending white racist rule in South Africa and (2) accelerating economic development throughout the African continent. To influence U.S. policy toward Africa in these areas, Diggs suggests, among other things, that blacks in the United States must follow foreign policy developments diligently, demonstrate their displeasure through voting, put effective pressure on their elected representatives in Washington, and use their $50 billion purchasing power to exert leverage. These are sound ideas, except that they have not been translated into reality. Africa continues to remain the unchallenged occupant of the bottom rung of U.S. foreign policy priorities. How do we explain U.S. interest in Africa and the apparent lack of effective policy? First, let's re-examine U.S. interest in Africa.

In a speech by then Secretary of State George Shultz at the World Affairs Council in Boston, on February 15, 1984, the secretary pointed out four major interest areas:

First, we have a significant geopolitical stake in the security of the continent and the seas surrounding it. Off its shores lie important trade routes, including those carrying most of the energy resources needed by our European allies. We are affected when Soviets, Cubans, and Libyans seek to expand their influence on the continent by force, to the detriment of both African independence and Western interests.

Second, Africa is part of the global economic system. If Africa's economies are in trouble, the reverberations are felt here. Our exports to Africa have dropped by 50% in the last three years; American financial institutions have felt the pinch of African inability to repay loans. And Africa is a major source of raw materials to the world economy.

Third, Africa is important to us politically because the nations of Africa are now major players in world diplomacy. They comprise nearly one-third of the membership of the United Nations, where they form the most cohesive voting bloc in the General Assembly.

Finally, Africa is important to us, most of all, in human terms. Eleven percent of America's population traces its roots to Africa; all of us live in a society profoundly influenced by this human and cultural heritage. The revolution of Africa's independence coincided with the civil rights revolution in this country. Perhaps it was not a coincidence. Both were among the great moral events of this century: a rebirth of freedom, summoning all of us to a recognition of our common humanity. Just as the continued progress of civil rights is important to the moral well-being of this country, so too the human drama of Africa—its political and economic future—is important to the kind of world we want our children and grandchildren to inherit.

Although Africa is taking on increasing importance in several respects, many Americans, according to former Secretary Schultz, have images of Africa that are anachronistic, partial, and often inaccurate. He went on to say, "The perception of Africa that most of us grew up with—unknown lands somehow exotic and divorced from the rest of the world—has unfortunately persisted in some quarters despite the last nearly 40 years of Africa's independence and increasing presence on the world stage. It is a misperception that ignores compelling realities." The compelling realities were probably better explained by Vice President George Bush during his 1982 tour of Africa. In his speech to the Kenya Chamber of Commerce in Nairobi on November 19, 1982, the vice president indicated U.S. interest in what he called "constructive change in southern Africa" when he said:

We will not ignore or disguise our strong belief in the importance of justice and equality before the law. Apartheid is wrong. It is legally entrenched racism—inimical to the fundamental ideals of the United States. America's history and America's future can only be understood in terms of our commitment to a multiracial democracy in which all citizens participate and from which all benefit. Will black Americans play a role in meeting this commitment? Are there constraints and/or promises for black Americans in developing more aggressive and productive American foreign policy toward Africa? Is race an issue in U.S. policy toward Africa? What theoretical models should we explore for African-American effective involvement in American foreign policy issues, particularly in Africa? (U.S. Department of State, 1984)

An important aspect of black history since the 1960s is the increased interest of black Americans in Africa and African affairs. This is not to suggest that they had no interest in Africa until the 1960s. On the contrary, black Americans have always been interested in their roots in Africa. The difference now, it seems, is that they are more aware than ever of the bonds that link them to the continent of their origin. This new awakening may be attributable in part to African-American interest in Africa, as demonstrated in the early struggle for African independence prior to the 1960s. This interest and series of activities are generally referred to as the *Pan-African movement*.

THE PAN-AFRICAN MOVEMENT

In the context in which Pan-Africanists use it, the term "Pan-Africanism," or the "Pan-African movement," refers to belief in the uniqueness and spiritual unity of all black people, the concurrent demand for self-determination in Africa for Africans, and the demand for equal and dignified treatment for blacks throughout the world community. W.E.B. Du Bois, one of the pioneers of the Pan-African movement, drew an interesting parallel between Zionism and Pan-Africanism: "The African movement means to us what the Zionist movement must mean to the Jews, the centralization of race effort and the recognition of a social fount" (Davis, 1987).

Pan-Africanism began not in the "homeland," Africa, but in the "diaspora." Zionism had its origins in Central and Eastern Europe; Pan-Africanism had its roots in the New World. It developed through a complicated trans-Atlantic triangle of influences: the Americas, Europe, and Africa. In its early phase—the middle of the nineteenth century to the turn of the twentieth century—the inhabitants of Africa imbibed these new ideas mainly from their studies in the United States and Britain.

The emotional impetus for the Pan-African concept flowed from the experiences of a widely dispersed people of African stock who felt themselves to have lost their homeland, either physically through dispossession or slavery, or socially, economically, politically, and mentally through colonialism. With this loss came enslavement, persecution, inferiority, discrimination, and dependency. It involved a loss of independence, freedom, and most especially *dignity*. Dignity is a majestic, magical word in the vocabulary of Pan-Africanists; to regain dignity is the mainspring of all their actions.

Alienation and Exile

The intellectual superstructure of Pan-Africanism has meaning only if we keep constantly in mind that at its roots these deep feelings of dispossession, oppression, persecution, and rejection. This complex of emotion—the "alien and exile" theme—is one of the primary strands in the growth of Pan-Africanist ideas. It is typified by the twentieth-century black American writer Claude McKay's (1953) poem "Outcast":

Under the white man's menace, out of time.

Ambivalence Toward the West

McKay's deservedly famous sonnet is rich in other emotions that reflected and forecast political ideas. There is the ambivalent struggle with "the great western world" from whose "fee" there is no hope of ever obtaining "full release." Africa calls, but there is no going back; having bent the knee to "alien gods" he is an inner exile, forever lost—"a ghost," "a thing apart." This ambivalence proclaims the inability of black Americans to disengage themselves from the West, even for those who feel their rootlessness within its society. Here is one of the powerful internal conflicts that explains the appeal of Marcus Garvey's "Back to Africa" movement in the 1920s. It is a potent emotion, but an impotent political force.

Black Solidarity

In the poetry of McKay's contemporary, Langston Hughes, we find the strong chords of a third persistent theme: the wish to create a common identity among all those of Negro stock; to establish a greater sense of solidarity and security; to achieve a sense of political belonging among the isolated, uprooted communities of the diaspora, first with one another and then with Africa (Hughes, 1940).

Hughes, himself of mixed descent, was so light of color that he was regarded in Africa as "a white man." But he was deeply color-conscious, as he writes about being a Negro (1974):

Black like the depths of my Africa.

It is when he writes of his sense of color, of blackness, that he expresses what is undoubtedly the dominant theme in Pan-Africanism: race-consciousness born of color. This is a theme that runs powerfully through the story of Pan-Africanism's growth.

Feelings of Inferiority

"Negro, black like grief. . . ." In this line by the Senegalese poet, David Diop (1973), we find all there is to know about the equation between black and grief, suffering and submissiveness. For centuries, the Jews had kept alive their belief and confidence in themselves through the biblically rooted faith that God had chosen than for a special mission to the world. Even so, many Jews came to accept the judgment of inferiority passed on them by gentiles. Blacks, especially those living in the diaspora, had no such biblical myth to sustain them. The extent to which they themselves came to accept the verdict of whites is clearly shown in the extremely valuable studies made by Harold R. Isaacs and others about the way black children have seen themselves. Isaacs, the author of *Five Writers and Their African Ancestors,* gives this example from a schoolchild:

In the fourth grade, those pictures of the races of man . . . with a handsome guy to present the whites, an Indian and then a black, kinky-haired specimen—that was me, a savage, a cannibal, he was just the tail end of the human race . . . he was at the bottom. . . . That picture in the book was the picture of where and what I came from. . . . (James, 1963)

African Personality

In a poem by Dalmas we find the nascent idea of an African personality: "to feel myself . . . a new self from the one I was yesterday . . . when the hour of uprooting came" (see Legum, 1962). "I am a Negro and all Negro. I am black all over, and proud of my beautiful black skin," proclaimed the American Negro, John Edward Bruce, in response to Majola Agbebi, a Yoruba Baptist, in 1902 when Agbebi inaugurated what was probably the first independent Native African Church in West Africa (see Asante, 1985). It was to Agbebi that the distinguished West Indian, Edward Blyden, first applied the term "African Personality," which he explained by saying that "Africa is struggling for a separate personality." Agbebi's inaugural address made such a profound impression on Bruce (1856–1924), a New York journalist and co-founder of the Negro Society for Historical Research, that he led a deputation of New York Negroes to have October 11 observed as "Majola Agbebi Day" to immortalize him an African Personality. Bruce was much influenced by Blyden's ideas of an emerging, distinctive African personality.

Fears that uncritical absorption of Western ideas would in time destroy the distinctive personality of Africans were voiced by Edward Blyden's kinsman, Dr. Edward W. Blyden, in his presidential address at the opening of the Liberian College in 1881. There is little of the more recent, sophisticated intellectualization and political ideology about the African personality in Dr. Blyden's seminal speech. Its importance lies in the stress he laid on the desirability of controlling the process of acculturation between the West and Africa:

The African must advance by methods of his own. He must possess a power distinct from that of the European. It has been proved that he knows how to take advantage of European Culture and that he can be benefited by it. Their proof was perhaps necessary, but is not sufficient. We must show that we are able to go alone, to carve out our own way. We must not be satisfied that, in this nation [Liberia], European influence shapes our polity, makes our laws, rules our tribunals and impregnates our social atmosphere. . . . (Blyden, 1881)

Thus far we have been concerned mainly with trying to discover the roots of the forces that produced Pan-Africanism. Their common denominator is a revolt by black people against what Aimé Césaire (1972) has called "the influence of the colonial, semi-colonial, or para-colonial situation." The situation existed in the New World and Europe no less than in Africa, and, hence, the trans-atlantic triangle of influences that nurtured Pan-Africanism.

W.E.B. Du Bois

Following the end of World War I, the Western colonial powers gradually lost control over the colonies that they had built during the previous century. In Africa, the nationalist movements that helped bring this about were strongly influenced by the Pan-African movement led by the American, W.E.B. Du Bois.

Beginning in 1900, Du Bois was active the rest of his life as a Pan-Africanist, organizing five Pan-African Congresses: Paris, 1919; London and Brussels, 1921; London and Lisbon, 1923; New York, 1927; and Manchester (England), 1945. He resigned his positions at the NAACP in 1934, because he had come to advocate black nationalism in opposition to the NAACP's commitment to integration. Returning to work with the NAACP from 1944–1948, Du Bois served as a consultant to the founding convention of the United Nations and was active in calling the attention of the Untied Nations to the plight of black Americans. Politically a socialist most of his adult life, he ran on a socialist ticket for the U.S. Senate from New York in 1950 and visited and observed socialist countries in his travels. In 1961, deeply disillusioned with the painfully slow and hard-won pace of improvement in the United States after a long life of totally committed struggle for African-American rights, Du Bois joined the Communist Party and moved to Ghana, where he died in 1963.

Pan-Africanism

W.E.B. Du Bois was introduced to Pan-Africanism in London in 1900 at the first conference ever held to propagate its ideas. Its sponsor was a Trinidad lawyer, H. Sylvester Williams, who, so far as is known, was the first person to talk about Pan-Africanism—although in 1897 Du Bois had said that "if the Negro were to be a factor in the world's history it would be through a Pan-Negro movement." Williams' chief collaborator was Bishop Alexander Walters of the African Methodist Episcopal Zion Church, who provides an important link between this independent religious movement and Pan-Africanism.

At the conclusion of the first conference a memorial was addressed to Queen Victoria. It is sobering to recall that at that time, almost a hundred years ago, they were protesting against the treatment of Africans in South Africa and Rhodesia. It was at this conference that Du Bois spoke what turned out to be prophetic words: "The problem of the twentieth century is the problem of the color line— the relation of the darker to the lighter races of men in Asia and Africa, in America and the islands of the sea" (Du Bois, 1900).

The second Pan-African Congress, the first under Du Bois' leadership, was held at the same time as the Peace Conference in Paris in 1919 following World War I. Du Bois was determined "to have Africa in some way voice its complaints to the world." The congress adopted a lengthy resolution that nowhere spoke of the Africans' right to independence. It proclaimed the need for international laws to protect the natives; for land to be held in trust; for the prevention of exploitation by foreign capital; for the abolition of slavery and capital punishment; for the right of education. Finally, it insisted that Africans had the right to participate in the government as soon as it was feasible.

These reformist ideas of Pan-Africanism had not moved much further by the time the third congress was held in London and Brussels in 1921. Du Bois' address to the third congress helped establish another of the emerging themes of Pan-Africanism: an emphasis on interracialism and the establishment of democratic institutions among oppressed peoples. The fourth congress, held in 1923 in London and Lisbon, continued the reformist approach, reiterating earlier congress' resolutions and calling for Africans to have meaningful participation in the government of their countries.

The fourth Pan-African Congress, directly led by Dr. Du Bois, was held in New York in 1927. Here a major idea toward a new form of Pan-Africanism was introduced: that Africans must find their own way toward unity and freedom. Black Americans could help, but their problems were different; they could not lead Africa. In this new form, the Pan-African idea grew into a much more directly *African* idea. This form would reach its full development only with the fifth Pan-African Congress, held in Manchester (England) in 1945, when leading African nationalists presented new demands for African independence. The Second World War had fundamentally altered the world situation and marked the beginning of the end of the European colonial empires, notably the British and the French. Attending the sixth congress were many new, younger African leaders, such as Kwame Nkrumah of Ghana and Jomo Kenyatta of Kenya, who would go on to play important roles in winning independence for, and participating in, the governing of their countries in the following decades.

The central dilemma for the sixth congress, facing a post-war world, was the problem of using violence to back up its challenge, "We are determined to be free." The congress issued a threat: "If the Western World is still determined to rule Mankind by force, then Africans, as a last resort, may have to appeal to force in the effort to achieve freedom, even if force destroys them and the world." But, pending the "last resort," the congress opted for "positive action" based on Gandhi's teaching of nonviolent resistance. There were other signposts in the growth of Pan-African ideas at the sixth congress: a One man, one vote" was recognized in a resolution demanding universal franchise. Socialism was not mentioned, but there was an assertion that "economic democracy is the only real democracy" and condemnation of "the rule of private wealth and industry for private profit alone." Also, the nascent Bandung spirit was acknowledged: "Congress expressed the hope that before long the peoples of Asia and Africa would have broken their centuries-old chains of colonialism. Then, as free nations, they would stand united to consolidate and safeguard their liberties and independence from the restoration of Western imperialism, as well as the danger of Communism."

It was not until 1958, when Dr. Kwame Nkrumah sponsored the First Conference of African States in Accra, Ghana, that the Pan-African Conference met in Africa. At the Accra conference the African states present concentrated on the independence of Africa and the possibility of African unity. What emerged from the Accra conference fell short of a political "United States of Africa"; rather, it was an agreement to experiment with regional unity among African states. Thus, many regional conferences took place before the Addis Ababa (Ethiopia) Conference of 1961, which established a charter for African cooperative ventures. Subsequently, in 1963, the Organization of African Unity (OAU) was created at another Addis Ababa All-African Summit. Today, the OAU has its headquarters at Addis Ababa with a Secretary General. Among other concerns, the OAU works toward African cooperation in socio-cultural, political, and educational affairs, and African economic development.

Institutionalization of interest is a critical measure of these developing orientations. The founding in 1962 of the American Negro Leadership Conference in Africa—it has since disbanded—by black elites in the civil rights movement signaled the institutionalization of African-American pressure to protect and enhance African interests.

That trend has continued to develop, most notably in the creation of the lobby, TransAfrica. In that body we find an interest in enhancing professionalism (as an organized lobby with a research staff and the recent addition of a research and educational affiliate called TransAfrica Forum); in developing specialized talents (as a full-time lobby with full-time concern with the "outer" black world); and in extending vision beyond a purely African one, to include a Caribbean focus. Perhaps the fact that TransAfrica and similarly situated interests have not yet been able to affect the foreign policy process meaningfully less important than the fact that the task of serious foreign policy political mobilization is under way in black America.

The extent to which black bureaucrats and diplomats have been able to exert significant influence on the foreign policy process, in the sense of being architects as opposed to being instruments, remains an open question. Certainly the kind of influence that Andrew Young was able to exert, at least for a while, was unique; and it is perhaps more significant that he was removed prematurely. It is of significance, however, that in February 1983 another institutional expression of this rising black American concern appeared, in the form of an organization of black ambassadors, created for the long-term purpose of heightening an interest in foreign policy within the black community and encouraging young blacks to consider foreign service careers.

In a sense, these developing expressions of a linkage of interest with Africa through a foreign policy focus may be perceived as another stage in the fulfillment of a historic U.S. pattern of ethnic groups bringing their influence to bear on matters affecting their ancestral lands. Such developments are consistent with what may be formulated as a general rule: that the more heightened a sense of racial or ethnic identity, the greater the propensity for such expressions of linkage to transcend national boundaries.

But there is a particularly sharp edge to the rising African-American identification with African causes. There is, so to speak, a dual, racially significant attachment. Here, we have a developing relationship not only conditioned by the facts of common racial origin but also impregnated with the realities of common racial traumas. One must pause here to question the impact of this dualism—what Du Bois called "twoness"—on the African-American role in U.S. foreign policy processes. It is equally important to note that black Americans do not have a monopoly on racial dualism. White Americans from Europe have a similar historical experience—the European soul and the American soul in one body. In this context, the U.S. soul prevails in the interest of national security. Black Americans are no exception.

TRANSAFRICA

The TransAfrica organization provides a model for understanding African-American leadership in American foreign affairs, especially in Africa and the Caribbean.

The idea of a foreign policy lobby germinated at the Black Leadership Conference convened by the Congressional Black Caucus on September 25–26, 1976. The 130 leaders attending the conference concluded that the conspicuous absence of African-Americans in high-level international affairs positions, and the general subordination, if not neglect, of African-Caribbean priorities, could be corrected only by the establishment of a private advocacy organization. An *ad hoc* committee of Randall Robinson, Herschelle Challenor, and Willard Johnson, formulated an organization design and investigated funding possibilities for such an organization.

On July 1, 1977, TransAfrica, a nonprofit organization, was incorporated in Washington, D.C., with Randall Robinson as executive director and support staff member. Start-up funding came from the National Council of Churches, the Board of Global Ministries/United Methodist Church, and the Ford Foundation. In the last twenty years, the membership has grown to over 40,000 supporters (Robinson, 1998).

TransAfrica is dedicated to the mission of monitoring legislative activities and lobbying for more progressive U.S. foreign policy toward Africa and the Caribbean. It has matured into the leading foreign policy organization on issues about Africa, the Caribbean, human rights, democracy, and economic, political, and social concerns of developing and underdeveloped countries. Another critical part of TransAfrica's mandate is to foster a closer alliance among African-Americans and Africans and Caribbeans through activities that promote political awareness and involvement in foreign affairs.

During its twenty-year history, TransAfrica has served as a force for political action by persuading presidential administrators and congressional leaders to review and revise their policy imperatives. Through contact with print and broadcast media, this organization has successfully raised the profile of issues related to all of Africa and the Caribbean that would otherwise go unnoticed by mainstream America. Seven chapters located across the nation have been organized in an effort to cultivate an interest in foreign affairs on the local level.

TransAfrica meets regularly with members of Congress, testifies at congressional hearings, conducts press conferences, contributes articles to media outlets, and publishes policy statements, reports, and newsletters on issues related to Africa and the Caribbean.

In the last twenty years TransAfrica has:

- Mobilized opposition to U.S. support of apartheid so successfully that the Anti-Apartheid Act of 1986 was passed despite President Reagan's veto.
- Helped establish and coordinate the Free South Africa Movement, for which it organized protests for one year in front of the South African embassy (more than 5,000 people were arrested).
- Spoken out against human rights violations in Liberia, Zaire, Kenya, Haiti, Malawi, and Ethiopia.
- Spearheaded the struggle to maintain economic sanctions against Rhodesia (now Zimbabwe).
- Created the Action Alert letter writing system which generates a very large volume of mail on issues of concern in selected congressional districts.
- Facilitated meetings between American policy-makers and foreign leaders, including Nelson Mandela, Jamaican Prime Minister Michael Manley, and the late Maurice Bishop, prime minister of Grenada.
- Addressed the plenary session at the OAU conference in Nairobi.
- Organized meetings between African-American leaders and then Secretary of State James Baker on apartheid, famine relief, and human rights.
- Established a Foreign Institute in 1993 to mobilize a black "Think Tank" to focus on American policies on Africa and the Caribbean.

Current TransAfrica priorities include pressing for democracy in Nigeria, allaying problems in the Caribbean banana trade, and increasing foreign aid to some countries and decreasing it to others based on performance in human rights and democratic ideas. Under the leadership of its executive director, Randall Robinson, the organization will pursue all opportunities to create an understanding among policy-makers and assist in the formulation of constructive U.S. foreign policy as it affects Africa and the Caribbean.

BLACK AMBASSADORS/DIPLOMATS

Between 1949 and 1996, more than ninety black Americans served as U.S. ambassadors and/or foreign service officers. It should also be noted that several blacks served in similar capacities between 1896 and 1949. For example, between 1869–1913 eight blacks, including Frederick Douglass, represented the United States in Haiti with a ministerial rank (Miller, 1978). Several other black diplomats of ministerial rank served in Liberia, West Africa, during the same period. Collectively, these men and women served all over the world, especially in Africa, Asia, the Caribbean, Latin America, the United Nations, and Europe (see Appendix D for a complete list). One of these foreign diplomats was Ralph Johnson Bunche. His accomplishments exemplify the kind of leadership provided by African-Americans in the international arena.

Ralph Bunche

Ralph Johnson Bunche (1904–1971), diplomat, was born the grandson of a slave. He was orphaned at age fourteen. He attended Jefferson High School in Los Angeles, where he was valedictorian of his class in 1922. He won an athletic scholarship to the University of California–Los Angeles (UCLA), where he starred in football, baseball, and basketball while being the sports editor of the college yearbook. He also worked as a janitor in the women's gym and spent his summers as a mess boy on a coastal steamer, in order to earn extra money for his support.

He graduated summa cum laude with a bachelor's degree in international relations. He then went to Harvard University and received his master's degree in government in 1928. In that same year, he became head of the Political Science Department at Howard University and continued teaching until 1932. In that year, he received a Rosenwald grant and went back to work for his doctor of philosophy degree at Harvard (Urquhart, 1993).

His thesis for his Ph.D. degree was "French Administration in Togoland and Dahomey." For research, he traveled through the interior of both Togoland and Dahomey by truck. He saw colonial life in Africa, and his thesis was so finely done that he won the Tappan Award for the best essay of its kind in the social sciences.

Dr. Bunche received a two-year post-doctoral fellowship in anthropology and colonial policy from the Social Science Research Council. He studied at Northwestern University in 1936 and at the London School of Economics in 1937, and later, in 1937, he studied at South Africa's Capetown University.

Upon his return trip to Africa, Dr. Bunche became an honorary citizen of the Kikuyu tribe. He earned the name "Karioki," which means "He who has returned from the dead." That ceremony, or induction, into the tribe, made a very deep impression upon him. The chief said, when he welcomed Dr. Bunche, that many of his former relatives had been captured by slave traders and he had never seen them again. "I prayed for the day when one would return, and today you are the one that returned and therefore, I have given you this name of Karioki."

Dr. Bunche then joined the Carnegie Corporation as the chief aide to Gunnar Myrdal, the Swedish sociologist who was working on a cultural survey of Negro life in America. The result was the most excellent study, a classic, entitled *An American Dilemma*. It was a very difficult piece of work, and it was very hazardous. Dr. Bunche remembered going with Gunnar Myrdal into the small towns of the South and being ordered out by the sheriff, though Myrdal explained that they were there just to ask people questions. When they did approach people, they found that the people were afraid to talk. Everyone tried not to become involved in the study.

When World War II broke out, Dr. Bunche became the senior social science analyst for the office of the Coordinator of Information in African and Far Eastern Affairs. In 1942, he was assigned to the African section of the Research and Analysis Branch of the Office of Strategic Services. His first assignment was as a principal research analyst, and then later as chief of the section. After two years he joined the State Department, where he held number of positions successively. These included area specialist in the Division of Territorial Studies; acting associate chief, Division of Dependent Area Affairs; Office of Special Political Affairs, and associate chief and acting chief of the Division of Dependent Area Affairs.

In 1942, he helped draw up the territories and trusteeships sections of the United Nations Charter and served as technical expert on trusteeship for the United States Delegation to the Dumbarton Oaks Conference. The outline for what became the United Nations was drawn up at a conference held at Dumbarton Oaks, a mansion in Washington, D.C. Here, during August through October 1944, it was proposed that the unit to preserve world peace would be the Security Council, a body in which the "big five"—China, France, the Soviet Union, the United Kingdom, and the United States—would be permanently represented.

At Yalta in February 1945, Franklin D. Roosevelt, Winston Churchill, and Joseph Stalin agreed that a conference of united nations should be called to meet in San Francisco in the United States on April 25, 1945, to prepare the charter of an organization along the lines proposed in the informal conversations of Dumbarton Oaks. This organization was to be the United Nations. And so, fifty nations sent delegates to San Francisco between April 25 and June 26, 1945, to implement the Dumbarton Oaks proposals, the Yalta agreement, and other amendments proposed by various other governments.

Dr. Bunche first entered the United Nations "on loan" from the State Department in May 1946, when he joined the secretariat as director of the Trusteeship Division. The following year, he resigned from the State Department to accept a permanent post with the secretariat. In 1948, he was appointed chief assistant to Count Folke Bernadotte, United National mediator for the Palestine situation. This brought Dr. Bunche's name before the public. When Count Bernadotte was assassinated on September 17, 1948, Dr. Bunche had to continue the cease-fire negotiations with Egypt and Israel. On the day of the assassination, Bunche denounced the crime as an outrage against the international community. He had to assume a great responsibility under sorrowful circumstances. After forty-two days of negotiations, Dr. Bunche reported to the Security Council on January 7, 1949, with the agreements for a permanent cease fire and for a peace settlement (Urquhart, 1993).

It was at this point that the entire world became aware of Dr. Bunche. In 1950, Dr. Bunche was awarded the Nobel Peace Prize, and when it was presented to him at Oslo, he said,

In these critical times—times which test to the utmost the good sense, the forbearance and the morality of every peace-loving people—it is not easy to speak of peace with either conviction or reassurance. True it is that statesmen the world over, exalting lofty concepts and noble ideals, pay homage to peace and freedom in a perpetual torrent of eloquent phrases. But the statesmen also speak darkly of the lurking threat of war; and the preparations for war ever intensify, while strife flares or threatens in many localities.

In 1955, Dr. Bunche was promoted in his position in the secretariat, working directly under the U.N. secretary-general. During 1954 and 1962, becoming concerned, he worked with the U.N. International Conference to promote peaceful uses of atomic energy, and helped draft the statute of the International Atomic Energy Agency, while also working in the organization of that agency. In 1960, when the Congo erupted, Bunche rushed in to help Dag Hammarskjold, then U.N. secretary-general, to oversee the U.N. civilian and military operations in strife-torn Africa.

Until Bunche's retirement on October 1, 1971, he had been the highest-ranking American in the U.N. secretariat. He was under-secretary in charge of political affairs (Bunche, 1952). He was inactive in world politics after the summer of 1971 because of various ailments and a broken right wrist, which he suffered in a fall at his home. He had been suffering from kidney malfunction, advanced diabetes, and heart disease for several months before death came at 12:40 a.m. on December 10, 1971.

President Nixon telephoned Bunche's widow to express his sympathy. The president also issued a statement praising the diplomat as "one of the greatest architects of peace in our time. America is deeply proud of this distinguished son and profoundly saddened by his death, but we are also strengthened by the inexhaustible measure of dedication and creative action that spanned his splendid career" (Rivlin, 1990).

Related to black American leadership contributions to American foreign affairs is the role of blacks in the American armed forces. Black military history and the role of blacks in American foreign affairs have been relatively well documented in recent years (Hawkins, 1993; Putney, 1992; Buchanan, 1977; Johnson, 1974; Greene, 1974; Urquhart, 1993; Miller, 1978; and Gordon, 1991).

The military heritage of black Americans is as long-standing as the history of the black presence in North America. From the first recorded visit of a black person to what is now the United States in 1528 (Hawkins, 1993), blacks— both the enslaved and the free—have participated in military or quasi-military actions. It should be noted, however, that such participation has certainly not been undertaken without difficulty. Since its modest 1528 beginning, blacks have served and attained the rank in the armed forces of general, and its naval equivalent. They have also served as general of the Army and Air Reserves as well as the National Guard. Not until 1940 was a black officer in the U.S. Army promoted to general. Since Benjamin O. Davis, Sr., attained that rank, about 120 others have risen to it or its equivalent in various branches of the military, either as an active duty or reserve officer.

For the purpose of this chapter, a brief summary of blacks who became the first to occupy high military leadership positions has been included. No attempt was made to chronicle the full range of the contributions of these leaders. Rather, the list presents them and the roles they played in changing the image of the U.S. military organizations. They have made major contributions, set many precedents, and earned many military awards and decorations.

FIRSTS IN THE MILITARY

First West Point Graduate: In 1887, Henry Ossian Flipper became the first African-American to be graduated by the United States Military Academy at West Point; he then became the first African-American commissioned officer in the U.S. Army.

First Annapolis Man: In 1949, Wesley A. Brown became the first African-American to graduate from the United States Naval Academy at Annapolis.

First World War II Hero: By downing four Japanese planes during the attack on Pearl Harbor, Messman First Class Dorie Miller became the first American hero of World War II. He was awarded the Navy Cross.

First Female Army Nurse: When she was commissioned a lieutenant, Susie King became the U.S. Army's first African-American nurse. Born a slave in Georgia, she wrote her memoirs in 1902, which are the only record of African-American nurses in the Civil War.

First General: The grandson of a slave, Benjamin O. Davis in 1940 became the first African-American to be a general in the United States Army. He had served in three wars.

First Female General: Born in 1927 and trained as a nurse in Harlem Hospital, Hazel Johnson went on to become the first African-American female general in the United States Army.

First Admiral: Born in 1922, Samuel Gravely, Jr., rose in the Navy to become the first African-American to command a U.S. warship, the destroyer escort *Falgout;* in 1971, he became the first African-American admiral in naval history.

First Medal of Honor Winner: Born a slave, William H. Carney enlisted in the fifty-fourth Massachusetts Colored Infantry in 1863. In July of that year, he led a heroic assault on Fort Wagner, South Carolina, and became the first African-American to receive the Medal of Honor.

First Chairman of the Joint Chiefs of Staff: Born April 5, 1937 in New York City, General Colin L. Powell was confirmed by the U.S. Senate in October 1989. In his position, he became the first black to serve as principal military advisor to the president, the National Security Council, and the Secretary of Defense.

There are reasons to believe that the future role of black leadership in the global arena will continue to grow. For one thing, the globalization of the U.S. economy will enhance greater opportunities for black Americans in the international community. A second reason is the reception that black Americans now enjoy in the Clinton Administration, along with Clinton's recent visit to Africa and several appointments of black Americans as ambassadors. The last (but not least) reason is Rev. Jesse Jackson's recent role in winning freedom for three captured Americans held as prisoners of war in Yugoslavia. They were Steven M. Gonzales, 22; Christopher J. Stone, 25; and Andrew A. Ramirez, 24. Jackson launched his four-day mission to recover the soldiers despite the State Department's lack of approval and the department's warnings about the dangers to the personal safety of Jackson's twenty-four-member interfaith delegation. Americans' freedom was the fruit of Rev. Jackson's heroic and determined efforts. These are clear reasons for future optimism.

13

The Future of Black Leadership

We realize that our future lies chiefly in our own hands. We know that neither institution nor friends can make a race stand unless it has strength in its own foundation; that races, like individuals, must stand or fall by their own merit; that to fully succeed they must practice the virtues of self-reliance, self-respect, industry, perseverance, and economy.

Paul Robeson

What is the future of black leadership in American society? Will black leadership endure? What are the major challenges for black leadership in the twenty-first century? To what extent will the color line be a factor in black leadership? Will black leadership effect social change? These are but a few questions that this chapter attempts to address.

Although it is difficult, if not impossible, to predict the future precisely, intelligent speculations about the future can be made. When Alvin Toffler (1972) and other futurists wrote about the future, their opinions were at first greeted with laughter. People thought that they were out of their minds. Today, however, much of the futurists' predictions about technological development and its impact on society are, for all practical purposes, a *fait accompli*. In fact, today the word "futurist" has leapt back into language—but with a new meaning. The term now denotes a growing school of social critics, scientists, philosophers, planners, and others who concern themselves with the alternatives facing the human race as it collides with an onrushing future.

The future of black leadership in America must be viewed in historical context. This context provides an understanding of the present state of black leadership. On the basis of our understanding of the present status of black leadership, it is possible to project what is likely to happen in the future. Indeed, this is what most historiographers (Nevins, 1938; Gottschalk, 1964) meant in the discourse on the function of history: fetching understandings from the past to understand the present and plan for the future. Simply put, Toffler (1970) wrote, "If we do not learn from history, we shall be compelled to relive it. . . . But if we do not change the future, we shall be compelled to endure it. And that could be worse." Toffler goes on to say that "we cannot humanize the future until we draw it into our consciousness and probe it with all the intelligence and imagination at our command." This is precisely what this chapter is all about—probing the future of black leadership.

In probing the future of black leadership in America, we have relied heavily on the historical trend of black leadership, the nature of the challenges that gave birth to this ethnic leadership, the current challenges, and a convenient national survey of American scholars in African-American studies disciplines. The survey included opinions of African-American leaders, ten leading black newspapers and magazines, and ten leading white newspapers and magazines. The data collection process involved mailing a brief questionnaire addressing three questions: (1) What are your views on black leadership in America? (2) What are some of the shortcomings of black leadership in America? (3) What are some of the prospects for black leadership in America, particularly in the twenty-first century? Follow-up interviews were made in several cases.

The goal of black leadership, as evidenced in this book, has been the uplifting of blacks through freedom, justice, and equal opportunities. Although black Americans share this common goal, there is clear evidence that black leaders, throughout their history, have not always agreed on a single leadership strategy. In fact, black leadership styles and tactics have wide variations. This is to be expected because, like other racial groups, the black groups are not homogenous. Indeed, blacks are heterogeneous. Contrary to most white stereotypes of blacks, all blacks are not alike, and certainly they all do not think the same way.

The accomplishments of black Americans, their leadership and, yes, the contributions of millions of white men and women of good will are worth noting. Slavery was abolished; blacks gained full citizenship; the doctrine of "separate but equal" was no longer the law of the land following the case of *Brown v. the Topeka Board of Education* in 1954; interracial mating is no longer a crime; several doors of opportunity have been opened in many aspects of American life. Thus, no one can deny that black Americans have made significant progress toward freedom and upward mobility, perhaps never dreamed of before. In fact, it has been estimated that black American annual income nationwide is in excess of $400 billion (Brown, 1995). This means that if black America were a nation, it would rank number seven in annual national income. All these gains are well and good. But the problems currently facing black America are disturbing. Practically, by any measure, a disproportionate number of black Americans are by far more at-risk than their white counterparts. In spite of numerous civil rights legislations, blacks are bleeding from the legacies of slavery and past and present discriminatory practices. Several annual Urban League publications on the status of black Americans for the eight years (1987–1994) suggest that blacks are being systematically relegated to a permanent underclass status. A recent publication, "Repairing the Breach" (Austin, 1996) provides other alarming data on the status of African-American men and boys. This national Task Force Report, under the sponsorship of the W.K. Kellogg Foundation, among other things, has concluded:

African-American males (and the larger African-American community) have faced continuous forms of mistreatment and oppression. The denial of the opportunity to vote, the denial of higher-paying industrial jobs, the denial of educational opportunities, and other related forms of racial discrimination all reflected practices and policies deeply rooted in American thought and traditions. And the consequences of these historical practices are still very much with us today.

Other sources of research data confirm the conclusion of the task force, as they reveal the following statistical overview of the status of African-American men and boys:

Population:

- Total U.S. population is 248,709,873. The total African-American population is 29,930,524 (12%). Of this latter number, 14,170,151 are males. (*Source*: U.S. Census, 1992)

Health:

- Black male life expectancy in 1991 was 64.6 years. White male life expectancy in 1991 was 72.9 years.
- The black male death rate from HIV in 1991 was 52.9 per 1,000. The white male death rate from HIV in 1991 is 16.7 per 1,000. (*Source*: National Center for Health Statistics, 1994)
- Black males are more likely to be born to unwed teenage mothers who themselves have limited education and even more limited life choices (Gibbs, 1988).

Homicide:

- Homicide rates in 1991 for African-American males were 72.5 per 100,000, nearly eight times higher than for white males. (*Source*: National Center for Health Statistics, 1994)

Poverty:

- The rate of poverty for all African-Americans is 29.5 percent compared to a 9.8 percent for whites. (*Source*: U.S. Census, 1992)
- Nearly half (42.7 percent) of black youth under the age of eighteen live in families below the poverty line. (*Source*: Curtis, 1996)

Family Life:

- Of the 7,055,063 black families, 3,045,283, or 43 percent are headed by black females. 26.3 percent of all black families live in poverty, compared to 7.0 percent of white families. (*Source*: U.S. Census, 1992)

Incarceration:

- Almost one in three (33 percent) black males between the ages of twenty and twenty-nine is under the control of the criminal justice system—in prison, jail, on probation, or on parole. This compares with one in sixteen white males and one in ten Hispanic males (Maurer, 1990).
- The number of African-American males in prison and jail exceeds the number of African-American males enrolled in higher education (Maurer, 1990).
- Black men in the United States are imprisoned at a rate four times that of black men in South Africa: 3,109 per 100,000 compared to 729 per 100,000 (Morton and Snell, 1992).
- Forty-four percent of all prisoners in the United States are black; black men make up 40 percent of the condemned on death row (Sentencing Project, 1990).

Education:

- More than 20 percent of the black male adolescents in the twelve to seventeen age group were unable to read at the fourth grade level (Brown, 1979).

Jobs:

- Unemployment black youth was 34 percent—twice the rate of 17.4 percent among all teenagers (Gibbs, 1988).

By most demographic indices—mortality rate, health, crime rate, homicide rate, life expectancy, income level, education level, unemployment level, and marital status—African-American men have the smallest chance to achieve the American dream. In fact, of the four comparison groups (black males, black females, white males, white females), social indicators show that black males experience the highest rates of health and social problems, including heart disease, hypertension, diabetes, homicide, suicide, unemployment, delinquency and crime, school drop out, imprisonment, and unwed teenage parenthood (Gordon and Majors, 1994). As Gibbs (1988) put it, black males have been miseducated by the educational system, mishandled by the criminal justice system, mislabeled by the mental health system, and misread by the social welfare system. In fact, she argues that black males have become rejects of the American affluent society and misfits in their own communities.

At the Tenth Annual Awards Dinner of the Urban Bankers Coalition in 1990, Clifton Wharton, Jr., provided another aspect of the obstacles to black progress. A trailblazer who opened a number of doors, Wharton became the first black to head a Fortune 100 company when, in 1987, he became chairman and CEO of the world's largest private pension fund, the Teachers Insurance Annuity Association/College Retirement Equities Fund. In 1987 he became the first black president of a major, predominantly white university, Michigan State University, and the world's largest university system, the State University of New York, in 1978. He was also the first black to be appointed deputy secretary of state of the U.S. Department of State, in 1993. In his speech to the Urban Bankers Coalition on April 26, 1990, Wharton (1990) had the following to say:

For almost four centuries in the United States, Blacks have wanted and aspired to full citizenship in society, culture, and the economy. The barriers to our participation have been such that to accomplish any given goal, Black men and women have had to run twice as fast, work twice as hard, and fight twice as valiantly as the white majority.

Yet we *have* run twice as fast. We *have* worked twice as hard. We *have* fought twice as valiantly. And again and again, we have risen to the challenges and accomplished our goals!

Yes, there has been marvelous progress in recent years—from entry-level positions to the board room. Although there is much distance yet to travel, one can read of the business success stories of Black Americans in *Black Enterprise* magazine, in *Ebony,* and yes, in the *Wall Street Journal* and the *New York Times.* More importantly, Blacks are taking their rightful place in mainstream jobs of true responsibility, rather than in positions that may have high visibility but lack decision-making or vertical mobility.

All right, there has been progress. That is the good news, even though it has been a long time coming. The bad news is that not only is there still so much to be done, but also that racial prejudice and stereotyping continue to be prevalent and an obstruction to progress.

I will not spend much time on the problem of outright prejudice that all of us have endured in myriad ways. There is not much we can do about it, anyway. We know it cannot be legislated out of existence. Prejudice is resident in the mind, and those who harbor it are always pleased to seize upon anything that reinforces their point of view, such as highly-questionable tracts like the recent book, *The Bell Curve.*

What is perhaps of more concern is the racial and ethnic stereotyping that often lies latent even in those who would describe themselves as liberal or unprejudiced. This often can be more of a problem than outright bias when well-meaning people see minorities through a stereotypical lens and apply different tests, attitudes, and expectations.

In his recent book on the use of politics by the black community, Robert C. Smith (1992) produces some gems of insight and theoretical importance. Smith's thesis is that struggle over racial meaning is a constant and dynamic tension between the black perspective and the attempt by whites to impose the dominant perspective on a racial event. Smith uses this paradigm to examine the civil rights movement in order to determine its impact on the political agenda of the 1970s, and concludes that the movement fell short in many respects. He suggests that the most significant impact is that the movement furthered the process of political incorporation to the point that a new generation of leaders has emerged within major American political institutions at every level of government. He goes on to conclude that this alone has not had much of an effect on the quality of life in the black community. It should also be noted, ironically, that the civil rights movement ushered in an electoral politics movement at a time when resources began to be withdrawn from major urban areas, where most blacks reside. In short, Smith has provided dismal evidence of the irrelevancy of black politics in producing in the last twenty-five years benefits for most blacks, especially the imperative to reconstruct and integrate the ghettos into the mainstream of American society. Jones (1981) has also alluded to this issue of increasing irrelevancy of black leadership in the paper he presented at the National Conference of Black Political Scientists.

Along this same line of argument, Harold Cruse (1990) not only discusses the crisis of black leadership, but concludes that African-Americans have no leaders. At a lecture at Prairie View A&M University in 1989, in response to a question asking him to evaluate black leaders, Cruse responded, "What leaders? We have no leaders." The apparent questioner responded by listing familiar names of the leaders of civil rights organizations, members of the Black Congressional Caucus, and black mayors. Cruse's response was that those persons listed by the questioner were not leaders, because they had no plan, no program of action, and no organization to mobilize or lead blacks in a direction. The acuity of Cruse's observations is of relevance to the discourse on the future of black leadership in America. Black America may elect black mayors in every city, and may elect congresspersons who are unable to deliver on promises and programs, and may force presidents to appoint black cabinet members and budget directors and civil rights organizations may operate more as relics of the past than instruments for action in the present and the future, in which case, of course Cruse's argument is correct. No doubt, this issue is a major challenge for black leadership now, and may remain so in the future, if black electorates fail to hold their leaders accountable.

Another area of concern is the relationship between black leaders and the American intellectuals, especially African-American intellectuals. James addresses this subject in her recent (1997) work, *Transcending the Talented Tenth*. Du Bois' gradual rejection of the "Talented Tenth" as race leaders has influenced contemporary blacks, elites, and academics such as Henry Louis Gates, Jr., Cornel West, and Angela Davis. The search for a common program among black Americans, one that recognizes and synthesizes struggles to dismantle sexism, heterosexism, and elitism alongside the battle for racial and economic justice is a part of the challenge that faces black leaders and American intellectuals in the future. Just how African-American intellectuals—as the postmodern Talented Tenth straddling the twentieth and twenty-first centuries (much as their predecessors bridged the nineteenth and twentieth centuries)—will manifest or falter as effective black leadership remains to be seen.

PERCEPTIONS AND REALITIES

Among the groups that either completed the questionnaires and/or received follow-up interviews for the survey of African-American studies mentioned earlier was the black leadership of the National African-American Male Collaboration. Although the group has a very short history, its participation in this study was about 90 percent of its membership (thirty-two program directors from all over the country).

In September 1993, the W.K. Kellogg Foundation launched the African-American Men and Boys (AAMB) initiative under the guidance of Dr. Bobby Austin, to address some of the challenges facing this group of males. Stage I included thirteen programmatic projects and two technical projects. In Stage II, an additional seventeen projects were added to create model collaborations that could bring about long-term structural interventions at the community level.

Three principles have guided this initiative:

1. Use leadership development, capacity-building, and skills-building to strengthen the leaders of the thirteen new or expanded programs;

2. Develop a model, free-standing collaboration for projects, to capitalize on each other's strengths and provide more resources and services than the projects would on their own, and, ultimately, achieve ways of sustaining themselves; and

3. Find additional successful projects, develop criteria for establishing models for replication, and focus on structures for leveraging funds that will lead to long-term sustainability and systems change.

The AAMB initiative strives to provide communities with a wide array of both effective programs (not merely focused drug prevention or anti-violence programs) and resources to meet the needs of young men. While many of the programs focus on a particular program of service, most include a wide array of opportunities for their participants. The strength of the AAMB initiative is the linking together of programs to form a network by which the programs can learn from each other and share resources and expertise in order to strengthen and expand their own programs. By doing so, the programs can all offer more holistic, comprehensive services to meet the needs of black males and to address complex and interconnected problems in their communities.

From the spirit of the AAMB initiative grew the National African-American Male Collaboration in the summer of 1995. This model collaboration has demonstrated the whole is truly greater than the sum of its parts. Each participating agency now has the capacity and ability to draw on services, expertise, and other resources from all other projects in the collaboration.

The National African-American Male Collaboration forms a network of support, resources, talents, and research to achieve a common purpose: *improving the quality of life for African-American males, developing healthy minds and bodies, and building leadership skills in youth.* It has three leadership emphases: personal and academic leadership, entrepreneurial leadership, and family and community leadership.

Other respondents to the survey, in addition to the aforementioned newspaper and magazine editors, African-American Studies scholars and black leadership practitioners, included students of my Black Leadership class at the University of Kansas. The groups' responses have been summarized in the following pages.

It should only get better for black leadership. Slowly, very slowly, resistance breaks down year to year. Black leaders emerge in great numbers as educated, accomplished individuals with each passing year. Also, we get farther away from the classic civil rights struggles of the 50s and 60s which led to a particular mindset among black leaders that may not be as relevant for the twenty-first century. Progress will be steady, but will also be slow. (*Boston Globe*)

As the twenty-first century approaches most importantly I feel will emerge a new black leadership that will remember the old days and the kind of work and sacrifice it took to bring its people up the ladder. This new leadership (NAACP-AAMB) will employ some of these old methods that have proven to work. This new leadership with renewed enthusiasm to make life better for the black race, so we may all look to having a better opportunity of sharing the wealth of a good and prosperous life will be what we will be looking for from our leaders of the next century. (Eddie Banks, Eisenhower Foundation)

To whom much is given, much is required. Those of us who have been blessed to be leaders must bear down and make sure that we have created *much* greater opportunities for those who come behind us. Our destiny is in our hands. (Charles H. Beady, Piney Woods School)

We need leaders that will direct us in the areas of family commitment and development, and leaders who emphasize the need for a technologically advanced race—we are going to be behind technologically if we don't get a foothold now, especially with our youth. (Linda Broadous Miles, Al Wooten Jr. Heritage Center)

Unless an older generation is willing to step aside, the prospects are poor. (Paul Brock, CRP, Inc., Kellogg Consultant)

We must in a sense return to the "old Landmark" in much of our principles, values, and overall foundation. We must help the generation of today and tomorrow to get on board. (Walter Darnell, Omega Little Brothers)

The prospects for leadership are vast, but only if existing black leadership is willing to open its ranks to new visions and strategies to resolve the complex problems facing African-Americans today and that will face them in the twenty-first century. Some of the most prominent among these problems are: growing poverty, inequality, and problems of literacy in an information-intensive economy. (Walter C. Farrell, Jr., Ph.D., Piney Woods Country Life School and University of Wisconsin-Milwaukee, School of Education)

The prospects [for black leadership in America] are: 1) better educated young blacks; 2) diminishing job opportunities; 3) entrepreneurial opportunities; and 4) White resistance to black progress. (Robert L. Green, Ph.D., Case Western Reserve University)

[The prospects for black leadership in America are poor], based on the American Dream illusion and paradigm from which African-American colleges and universities operate and miseducate. The Talented Tenth has become our own worst enemy. Marriage and having children is a low priority among them. The valuing of family and family leadership is lacking. (Paul Hill, East End Neighborhood House)

Excellent core of young blacks who must be given leadership opportunities. New generation (late 30s–early 40s) ready to work—also brilliant! (Spencer H. Holland, Ph.D., Project 2000, Inc.)

I believe black leadership will become more sensitive and caring. They will embrace the need to mentor young people and hold others accountable. They will come to the assistance of others when in distress. (Gordon Johnson, Jane Addams Hull House)

Until a resource base or means to establish the same from the African-American community is established, African-American leadership will remain theoretical, passive, and reactive. (Hurley Jones, Pathways Community Development Commission)

1. They [black leaders in America] are talented, well-educated, and appear to be highly committed to black Americans. However, they also appear to be less influential on the national level, and less effective locally. In addition, the Reagan revolution and the growing power of the Republican party in the U.S. Congress has eroded and undermined the power of the Congressional Black Caucus.
2. a) They are too detached physically and psychologically from the experiences and lives of average African-Americans; we have created an elitist professional leadership class.

   b) They have become too involved in the system and frequently have adopted attitudes and behaviors that distance them from African-Americans.

   On one hand, they are dim; for the reasons cited in #2. On the other hand, they are bright, for the reasons cited in #1. In spite of the fact that leadership development has become very popular we still have too few authentic leaders who emerge from local communities. In the future this will exacerbate the gulf between the leaders and black communities. This problem needs to be addressed in the future. (Anthony E.O. King, Ph.D., University of Alabama)

Until they refocus on building from our strong resource base we will continue to flounder and go in every direction. (Garry A. Mendez, Jr., Ph.D., The National Trust)

- [T]he fragmentation will continue
- [O]ne leader will emerge to galvanize and reinvigorate the community. Mfume seems to be one possibility. (John Payne, Duke Ellington School of the Arts)

- [Black leadership in America will] need to be more in89clusive, tolerant of diversity across marginalized groups (incl. women, new immigrants, gay/lesbian)
- Will also need to focus on high integrity, effective leadership (e.g., Kwiesi Mfume, Marion Wright Edelman, etc.) (John A. Rich, MD, Boston HealthCREW)

The prospects are bleak until there is a movement toward a more focused, values and culturally connected vision and the establishment of a commitment to change focused on real challenges and *real* solutions. (Horace H. Turnbull, The Boys Choir of Harlem)

As racial and other barriers continue to be broken and as black role models become more and more visible, the prospect for black leadership in medicine will continue to improve. At the same time, that progress is dependent on the critical effort to increase the number of African-American medical students and physicians. The AMA and other medical groups are working together to address this issue. The "3000 by 2000" program of the Association of American Medical Colleges—to increase the number of medical students to 3000 by the year 2000 along with the cross-organizational coalition of "Health Professionals for Diversity" and other projects are beginning to make a difference. We are confident that this trend will continue. While the challenges are monumental, the prospects for success are unlimited. (Frank E. Staggers, MD, American Medical Association, Chair, AMA Advisory Committee on Minority Physicians)

Well, I think [black leadership] is moving in various directions, and one is this conservative movement in the Republican party. I know that there are Black Republicans who are pleased with this in a way, but they are themselves not entirely comfortable with some of these black conservatives. There is the Million Man March and Louis Farrakhan and his movement, which is both very positive and a little bit scary. I think it's very positive in the sense that it is asking black men to accept their responsibilities as fathers and as husbands and as members of the community. It's a Puritanical movement so it tells people not to drink or do drugs and those are positive things as well. It talks about the need for blacks to build institutions in their communities: schools and churches and above all businesses, and I think that's positive as well. On the other hand, I think that Farrakhan at times has preached a message of hate, hatred of Jews, and I'm not convinced that he hasn't done that. He tried hard to convince people that he hadn't, I'm still not convinced. I have read some things that he has written and I've heard certain things that he has said that have kind of upset me. So, there's that leadership; conservative black leadership, the leadership that is kind of a moral crusade to clean up the community, the leadership of Louis Farrakhan and the Black Muslims. There is still the very powerful leadership of Jesse Jackson, trying to move the Democratic party to the left, trying to get more blacks elected to office, voter registration. The old kind of civil rights momentum and emphasis is evident in Jackson's politics, and that's where I would find myself more comfortable. He's a powerful moral leader, a powerful speaker, a powerful influence within the Democratic party. There are other blacks within the Democratic party who are very effective politicians, and I think they've gained some influence and some power as a result of that. People like William Gray who served in the Congress for a number of years and is president of the National Negro College Fund.

There are some blacks in business who hold high positions now. So there's not one black leader as there has been, I think, at certain times in the past. There are a number of black leaders moving in somewhat different directions. I think, though, that even if you go back to Du Bois and Washington moving in different directions, their ultimate goals, what they wanted in the end, were pretty much the same. And I think this is true for a lot of the black leaders today, even though they pursue these goals in different ways, I think most of them genuinely want racial equality, equality of opportunity, uplifting people or encouraging them to uplift themselves, working to strengthen the family, strengthen other community institutions, and most of all . . . I would mention a black woman who I think has provided real leadership and that's Marion Wright Edelman, concerned not only with families but with children and the next generation, and with succeeding generations, and I think she is making incredibly important contributions in that area. (William M. Tuttle, Jr., Ph.D., University of Kansas)

I suspect that black leadership will become even more important and diverse in the next century in terms of the issues and concerns needing attention. We will develop more militant leaders among working class black people and black women will become increasingly more powerful and demanding of social and economic justice. (Darlene Clark Hine, Michigan State University)

[Black leadership in America faces] [c]hallenges of economic shift, multiracial democracy, and cultural centeredness. (Molefi Asante, Ph.D., Temple University)

I think [black leadership] will change. The more we move to the twenty-first century, the less we will look to people who are civil rights oriented, but more toward people who can paint a vision and can articulate that vision. Today, black people think of leaders as civil rights leaders, and in the twenty-first century, that won't cut it.

The main obstacle to black leadership in the future will be the issue of being able to transcend blackness. For example, being Mayor of Kansas City, I had to receive 97% of the black vote and at least close to 40% of the white vote, and you've got to be able to be seen as someone who can perform well for the city, and not as someone who can perform well for black folks. Although when you perform well for city, it benefits black folks. The prospects are bright. We have young African-Americans today whose IQs are exploding off the chart, and if those of us already in positions of leadership can just continue to provide and counsel them and not hold them back, then the twenty-first century will be the best century for African-Americans. (Mayor Cleaver, Kansas City, Missouri)

I would argue that we need a full-scale blueprint for investing in the future: a comprehensive, national policy on minorities and the workforce.

We are at a particularly critical juncture in our nation's history. We face a call that demands a strong and sure response. The "call" is to help shape, nurture, and maintain a strong and vigorous minority community. A minority community where equal financial opportunity is not a dream, but a reality. It is a call to educate our young: to shape, nurture, and maintain their dreams—to breathe into their lives a renewed hope for the future. It is a call, clear and simple, to achieve the full and uncompromised equality each of us has a right to. Answering the call is no easy task.

In the past, for reasons we haven't been able to control, competitiveness has been our history—the competitiveness bred by having to fight twice as hard as our fellow citizens for every inch of progress.

Today, competitiveness has become our legacy—our special strength in a trying time.

Tomorrow? Perhaps tomorrow our competitiveness will turn out to be our destiny—the foundation of our strength and leadership in a new era.

In the Second Punic War, Hannibal took on the Roman Empire to protect his native Carthage. To achieve his goal, he scaled the heights of the Alps. Against all odds and expectations, he brought his forces through to victory. And today, when most of us have forgotten the names of his antagonists and hardly even recall what the conflict was all about, we still honor Hannibal for his courage, his resourcefulness, his fidelity, and his unflagging will to succeed.

I do not think I need to explain why Hannibal seems to me a fitting symbol for today's black professionals. (Clifton R. Wharton, Jr., Ph.D., Former U.S. Deputy Secretary of State)

The restoration of a healthy life in the 'hood requires an all-out war against the manipulative cosmopolitans who have been determining policy for the managerial elite. The black leadership's enchantment with radical leftwing ideologies has ended in the blind alley of the 'hood's misery, despair, and hopelessness. True, an enormous portion of those who vote for the Left do so for honorable reasons and think they are opposing "The Establishment," that is, the managerial elite. They have done their best to support the black struggle for justice and will continue to do so. Simultaneously, an enormous portion of those who vote for the Right do not wish black people ill and would welcome an alliance against that same Establishment, were the issues and lines to be drawn clearly.

No, I am not suggesting that blacks desert the Left for the Right, desert the Democratic Party for the Republicans. Nothing could be clearer than that blacks can, should, and will do their best to steer an independent course. But have black political leaders done that or have they in fact locked themselves into a coalition in which they get more and more clout with fewer and fewer desirable results? An independent perspective must be brought to both parties and, above all, political leaders must recognize and openly acknowledge that the black cause has potential allies, as well as dangerous enemies, in all ideological camps.

If victory in the Cultural War requires alliances even with, among others, the large anti-racist sections of the dreaded Christian Right, so be it. In politics you take your allies where you can find them, even if you must hold them at arm's length. To put it differently, if you want to go duck hunting, go where the ducks are. New wars require new alliances in accordance with new relations of forces. Neither blacks nor whites can go on fighting the last war and the wars before that without ending in a debacle. But that is precisely what our political and cultural leaders, both black and white, have been doing. And that, I believe, explains much of the current political paralysis inside and outside the 'hood. (Eugene D. Genovese, Ph.D., Professor Emeritus, Emory University)

BLACK LEADERSHIP SURVEY

1. What are your views on Black leadership in America?

2. What are some of the shortcomings of Black leadership in America?

3. What are some of the prospects for Black leadership in America, particularly in the twenty-first century? (Gordon 1997)

(Please attach additional pages if necessary)

Print Name: _____   Signature: _____

Institution: _____   Date: _____

☐ Please do not identify my name with the responses above in your publication.

Return to: The University of Kansas, Center for Multicultural Leadership, Schiefelbusch Institute for Life Span Studies, 1028 Dole Human Development Center, Lawrence, KS 66045

Student Responses

1. The motivation to become something better, example: progress.
2. Ambition.
3. Believing and having faith that positive outcomes will happen.
4. Persuasion, getting people involved.
5. Education.

1. When represented properly, the immediate outcomes are gratifiable (i.e., the Texaco incident where in 1996 Texaco agreed to pay $176.1 million to settle a 2-year-old race discrimination suit).
2. Because of black leadership, more blacks can be found to have or own their own businesses, more higher level involvement in the corporate world.

1. Black leadership is finally striving toward a possible monolithic leader in Farrakhan; and Jackson and Chavis are supporting him.
2. Black leadership is finally gaining economic strength with the rise of black companies in the Fortune 500 or blacks starting businesses.
3. Black leadership is gaining more political power by putting blacks in authoritative positions.
4. Black leadership now has somewhat of a striving toward a "talented tenth" with more blacks going to college, graduating, and pursuing advanced degrees.
5. Black leadership is moving away from the old ideological foundations of accommodation, separatist, and integration; and moving toward full equality, acceptance, and the betterment of its community in the interest of preserving humanity.

1. Jesse Jackson's affirmative action victory which will hopefully spread to blacks in all job opportunities.
2. Blacks going on to higher education is increasing more chances of a black leader emerging.
3. The presence of religion in oratory to rally and motivate their followers.
4. The fact that there hasn't been a leader in a while, remember—leadership has been reactionary in the past.
5. Black leaders able to demonstrate and protest peacefully.

1. Relative to the socio-political situation 3–4 decades ago, blacks have an [increasing] accessibility to the mainstream.
2. In terms of corporate America, blacks are finding more ways to achieve success—moving into the Fortune 500.
3. Also, with regards to corporate America, blacks are beginning to own more businesses.

4. In general, though, there is much still to be done, the condition of blacks has come a long way, which stands as proof that the labors of the black community to prosper and find justice, equality, and freedom can be fruitful.

1. More people are capable of having the characteristic of being a leader or having leadership qualities.
2. Leaders may be more likely to cooperate with other leaders.
3. Black leadership is changing the theme away from racism directly and look at the avenues that create it.
4. There seems to be more individuals who possess the ability to be a leader. Contain the ideological goals, etc.
5. Black leadership has grown to many areas, ideologies, etc. which makes a good leader able to be diverse and versatile in his or her presentation.

1. To become unified and have a determined goals, even with different leadership style, respect the other's objective and style of accomplishing it. Not separating like Martin Luther King and Malcolm X.
2. Being proactive to issues relating African-Americans and not being retroactive.
3. Being active, not passive, with your beliefs, ideas, and attitudes relating to the uplifting of African-Americans.
4. Reestablish the black community.
5. Go back to church.

1. That communities are trying to make the schools go far and better educationally.
2. [Blacks'] voice is being heard all over America because of their protests and marches are being recognized.
3. Wanting to help other blacks out by buying from blacks—more of an economic strength.
4. More blacks are being educated in a way because of affirmative action and striving for their goals and are going to achieve them.
5. More blacks are working to learn about their heritage.

1. We have more educated blacks.
2. More blacks own businesses (Wall Street).

1. Refocusing and revitalizing of key organizations [such] as NAACP.
2. Emergence of several leaders who may fill the void of a monolithic leader.
3. The fight for civil rights programs and leveling of the playing field.
4. The use of Black Studies programs.

1. We will be able to recognize potential leaders if we get out of the characteristics of traditional leaders.

2. Black leadership has always answered the community's call and will continue to do so.

3. We as black people are beginning to recognize the importance of political and economic status.

1. The prospects for black leadership are many. One prospect is [the emergence of] a leader for the lost youth. Who can they look up to, follow, and help achieve positive goals.

2. [There is a] need of a leader with vision for the future. A leader who can work in his/her external and internal environments very well. A wheeler and dealer like Booker T. Washington and someone not afraid to speak up on issues like Ida B. Wells . . . and all in one leader. A leader who can convey their vision and make it the vision of others. A vision that leads out of problems, not away from problems.

3. The census has shown that Caucasians are becoming the minority . . . in the United States. Leadership is needed in all communities to prepare for the challenges that lay ahead. Challenges in the area of local and national government, community economical health and well being, education, the welfare of the community, and many other areas.

4. One must also look at the prospect of uniting the black community. How can this be achieved? What goals need to be set? What information or education about these goals needs to be provided? What are the key elements to bringing a community together? How does one find these keys and use them?

5. [Efforts] are needed in the area of civil liberties and corporate structures. Anything can be written down and made into law if it is for the good of the people, but writing and law aren't enough. Leaders need to help see through the changes and help make effective the laws created for the good of the people. All kinds of leaders, from all different levels are needed to help push along the changes. Change may take time, but with commitment, direction, and push from black leaders of all levels, no matter where they lead at, change will come at a more reasonable rate.

What do all these responses mean? Certainly, these responses serve as indicators of perceptions and realities of black leadership's role in American life. They have many things in common, and two major conclusions that can be drawn: (1) that black leadership faces several formidable challenges in the twenty-first century, and (2) that social change in America is inevitable. A good example of the task that faces black leadership and indeed American leadership in general is a recent (1997) study on American public schools. According to the study, "Deepening Segregation in American Public Schools," schools around the nation are becoming more separate and unequal. Researchers Gary Orfield of Harvard University and Mark D. Bachmeir, David R. James, and Tamela Eitle of Indiana University found that the racial and ethnic segregation of black and Latino students has produced a deepening isolation from white students.

An expansion of segregation to the suburbs, particularly in larger metropolitan areas, was shown to be present by the study, as were segregation by class, family, and community educational background. This national study used data on race and poverty reported to the U.S. Department of Education by all states except Idaho.

On the other hand, the recent historic achievement of the golf sensation Tiger Woods keeps hope alive for millions of African-Americans. In 1997, Woods, became the youngest winner of the prestigious Masters golf tournament in Augusta, Georgia, at the age of 21, and the first black to claim a major professional golf championship. Woods finished at 18-under-par 270 at the Masters to earn the tournament's traditional Green Jacket and the $486,000 first-place prize.

In America, the country club and the golf course are major power houses. Traditionally, many major policies and decisions are made on the golf course and the historically lily-white country clubs. With Woods's admission into this American major league powerhouse, what will be his impact on American life? Can he or will he be allowed by the power structure to make a difference in African-American life? Will his power from the golf course power house trickle down to young blacks in the inner city who desperately need help? Just how will white America, black America, red America, and yellow America respond to all of these issues? It is perhaps too early to judge; time will tell. It is important to note, however, that if lessons from history are important, Woods, like his predecessors Jackie Robinson, Joe Louis, and Jesse Owens, to name a few, will no doubt make a difference. At a minimum, Woods will join his predecessors by opening the doors of different opportunities to people of color and will serve as a role model to American youth. It is this paradox in American history that deepens a better understanding of the "American dilemma," as Gunner Myrdal (1944, 1962) bluntly put it.

A MATTER OF PERSONAL CONCERN

This book has taken two years to complete. During this period I have had the opportunity to meet and have dialogue with many people, especially black leaders, as well as whites in leadership positions. Based on the responses and the lack of responses from black leaders and whites in general, some important compelling personal observations which have implications for the future of black leadership can be made.

Before criticizing anyone, we should all bear in mind that the crisis in the 'hood is only one manifestation, albeit the most ghastly, of an American national crisis, and that white leaders have been performing no better than black. While many black leaders, like many white, have revealed themselves as dubious and even unsavory characters, we may concern ourselves only with those who have been manning their posts honorably under excruciatingly difficult conditions. And we dare not forget that some of them fought heroically in the civil rights movement that decisively changed American society, made world history, and left a rich legacy on which to build.

The question remains: What has gone wrong? Martin Luther King, Jr., demonstrated the indispensability of a strategy that combined black autonomy and initiative with an understanding that the black struggle constitutes part of a larger struggle to reshape American national life, spiritually as well as socially. With a rare combination of wisdom and firm adherence to principle, he exposed as both wrong and self-defeating all attempts to allow the struggle to be propelled by hatred and violence. He grounded his political strategy in his religious thought and hammered at a central theme no longer popular:

As I have said in so many instances, it is not enough to struggle for the new society. We must make sure that we make the psychological adjustment required to live in that society. This is true of white people, and it is true of Negro people. Psychological adjustment will save white people from going into the new age with old vestiges of prejudice and attitudes of white supremacy. It will save the Negro from seeking to substitute one tyranny for another. (Washington, 1986)

As a matter of personal concern, it should be noted that in this study most black leaders and white leaders were either too busy to communicate—or simply avoided communicating—their reactions or views on the subject. Many black leaders told me that they could not afford to be critical about black leadership. Others simply did not want to say anything that might jeopardize their sources of income or political support base. Whites on the other hand either patronized black leadership in their responses or simply did not officially respond, for the fear of being charged as racists. The bottom line is that both whites and blacks in this context are either too busy to provide leadership or dishonest in facing their responsibilities as leaders. This behavior itself constitutes a major challenge for American leadership, especially black leadership in the future. Among other things, if black leadership for the future is to bring about social change in America in the new millennium, it must include the following characteristics: commitment, trust, dependability, accountability to its constituency, integrity, visionary moral values, faith, charisma, cultural sensitivity, knowledge of the issues, communication skills, and, above all, love. It is with this in mind that I feel compelled to conclude this work with a few recommendations.

RECOMMENDATIONS

A. Conduct more research in the field of black leadership, focusing on theoretical models as well as applied longitudinal research. Some selected research questions might include the following:
   1. How much power did various black leaders actually have?
   2. What were the sources and limits of that power, and how did black leaders use that power or influence in seeking to attain their goals?

3. To what extent was this power derived from black support, to what extent from white support, and to what extent from an organizational base or from a position in government?

4. To what extent did black leaders cooperate with each other, to what extent were they competing with each other, to what extent were their relationships marked by conflict, and how in turn did such patterns of cooperation, competition, and conflict shape the course of the leaders' careers and the degree to which the cause of black advancement was hindered or promoted?

5. To what extent were black leaders able to move beyond their role as leaders in the cause of black advancement to become leaders prominent in other broader and predominantly white social movements as well?

B. Black leadership should not be a Democratic Party-dominated group. Instead, it should be actively involved in the two-party system (Democratic and Republican parties). It is interesting to note that blacks were Republicans until 1935, when President Roosevelt promised a New Deal, which included the Welfare System. Today, blacks are being taken for granted by the Democratic Party. The Republican Party, on the other hand, does not seem to know how to redeem itself with blacks. If black reform is to be effective, it must function as power broker in all American major political parties and systems.

C. Black institutions of higher learning should provide rigorous leadership training for black youths and prepare them for the globalization of the American economy and international politics.

D. An annual Black Leadership Convention should be convened by the principal black leadership organizations such as the NAACP, the Urban League, Southern Christian Leadership Conference, black church national leadership, and black professional organizations like the National Bar Association, Black National Association of Journalists, National Medical Association, and so forth. The purpose of proposing such a convention is to work toward effective black leadership in various areas. The idea of a black national convention is not new. The "Negro Convention Movement" had its origin in the North during the early nineteenth century. In 1830, a group of "Free Negroes," seeking to devise ways and means for the bettering of their condition, met in Philadelphia in what is usually regarded as the first Negro Convention. For the next five years, annual national conventions were held, with subsequent conclaves (both on the national and state levels) meeting intermittently from 1835 until the late nineteenth century.

E. Black leadership must seek a better and more effective working relationship and collaboration with other ethnic leadership groups, working toward a goal of mutual interest. For example, the recent establishment of the Foundation for Ethnic Understanding by Rabbi Marc Schneier is a promising approach to enhancing black–Jewish relations in America.

For more than four centuries African-Americans have sought freedom, human dignity, and equal justice in America. Were they successful? The answer is Yes and No. "Yes," because the most inhumane institution of slavery was abolished and full citizenship became a *fait accompli* for blacks; many blacks shared in the American dream; they joined the rich, famous, and powerful; they even ran for the office of the American presidency, the highest leadership position in the world;

they became judges, lawyers, policy-makers, doctors, professors, astronauts, athletic and entertainment stars, and captains of industry. A recent study of the inside of America's black upper class by Graham (1999) reveals the untold stories of the black elite, including the first black millionaires of the 1880s. But we are also compelled to answer "No" for a variety of reasons. Among these are the resurgence of racism and discrimination in America, and, among blacks, a disproportionate poverty rate, high youth unemployment, low educational achievement, poor health status, low life expectancy, and a disproportionate incarceration rate, especially among African-American males. While America has experienced unprecedented economic prosperity in the 1990s, black Americans, as a group, have not had their fair share. These challenges are bound to create a new leadership in the twenty-first century. The nature of this leadership will depend, to a large measure, on how America responds to its changing demographics and the emerging new world order. Equally, and perhaps more importantly, will be the extent to which black Americans desire to use their well-deserved civil rights to achieve complete empowerment. If this empowerment is to be meaningful, it must be defined by black folks themselves. Simply put, the future of black leadership for social change is as bright as black Americans make it.

Appendices

Appendix A

Important Moments in African-American History

1619 Twenty Africans arrive in Jamestown, Virginia—North America's first slaves.

1739 The Cato revolt, the first uprising of slaves.

1775 Free African-Americans fight with the Minutemen at Lexington and Concord.

1777 Vermont becomes the first state to abolish slavery.

1787 The United States Constitution makes a male slave three-fifths of a man when determining representation.

1793 Congress passes the first Fugitive Slave Law.

1808 A federal law is passed prohibiting the importation of African slaves. It is disobeyed by almost all the importers.

1829 The first National Negro Convention meets in Philadelphia.

1831 Nat Turner leads a major slave revolt in Virginia.

1839 Slaves take over the Spanish slave ship *Amistad* and eventually win their freedom in court.

1849 Harriet Tubman escapes from slavery. She returns to the South several times to lead more than 300 slaves to freedom.

1857 The Dred Scott decision of the Supreme Court denies U.S. citizenship to African-Americans and forbids Congress to restrict slavery in any federal territory.

1862 African-Americans are allowed to enlist in the Union army. More than 186,000 serve in the Civil War and 38,000 die.

1863 The Emancipation Proclamation of Abraham Lincoln frees the slaves in the Confederate states.

1865 The Thirteenth Amendment to the Constitution, outlawing slavery, is ratified.

1868 The South Carolina House becomes the first state legislature to have a majority of African-Americans.

1870 The Fifteenth Amendment, which gives voting rights to all male American citizens of voting age, is ratified.

1875 Congress passes a law that bans discrimination in public places. Eight years later, the Supreme Court overturns the law.

1896 In *Plessy v. Ferguson,* the Supreme Court approves the concept of separate but equal public facilities.

1905 The Niagara Movement, prelude to the NAACP, is founded.

1910 The National Urban League is founded.

1925 A. Philip Randolph organizes the Brotherhood of Sleeping Car Porters.

1936 Jesse Owens wins four gold medals for track at the Olympic Games in Berlin.

1938 Joe Louis knocks out Max Schmeling to retain his heavyweight title, causing jubilation among African-Americans.

1940 Benjamin O. Davis becomes the first African-American general in the United States Army.

1944 The United Negro College Fund is founded.

1947 Jackie Robinson becomes the first African-American to play major league baseball.

1950 Ralph Bunche wins the Nobel Peace Prize, the first African-American to win a Nobel Prize.

1954 In *Brown v. Board of Education of Topeka, Kansas,* the Supreme Court strikes down "separate but equal" and rules that racial segregation in public schools is unconstitutional.

1955 African-American Rosa Parks refuses to change seats on a Montgomery, Alabama, bus. After her arrest, African-Americans boycott the city's bus system.

1956 The Supreme Court outlaws segregation on all modes of transportation.

1957 The Southern Christian Leadership Conference is formed, with Martin Luther King, Jr., as president.

1957 Congress passes the Voting Rights Act.

1960 Sit-ins at segregated lunch counters in Greensboro, North Carolina, trigger similar protests throughout the South.

1963 A summer march on Washington becomes the biggest civil rights demonstration in American history. Martin Luther King, Jr., gives his "I Have a Dream" speech.

1964 The Twenty-fourth Amendment, which forbids the poll tax, is ratified.

1965 Malcolm X is assassinated in New York City.

1965 Riots in the Watts section of Los Angeles cause thirty-four deaths, more than 3,500 arrests, and property damage of $225 million.

1966 The Black Panther Party is founded by Huey P. Newton and Bobby Seale in Oakland, California.

1967 The worst summer racial riots in American history take place.

1968 Martin Luther King, Jr., is assassinated and riots break out across America.

1969 The Supreme Court rules that school districts must end racial segregation "at once."

1973 African-Americans Thomas Bradley, Maynard H. Jackson, and Coleman A. Young are elected mayors of Los Angeles, Atlanta, and Detroit, respectively.

1974 Henry Aaron hits his 715th home run, breaking Babe Ruth's record.

1977 The final episode of the miniseries *Roots* receives the highest rating in television history.

1983 The state legislature of Louisiana repeals America's last racial classification law.

1986 The first national Martin Luther King, Jr., holiday is celebrated on January 20.

1988 Jesse Jackson receives 1,218 delegate votes at the Democratic National Convention.

1989 General Colin Powell is named Chairman of the Joint Chiefs of Staff.

1989 L. Douglas Wilder becomes the first African-American governor of Virginia.

1992 Carol Moseley Braun becomes the first African-American woman elected to the United States Senate.

1993 Writer Toni Morrison becomes the first African-American woman to win the Nobel Prize for Literature.

1996 The Million Man March goes to Washington, D.C., and African-American men re-dedicate themselves to both personal responsibility and rebuilding of their communities.

Source: Adapted from *Timelines of African-American History,* with other sources.

Appendix B

Major African-American Historical Landmarks in the United States

The Dexter Avenue Baptist Church in Montgomery, Alabama: It was here that Dr. Martin Luther King, Jr., organized the 1955 boycott of segregated Montgomery buses.

The Tuskegee Institute in Tuskegee, Alabama: Booker T. Washington's celebrated center for agricultural research, and the first school for African-Americans in the United States.

The Little Rock Central High School in Little Rock, Arkansas: In 1957, scene of the first major confrontation over executing the Supreme Court's 1954 outlawing of segregation in public schools.

Beckwourth Pass in Sierra Nevada Mountains: Running through California's Sierra Nevada range, the pass was discovered by James P. Beckwourth, the great African-American frontiersman.

The Mary McLeod Bethune Memorial in Washington, D.C.: The first monument to an African-American—and to a woman—erected in the nation's capital. Founder of the National Council of Negro Women, she became the first African-American to head the National Youth Administration's Division of Negro Affairs.

The Frederick Douglass Home in Washington, D.C.: Where the great nineteenth-century abolitionist lived for the last thirteen years of his life.

The Emancipation Statue in Lincoln Park, Washington, D.C.: Erected by former slaves, it is the oldest memorial to Lincoln in Washington.

The Carter G. Woodson House in Washington, D.C.: From 1915 until his death in 1950, this was the home of the man who founded the Association for the Study of Negro Life and History.

The Olustee Battlefield Historic Memorial in Olustee, Florida: The site of a bloody Civil War battle in which unseasoned African-American troops distinguished themselves.

The Martin Luther King, Jr., Historic District in Atlanta, Georgia: The district contains King's birthplace, grave site, and church where he served as an assistant pastor.

The Jean Baptiste DuSable Homesite in Chicago, Illinois: The place where DuSable established the first settlement of Chicago.

The Underground Railway Marker in Chicago, Illinois: An in-transit point for slaves escaping into Canada.

The Ida B. Wells-Barnett House in Chicago, Illinois: The home of the great crusader for the rights of African-American women.

Fort Leavenworth, Kansas: Home of the Tenth Cavalry, the first all-African-American unit, which fought with valor in both the Indian Wars and the Spanish-American War.

The Sunler Elementary School in Topeka, Kansas: The school that refused to enroll Linda Brown, triggering *Brown v. Board of Education* and the end of public school segregation in 1954.

The Port Hudson Siege Marker in Port Hudson, Louisiana: The scene of many acts of bravery by African-American troops in the Civil War.

The Matthew Henson Plaque in Annapolis, Maryland: *It* honors the first man of any color to reach the North Pole—on April 6, 1909.

Uncle Tom's Cabin in Rockville, Maryland: The site of the log cabin believed to be the birthplace of Josiah Henson, the escaped slave whose story was turned into *Uncle Tom's Cabin* by Harriet Beecher Stowe.

The Crispus Attucks Monument in Boston, Massachusetts: The site of the Boston Massacre, where Attucks was the first patriot to fall.

The William E. B. Du Bois Boyhood Homesite on Route 23 in Massachusetts: The boyhood home of the great civil rights leader.

The Jan Ernst Matzeliger Statue in Lynn, Massachusetts: It honors the inventor of the machine that revolutionized the American shoe industry.

The Sojourner Truth Grave in Battle Creek, Michigan: The burial place of the great nineteenth-century abolitionist.

The Carver National Monument in Diamond, Missouri: The place where the great black scientist George Washington Carver was born.

The Scott Joplin Residence in St. Louis, Missouri: The last home of the King of Ragtime.

Zuni Pueblo in Zuni, New Mexico: The place discovered in 1539 by Estevanico, a Moorish slave, who is credited with the discovery of territory that is now the states of Arizona and New Mexico.

The Harriet Tubman Residence in Auburn, New York: A monument to the woman who led approximately 300 slaves to freedom on the Underground Railroad.

The Amsterdam News Building in Harlem: The home of the largest African-American weekly newspaper in the United States.

The Apollo Theatre in Harlem: One of America's last great vaudeville houses, it has presented legendary African-American stars.

The Louis Armstrong Residence in Queens, New York City: The home of the world's most famous jazz musician.

The Ralph Bunche House in Queens, New York City: The home of the distinguished winner of the Nobel Peace Prize.

The Edward Kennedy "Duke" Ellington Residence in Harlem: You get here by taking the A train.

The James Weldon Johnson Residence in Harlem: For thirteen years, the home of the noted African-American composer and civil rights activist.

The Paul Robeson Residence in Harlem: The home of the great African-American actor and singer.

The Jackie Robinson Residence in Brooklyn, New York City: The home of the man who broke the color line in professional baseball, not far from where he played.

The Paul Laurence Dunbar Home in Dayton, Ohio: The home of the first African-American poet after Phyllis Wheatley to gain a national reputation.

The 101 Ranch Historic District in Marland, Oklahoma: Where Bill Pickett, the African-American cowboy who is in the Cowboy Hall of Fame, invented steer wrestling.

The Frances Ellen Watkins Harper House in Philadelphia, Pennsylvania: The home of the nineteenth-century abolitionist and fighter for women's suffrage.

The Mother Bethel African Methodist Episcopal Church in Philadelphia, Pennsylvania: The first church in the AME, one of the largest African-American denominations in the United States, and the site where Richard Allen founded the Free African Society in 1787.

The Henry O. Tanner Homesite in Philadelphia, Pennsylvania: The boyhood home of the first great African-American painter, Henry O. Tanner, the first African-American elected to the National Academy of Design.

Site of the Battle of Rhode Island in Portsmouth, Rhode Island: The site of the only Revolutionary War battle in which an all-African-American unit, the First Rhode Island Regiment, participated.

The Dubose Hayward House in Charleston, South Carolina: The home of the author of *Porgy*, the book upon which George Gershwin based his opera *Porgy and Bess*.

The Joseph H. Rainey House in Georgetown, South Carolina: A former slave, he was the first African-American to serve in the U.S. House of Representatives.

The Beale Street Historic District in Memphis, Tennessee: The site of the birth of the blues, a unique African-American contribution to American music.

W. C. Handy Park in Memphis, Tennessee: It pays tribute to the Father of the Blues, the composer of "St. Louis Blues."

The Benjamin Banneker Boundary Stone in Washington, D.C.: It commemorates the man who helped survey the city of Washington, D.C., and who was the most famous African-American in colonial America.

The Charles Richard Drew House in Washington, D.C.: The home of the African-American physician who did pioneering work in discovering how to preserve blood plasma.

The Hampton Institute in Hampton, Virginia: One of the earliest institutions of higher learning for African-Americans in the United States, it was attended by Booker T. Washington before he went to Tuskegee.

The Jackson Ward Historic District of Richmond, Virginia: The foremost African-American community of the nineteenth and early twentieth centuries.

The Maggie Lena Walker House in Richmond, Virginia: The home of the first woman of any color to establish and head a bank, the Saint Luke Penny Savings Bank.

The Booker T. Washington National Monument in Rocky Mount, North Carolina: On the site of the Burroughs plantation, where Booker T. Washington was born a slave in 1856.

The Harpers Ferry National Monument in Harpers Ferry, Virginia: Where John Brown and eighteen men, five of whom were African-American, made the famous anti-slavery raid in 1859.

Source: Adapted from the *Negro Almanac*.

Appendix C

African-Americans Honored on U.S. Postage Stamps

Matthew Henson: Explorer; co-discoverer of the North Pole.

Ida B. Wells-Barnett: Newspaper publisher.

George Washington Carver: Agricultural scientist.

James Weldon Johnson: Educator.

Dr. Charles R. Drew: Hematologist; blood plasma pioneer.

Paul Laurence Dunbar: Poet.

Booker T. Washington: Educator; founder of a college.

Peter Salem: Revolutionary War patriot.

W.C. Handy: Composer; father of the blues.

Henry O. Tanner: Painter.

Bessie Coleman: Aviator.

Jesse Owens: Olympic track champion.

Dr. Allison Davis: Educator.

Bessie Smith: Singer.

Muddy Waters: Singer.

Ma Rainey: Singer.

Billie Holiday: Singer.

Jimmy Rushing: Singer.

Howlin' Wolf: Singer.

Ethel Waters: Singer, actress.

Nat "King" Cole: Pianist, singer.

James P. Beckwourth: Explorer.

Scott Joplin: Composer; father of ragtime.

Jackie Robinson: Hall of Fame baseball player.

Percy Lavon Julian: Chemist.

Joe Louis: Heavyweight champion.

Roberto Clemente: Hall of Fame baseball player.

W. E. B. Du Bois: Writer; father of the NAACP.

Jan E. Matzeliger: Inventor.

Sojourner Truth: Abolitionist; civil rights leader.

Salem Poor: Revolutionary War patriot.

Frederick Douglass: Abolitionist.

Benjamin Banneker: Inventor.

A. Philip Randolph: Union leader.

Dr. Martin Luther King, Jr.: Civil rights leader.

Dr. Whitney Moore Young, Jr.: Civil rights leader.

Jean-Baptiste Pointe DeSable: Founder of Chicago.

Dr. Ralph J. Bunche: Statesman.

Mary McLeod Bethune: Educator.

Louis Armstrong: Musician.

Jelly Roll Morton: Musician.

Thelonious Monk: Musician.

Charlie Parker: Musician.

James P. Johnson: Musician.

Eubie Blake: Musician.

Charles Mingus: Musician.

Erroll Garner: Musician.

John Coltrane: Musician.

Coleman Hawkins: Musician.

Clyde McPhatter: Singer.

Buffalo Soldiers: U.S. Army Western cavalry.

Source: Constance Smith, Special Events Unit, U.S. Postal Service.

Appendix D

Black Chiefs of Mission
(by year of appointment)

Year	Name	Country
1949	Edward R. Dudley	Liberia
1953	Jessie D. Locker	Liberia
1955	Richard L. Jones	Liberia
1959	John Howard Morrow	Guinea
1961	Clifton R. Wharton*	Norway
	Mercer Cook	Niger
1963	Carl T. Rowan	Finland
1964	Mercer Cook	Senegal
	Clinton E. Knox*	Dahomey
1965	Mercer Cook	Gambia
	Patricia Roberts Harris	Luxembourg
	Hugh Smythe	Syrian Arab Republic
	Franklin H. Williams	Ghana
1966	Elliot P. Skinner	Upper Volta
1967	Hugh Smythe	Malta
1968	Samuel C. Adams	Niger
1969	Clinton E. Knox*	Haiti
	Terence A. Todman*	Chad
	Samuel Z. Westerfield*	Liberia
1970	Jerome Heartwell Holland	Sweden
	Clarence Clyde Ferguson Jr.	Uganda
1971	Charles J. Nelson	Botswana, Lesotho, and Swaziland
	John E. Reinhardt*	Nigeria
1972	W. Beverly Carter***	Tanzania
	Terence A. Todman*	Guinea
1973	O. Rudolf Aggrey**	Senegal and Gambia

1974	David B. Bolen*	Botswana, Lesotho, and Swaziland
	Theodore R. Britten, Jr.	Barbados and Grenada
	Terence A. Todman*	Costa Rica
1976	W. Beverly Carter**	Liberia
	Ronald D. Palmer*	Togo
	Charles A. James***	Niger
1977	Andrew Young	USUN
	Wilbert LeMelle	Kenya
	Ulrich St. Clair Haynes, Jr.	Algeria
	Mabel M. Smythe	Cameroon
	Richard K. Fox, Jr.*	Trinidad and Tobago
	David B. Bolen*	German Democratic Republic
	William B. Jones*	Haiti
	Maurice D. Bean*	Burma
	O. Rudolph Aggrey***	Romania
1978	Terence A. Todman*	Spain
1979	Donald F. McHenry	USUN
	Horace G. Dawson**	Botswana
	Anne F. Holloway	Mali
1980	Walter C. Carrington	Senegal
	Barbara Watson	Malaysia
1981	John A. Burroughs, Jr.*	Malawi
	Ronald D. Palmer*	Malaysia
	Melvin H. Evans	Trinidad and Tobago
	Gerald E. Thomas	Guyana
1982	Howard K. Walker*	Togo
1983	Arthur W. Lewis**	Sierra Leone
	Terence A. Todman*	Denmark
	Gerald E. Thomas	Kenya
	George E. Moose*	Benin
1985	Edward J. Perkins*	Liberia
	Irvin Hicks*	Seychelles
1986	Ronald D. Palmer*	Mauritius
	Cynthia S. Perry	Sierra Leone
	Edward J. Perkins*	South Africa
1988	John A. Burroughs, Jr.*	Uganda
	George E. Moose*	Senegal
	Leonard O. Spearman, Sr.	Rwanda
1989	Cynthia Shepard Perry	Burundi
	J. Steven Rhodes	Zimbabwe
	Terence A. Todman*	Argentina
	Howard K. Walker*	Madagascar
	Ruth V. Washington****	Gambia
	Johnny Young*	Sierra Leone
1990	Aurelia Erskine Brazeal*	Micronesia
	Arlene Render*	Gambia
	Leonard O. Spearman, Sr.	Lesotho

1991	Charles R. Baquet, III*	Djibouti
	Johnnie Carson*	Uganda
1992	Ruth A. Davis*	Benin
	Kenton Wesley Keith**	Qatar
	Edward J. Perkins*	USUN
	Joseph Monroe Segars*	Cape Verde
1993	Aurelia Erskine Brazeal*	Kenya
	Walter C. Carrington	Nigeria
	Edward J. Perkins*	Australia
	Leslie M. Alexander*	Mauritius
	Howard F. Jeter*	Botswana
1994	Sidney Williams	Bahamas
	Irvin Hicks*	Ethiopia
	Johnny Young*	Togo
	Carl B. Stokes	Seychelles
	Jerome Gary Cooper	Jamaica
1995	Johnnie Carson*	Zimbabwe
	Bismarck Myrick*	Lesotho
	Mosina H. Jordan***	Central African Republic
	James A. Joseph	South Africa
1996	Leslie M. Alexander*	Ecuador
	John F. Hicks, Sr.***	Eritrea
	Arlene Render*	Zambia
	Sharon P. Wilkinson*	Burkina Faso
1997	Brenda B. Schoonover*	Togo
	George E. Moose*	U.N.–Geneva
	Johnny Young*	Bahrain
1998	Shirley E. Barnes*	Madagascar
	William D. Clarke*	Eritrea
	Betty Ellen King	US Representative to ECOSOC
	Charles R. Stith	Tanzania
	George W. Boyce Haley	Gambia
	Robert C. Perry*	Central African Republic
	Elizabeth McKune*	Qatar
1999	Johnnie Carson*	Kenya
	Bismarck Myrick*	Liberia
	Diane Watson	Micronesia

All names listed are political appointments except as noted below:

   * Career Foreign Service Officer
  ** Career Foreign Service Information Officer
 *** Career Foreign Service A.I.D. Officer
**** Killed in auto accident en route to post.

Prepared by S/EEOCR, 7/2/99
Source: PA/HO and GD/PAS

Appendix E

Congressional Black Caucus Members, 105th Congress (listed alphabetically)

U.S. House of Representatives

Rep. Sanford D. Bishop, Jr., 2nd Congressional District, Georgia
    1433 Longworth House Office Building, Washington, D.C. 20515 202-225-3631

Rep. Corrine Brown, 3rd Congressional District, Florida
    1610 Longworth House Office Building, Washington, D.C. 20515 202-225-0123

Rep. Julia Carson, 10th Congressional District, Indiana
    1541 Longworth House Office Building, Washington, D.C. 20515 202-225-4011

Rep. Donna M. Christian-Green, Delegate, Virgin Islands
    1711 Longworth House Office Washington, D.C. 20515 202-225-1790

Rep. William Clay, 1st Congressional District, Missouri
    2306 Rayburn House Office Building, Washington, D.C. 20515 202-225-2406

Rep. Eva Clayton, 1st Congressional District, North Carolina
    2440 Rayburn House Office Building, Washington, D.C. 20515 202-225-3101

Rep. James E. Clyburn, 6th Congressional District, South Carolina
    319 Cannon House Offfice Building, Washington, D.C. 20515 202-225-3315

Rep. John Conyers, Jr., 14th Congressional District, Michigan
    2426 Rayburn House Office Building, Washington, D.C. 20515 202-225-5126

Rep. Elijah E. Cummings, 7th Congressional District, Maryland
    1632 Longworth House Office Building, Washington, D.C. 20515 202-225-4741

Rep. Danny K. Davis, 7th Congressional District, Illinois
    1218 Longworth House Office Building, Washington, D.C. 20515 202-225-5006

Rep. Ronald V. Dellums, 9th Congressional District, California
    2108 Rayburn House Office Building, Washington, D.C. 20515 202-225-2661

Rep. Julian C. Dixon, 32nd Congressional District, California
2252 Rayburn House Office Building, Washington, D.C. 20515 202-225-7084

Rep. Chaka Fattah, 2nd Congressional District, Pennsylvania
1205 Longworth House Office Building, Washington, D.C. 20515 202-225-4001

Rep. Floyd H. Flake, 6th Congressional District, New York
1035 Longworth House Office Building, Washington, D.C. 20515 202-225-3461

Rep. Harold E. Ford, Jr., 9th Congressional District, Tennessee
1523 Longworth House Office Building, Washington, D.C. 20515 202-225-3265

Rep. Alcee L. Hastings, 23rd Congressional District, Florida
1039 Longworth House Office Building, Washington, D.C. 20515 202-225-1313

Rep. Earl F. Hilliard, 7th Congressional District, Alabama
1314 Longworth House Office Building, Washington, D.C. 20515 202-225-2665

Rep. Jesse L. Jackson, Jr., 2nd Congressional District, Illinois
313 Cannon House Office Building, Washington, D.C. 20515 202-225-0773

Rep. Sheila Jackson-Lee, 18th Congressional District, Texas
410 Cannon House Office Building, Washington, D.C. 20515 202-225-3816

Rep. William J. Jefferson, 2nd Congressional District, Louisiana
240 Cannon House Office Building, Washington, D.C. 20515 202-225-6636

Rep. Eddie Bernice Johnson, 30th Congressional District, Texas
1123 Longworth House Office Building, Washington, D.C. 20515 202-225-8885

Rep. Carolyn C. Kilpatrick, 15th Congressional District, Michigan
503 Cannon House Office Building, Washington, D.C. 20515 202-225-2261

Rep. John Lewis, 5th Congressional District, Georgia
229 Cannon House Office Building, Washington, D.C. 20515 202-225-3801

Rep. Cynthia A. McKinney, 4th Congressional District, Georgia
124 Cannon House Office Building, Washington, D.C. 20515 202-225-1605

Rep. Carrie P. Meed, 17th Congressional District, Florida
401 Cannon House Office Building, Washington, D.C. 20515 202-225-4506

Rep. Juanita Millender-McDonald, 37th Congressional District, California
419 Cannon House Office Building, Washington, D.C. 20515 202-225-7924

Rep. Eleanor Holmes Norton, Delegate, District of Columbia
1424 Longworth House Office Building, Washington, D.C. 20515 202-225-8050

Rep. Major R. Owens, 11th Congressional District, New York
2305 Rayburn House Office Washington, D.C. 20515 202-225-6231

Rep. Donald M. Payne, 10th Congressional District, New Jersey
2244 Rayburn House Office Building, Washington, D.C. 20515 202-225-3436

Rep. Charles B. Rangel, 15th Congressional District, New York
2354 Rayburn House Office Building, Washington, D.C. 20515 202-225-4365

Rep. Bobby L. Rush, 1st Congressional District, Illinois
131 Cannon House Office Building, Washington, D.C. 20515 202-225-4372

Rep. Robert C. Scott, 3rd Congressional District, Virginia
2464 Rayburn House Office Building, Washington, D.C. 20515 202-225-8351

Rep. Louis Stokes, 11th Congressional District, Ohio
2365 Rayburn House Office Building, Washington, D.C. 20515 202-225-7032

Rep. Bennie G. Thompson, 2nd Congressional District, Mississippi
1408 Longworth House Office Building, Washington, D.C. 20515 202-225-5876

Rep. Edolphus Towns, 10th Congressional District, New York
2232 Raybury House Office Building, Washington, D.C. 20515 202-225-5936

Rep. Maxine Waters, 35th Congressional District, California
2344 Rayburn House Office Building, Washington, D.C. 20515 202-225-2201

Rep. Melvin L. Watt, 12th Congressional District, North Carolina
1230 Longworth House Office Building, Washington, D.C. 20515 202-225-1510

Rep. Albert R. Wynn, 4th Congressional District, Maryland
407 Cannon House Office Building, Washington, D.C. 20515 202-225-8699

U.S. Senate

Sen. Carol Moseley-Braun, Illinois
320 Hart Senate Office Building, Washington, D.C. 20510 202-224-2854

Officers

Rep. Maxine Waters, Chair

Rep. Earl Hilliard, First Vice Chair

Rep. Eddie Bernice Johnson, Second Vice Chair

Rep. Corrine Brown, Secretary

Rep. Sheila Jackson-Lee, Whip

References

INTRODUCTION

American Association of Retired Persons. 1996. *Appreciating Diversity*. Washington, DC: AARP Minority Affairs.

Burns, James. 1978. *Leadership*. New York: Harper & Row.

Franklin, John Hope, and August Meier. 1982. *Black Leaders of the Twentieth Century*. Urbana: University of Illinois Press.

Harrington, James. 1992. *Commonwealth of Oceans*. New York: Cambridge University Press.

Hartz, Louis. 1955. *The Liberal Tradition in America*. New York: Harcourt, Brace Printing.

Ladd, E. 1966. *Negro Political Leadership*. Ithaca: Cornell University Press.

Locke, John. 1690. *An Essay Concerning the True Original Extent and End of Civil Government*. Reprint, Boston: Edes and Gill, 1773.

Marable, Manning. 1998. *Black Leadership*. New York: Columbia University Press.

Myrdal, G. 1944. *An American Dilemma: The Negro Problem and American Democracy*. New York: Harper & Row. Reprinted 1962.

Persons, Georgia A. 1993. *Dilemmas of Black Politics*. New York: HarperCollins College Publishers.

Rabinowitz, Howard N., ed. 1982. *Southern Black Leaders of the Reconstruction Era*. Urbana: University of Illinois Press.

Redford, Emmette. 1966. *The Role of Government in the American Economy*. New York: Macmillan Press.

Tocqueville, Alexis de. 1938. *Democracy in America*. Translated by Henry Reeve, 1988. Birmingham, AL: Legal Classics Library.

U.S. Bureau of the Census. 1991. *Census Bureau Releases—1990 Census Counts on Specific Racial Groups*. Washington, D.C.: U.S. Department of Commerce News, June 12, p. 3.

White, John. 1985. *Black Leadership in America 1895–1968*. New York: Longman.

PART I

Bass, Bernard M. 1973. *Leadership, Psychology and Organizational Behavior*. Westport, CT: Greenwood Press.

Bolce, L. H., and J. H. Gray. 1979. "Blacks, Whites, and 'Race Politics.'" *Public Interest* (Winter): 61–75.

Bracey Jr., John, August Meier, and Elliott Rudwick. 1970. *Black Nationalism in America*. Indianapolis and New York: The Bobbs-Merrill Company, Inc.

Burgess, M. 1962. *Negro Leadership in a Southern City*. Chapel Hill: University of North Carolina Press.

Burns, James. 1978. *Leadership*. New York: Harper & Row.

Carnahan, Smith, and Gunter, Inc. 1994. *Turning the Pyramid Upside Down: Leadership in Transition*. Alexandria, VA: Unabridged Communications.

Carnahan, Smith, and Gunter, Inc. 1996. *Who Leads?* Alexandria, VA: Unabridged Communications.

Cole, L. 1976. *Blacks in Power: A Comparative Study of Black and White Elected Officials*. Princeton: Princeton University Press.

Cox, O. 1965. "Leadership among Negroes in the United States." In A. Gouldner (ed.) *Studies in Leadership*. Harper & Row.

Delaney, P. 1978. "Middle Class Gains Create Tension in Black Community." *New York Times*, February 28.

Du Bois, W. E. B. 1903. *The Souls of Black Folk*. New York: The New American Library.

Forsythe, D. 1972. "A Functional Definition of Black Leadership." *Black Scholar* (3): 18–26.

Franklin, John Hope, and August Meier. 1982. *Black Leaders of the Twentieth Century*. Chicago: University of Illinois Press.

Froman, P. 1948. "The Theory of Case Studies." *Social Forces* 26: 408–419.

Gardner, John. 1990. *On Leadership*. New York: Free Press.

Glasgow, D. 1980. *The Black Underclass*. New York: Vintage Books.

Gowin, E. B. 1915. *The Executive and His Control of Men*. New York: Macmillan.

Greenberg, S. 1980. *Race and State in Capitalist: Comparative Perspectives*. New Haven: Yale University Press.

Hamilton, C. 1973. "Full Employment as a Viable Issue." In *When the Marching Stopped: An Analysis of Black Issues in the 70s*. New York: National Urban League.

Hamilton, C. 1981. "The Status of Black Leadership." *New Directions* April: 7–9.

Heath, C. W., and L. W. Gregory. 1946. "What It Takes to Be an Officer." *Infantry Journal* 58: 44–45.

Higham, J. 1978. *Ethnic Leadership in America*. Baltimore: Johns Hopkins.

Hogan, Robert, Gordon J. Curphy, and Joyce Hogan. 1994. "What We Know About Leadership: Effectiveness and Personality." *American Psychologist* June, 49(6): 493–504.

Holden, M. 1973. *The Politics of the Black "Nation."* New York: Chandler.

Jenkins, W. O. 1947. "A Review of Leadership Studies with Particular Reference to Military Problems." *Psychology Bulletin* 44: 54–79.

Jones, A. J. 1938. *The Education of Youth for Leadership*. New York: McGraw-Hill.

Jones, M. 1972. "A Frame of Reference for Black Politics." In L. Henderson (ed.), *Black Political Life in the United States*. San Francisco: Chandler Pub. Co.

Jones, M. 1978. "Black Political Empowerment in Atlanta: Myth and Reality." *Annals* 439: 90–117.

Katznelson, I. 1971. "Social Policy." In T. Ferguson and J. Rogers (eds.), *The Hidden Election: Politics and Economics in the 1980 Presidential Campaign.* New York: Pantheon Books.

Kaufman, H. 1958. "The Next Step in Case Studies." *Public Administration Review* (Winter): 52–95.

Kilson, Martin. 1995. "Paradoxes of Black American Leadership," *Dissent* (Summer): 368–377.

Ladd, E. 1966. *Negro Political Leadership.* Ithaca: Cornell University Press.

Lassey, William R., and Marshall Sashkin. 1983. *Leadership and Social Change.* San Diego: University Associates, Inc.

Lawson, John, Leslie Griffin, and Franklin Donant. 1976. *Leadership is Everybody's Business.* San Luis Obispo, CA: Impact Publications.

Matthews, Donald R., and James W. Prothro. 1966. *Negroes and the New Southern Politics.* New York: Harcourot, Brace, and World.

Matthews, Donald R., and James W. Prothro. 1971. *The Negro Political Participation Study.* Ann Arbor, MI: Inter-University Consortium Political Research.

McFarlin, Annjennette S. 1976. *Black Congressional Reconstruction Orators and Their Orations.* Metuchen, NJ: The Scarecrow Press, Inc.

Moms, M. 1975. *The Politics of Black America.* New York: Harper & Row.

Myrdal, Gunnar. 1944, 1962. *An American Dilemma: The Negro Problem and American Democracy.* New York: Harper & Row.

Roucek, J. 1956. "Minority–Majority Relations in Their Power Aspects." *Phylan* First Quarter: 24–30.

Salamon, L. 1973. "Leadership and Modernization: The Emerging Black Political Elite in the American South." *Journal of Politics* 35: 615–646.

Scoble, H. 1968. "The Effects of the Riots on Negro Leadership." In. L. Massoti and D. Bowen, (eds.), *Riots and Rebellion; Civil Violence in the Urban Community.* Beverly Hills: Sage.

Smith, H. L., and L. M. Krueger. 1933. "A Brief Summary of Literature on Leadership." *Bull. Sch. Educ.* 9(4).

Smith, Robert C. 1981. "The Black Congressional Delegation." *Western Political Quarterly* 34: 203–21.

Smith, Robert C. 1976. *Black Elites and Black Groups in the Federal Policy Process: A Study in Interest Articulation.* Doctoral dissertation, Howard University.

Starch, D. 1943. *How to Develop Young Executive Ability.* New York: Harper.

Stogdill, Ralph M. 1948. "Personal Factors Associated with Leadership: A Survey of the Literature." *The Journal of Psychology* 25: 35–71.

Stogdill, Ralph M. 1974. *Handbook of Leadership.* New York: Free Press.

Thompson, D. 1963. *The Negro Leadership Class.* Englewood Cliffs, NJ: Prentice-Hall.

Walton, H. 1972. *Black Politics: A Theoretical and Structural Analysis.* New York: J. B. Lippincott.

Wilson, J. 1960. *Negro Politics: The Search for Leadership.* New York: The Free Press.

Wilson, W. 1972. *The Declining Significance of Race.* Chicago: University of Chicago Press.

PART II

Abbott, Martin. 1959. "County Officers in South Carolina in 1868." *South Carolina Historical Magazine* 60: 30–40.

African Colonization Society. 1826. *African Repository and Colonial Journal*. Washington City: Way & Gideon, Printers.

The African Repository. v. 53, April 1877. Washington: American Colonization Society, 75.

The African Repository. v. 56, July 1880. Washington: American Colonization Society, 73–74.

Afro-American Encyclopedia Vol. 4. 1974. North Miami: Educational Book Publishers, Inc., 1115.

Allen, Richard. 1880. *The Life, Experience, and Gospel Labors of the Rt. Rev. Richard Allen*. Philadelphia: F. Ford and M. A. Riply.

Allen, Richard. 1960. "An Address to Those Who Keep Slaves and Approve the Practice." *The Life Experience and Gospel Labors of the Rt. Rev. Richard Allen* with an introductrion by George A. Singleton. New York: Abingdon Press.

Arnold, Thomas St. John. 1990. *Buffalo Soldiers: The 92nd Infantry Division and Reinforcements in World War II, 1942–1945*. Manhattan, KS: Sunflower University Press.

Banneker, Benjamin. 1792. *Copy of a Letter from Benjamin Banneker to the Secretary of State, with His Answer*. Philadelphia: Printed and sold by Daniel Lawrence.

Barr, Alwyn. 1986. "Black Legislators of Reconstruction Texas." *Civil War History* 32 (December): 340–52.

Bennett Jr., J. H. 1958. *Bondsmen and Bishops: Slavery and Apprenticeship in the Codrington Plantation, 1710–1830*. Berkeley: University of California Press.

Bennett, Levone. 1969. *Before the Mayflower*. Chicago: Johnson Publishing Company.

Bentley, George R. 1970. *A History of the Freedmen's Bureau*. New York: Octagon Books.

Billington, Monroe Lee. 1989. "Civilians and Black Soldiers in New Mexico." *Military History of the Southwest* 19(1): 71–82.

Billington, Monroe Lee. 1991. *New Mexico's Buffalo Soldiers, 1866–1900*. Niwot: University Press of Colorado.

Brewer, J. Mason. 1935. *Negro Legislators of Texas*. Dallas: Mathis.

Brock, Eulin. 1981."Thomas W. Cardozo: Fallible Black Reconstruction Leader." *Journal of Southern History* XLVII (May).

Caldecott, A. 1896. *The Church in the West Indies*. London: Society for the Propagation of the Christian Knowledge.

Cugoano, Ottobah. 1787. *Thoughts and Sentiments on the Evils of Slavery*. London: Printed for and sold by the author.

Davidson, Basil. 1970. *The Lost Cities of Africa*. Boston: Little, Brown Co.

Douglass, Frederick. 1884. *Life and Times of Frederick Douglass*. New York: Bonanza Books. Reprinted 1962, with an introduction by Rayford W. Logan.

Ebony. 1995. Chicago: Johnson Publishing.

Equiano, Olaudah. 1967. *The Interesting Narrative of the Life of Olaudah Equiano or Gustavus Vassa, the African*. Abridged and edited by Paul Edwards. New York: Praeger.

Factor, Robert. 1970. *The Black Response to America—Men, Ideas, and Organizations from Frederick Douglass to the NAACP*. Menlo Park, CA: Addison-Wesley Publishing Company.

Franklin, John Hope 1994. *From Slavery to Freedom,* 7th ed. New York: McGraw-Hill, Inc.

Franklin, John Hope. 1985. *George Washington Williams.* Chicago: University of Chicago Press.

Franklin, John Hope, and August Meier, eds. 1982. *Black Leaders of the Twentieth Century.* Urbana: University of Illinois Press.

Frazier, E. Franklin. 1962. *Black Bourgeoisie.* New York: Collier Books.

Gordon, Jacob. 1993. *Narratives of African Americans in Kansas, 1870–1992: Beyond the Exodus Movement.* Lewiston, NY: Edwin Mellen Press, Ltd.

Grimké, Francis J. 1885. "Colored Men as Professors in Colored Institutions." *AME Church Review* IV (July): 142–149.

Haley, Alex. 1976. *Roots.* Garden City, N.Y.: Doubleday.

Hargrove, Hondon B. 1985. *Buffalo Soldiers in Italy: Black Americans in World War II.* Jefferson, NC: McFarland.

Harlan, John Marshall. 1997."Justice Harlan Dissenting" reprinted in L. Mpho Mabunda's (ed.) Reference Library of Black America, Vol. 1, Detroit, MI: Gale Research. 140–144.

Holland, Frederic May. 1891. *Frederick Douglass: The Colored Orator.* New York: Funk & Wagnalls.

Horton, George Mason. 1838. "Poems by a Slave." In Phillis Wheatley's *Memoir and Poems of Phillis Wheatley, a Native African and Slave.* Boston: I. Knapp.

Huggins, Nathan Irvin. 1990. *Black Odyssey: The African-America Ordeal in Slavery.* New York: Vintage Books.

Jordan, Winthrop. 1968. *"White Over Black"—American Attitudes Toward the Negro, 1550–1812.* Chapel Hill: University of North Carolina Press.

July, Robert William. 1968. *The Origins of Modern African Thought: Its Development in West Africa During the Nineteenth and Twentieth Centuries.* London: Faber.

Katz, William L. 1971. *The Black West: A Documentary and Pictorial History of African Americans in the Westward Movement.* Garden City, N.Y.: Doubleday.

Kilson, Martin. "Paradoxes of Black American Leadership." *Dissent* Summer: 368–372.

King, Edward. 1875. *The Great South.* Hartford, CT: American Publishing Company.

Knapp, George E. 1992. "Buffalo Soldiers: 1866 Through 1890." *Military Review* 72(7): 65–71.

Locke, Alain. 1925. *The New Negro; an Interpretation.* New York: A. and C. Boni.

Lowe, Richard. 1995. "Local Black Leaders During Reconstruction in Virginia." *The Virginia Magazine of History and Biography* 103(2).

Magdol, Edward. 1974. "Local Black Leaders in the South, 1867–75: An Essay Toward the Reconstruction of Reconstruction History." *Societas* 4: 81–110.

Moses, Wilson J. 1989. *Alexander Crummell.* New York: Oxford University Press.

Payne, Daniel A. 1891. *History of the African Methodist Episcopal Church.* Nashville, TN: Publishing Home of the A.M.E. Reprinted 1968, New York.

Pitre, Merline. 1997. *Through Many Dangers, Toils, and Snares: Black Leadership in Texas.* Austin, TX: Eakin Press.

Porter, Kenneth. 1971. *The Negro on the American Frontier.* New York: Arno Press.

Rabinowitz, Howard N. (ed.) 1982. *Southern Black Leaders of the Reconstruction Era.* Urbana: University of Illinois Press.

Ramos, George. 1996. "Reflection on Ironies of an Activist's Life," *Los Angeles Times* 17 April.

Rankin, David C. 1974. "The Origins of Black Leadership in New Orleans During Recon-
     struction." *Journal of Southern History* 40: 417–40.
Reynolds, L. H. 1887. "Why Negro Churches are a Necessity." *A.M.E. Church Review IV.*
Roman, C. V. 1911. *A Knowledge of History is Conducive to Racial Solidarity, and Other
     Writings.* Nashville, TN: Sunday School Union Print.
Russwurm, John, and Samuel Cornish. 1827. *Freedom's Journal.* New York.
Sancho, Ignatius, ed. 1782. *Letters of the Late Ignatius Sancho, An African: To Which are
     Prefixed Memories of His Life.* 2 vols. London: J Nichols.
Savage, W. Sherman. 1976. *Blacks in the West.* Westport, CT: Greenwood Press.
Schubert, Frank N. 1993. *Buffalo Soldiers, Braves and the Brass: The Story of Fort Robin-
     son, Nebraska.* Shippensburg, PA: White Mane.
Senate Report No. 693, Part 2, Forty-sixth Cong., 2nd sess. 1880. Washington, DC: U.S.
     Government Printing Office, 101–105, 108–111.
Smith, Elaine, and Audrey Thomas McCluskey. 2000. *Mary McLeod Bethune: Building a
     Better World.* Bloomington: Indiana University Press.
Thompson, Vincent B. 1993. "Leadership in the African Diaspora in the Americas Prior
     to 1860." *Journal of Black Studies* 24(1): 42–76.
Tocqueville, Alexis de. 1845. *Democracy in America.* New York: J. & H. G. Langley.
Turner, Frederick. 1920. *The Frontier in American History.* Huntington, N.Y.: R. E. Krieger
     Pub. Co.
Turner, Henry M. 1898. "God Is A Negro." *Voice of Missions.* February 1.
United States Supreme Court. 1860. *The Case of Dred Scott in the United States Court.
     The Full Opinions of Chief Justice Taney and Justice Curtis.* New York: The Tri-
     bune Association.
Wesley, C. H. 1935. *Richard Allen: Apostle of Freedom.* Washington, D.C.: Associated
     Publishers.
White, John. 1985. *Black Leadership in America, 1895–1968.* London: Longman.
Williams, George Washington. 1990. *History of the Negro Race in America, 1619–1880.*
     New York: Vintage Books.

PART III

Aptheker, Herbert. 1945. *American Negro Slave Revolts.* New York: Columbia University
     Press.
Asante, Molefi Kete. 1985. *African Culture.* Westport, CT: Greenwood Press.
Austin, Bobby (ed.). 1996. *Reparing the Breach: Key Ways to Support Family Life, Reclaim
     Our Streets, and Rebuild Civil Society in America's Communities.* Chicago: Noble
     Press.
Blyden, Edward. 1881. "The Aims and Methods of a Liberal Education for Africans." Inau-
     gural address as President of Liberia College, Liberia, West Africa, January 5.
     Quoted by Edward Blyden in *Christianity, Islam, and the Negro Race.* 1887. Lon-
     don: Whittingham.
Brown, S. 1979. "The Health Needs of Adolescents." In *Healthy People: The Surgeon Gen-
     eral's Report on Mental Health Promotion and Disease Prevention.* Publication 79-
     55071A. Washington, D. C.: U.S. DHEW.
Buchanan, A. Russell. 1977. *Black Americans in World War II.* Santa Barbara, CA: Clio
     Books.

Bunche, Ralph Johnson. 1950. Acceptance of Nobel Peace Prize. Oslo.

Bunche, Ralph J. 1952. *Peace and the United Nations*. Leeds: University of Leeds.

Butler, John Sibley. 1991. *The Entrepreneurship and Self-Help Among Black Americans*. New York: State University of New York Press.

Carson, Clayborne. 1982. *In Struggle: SNCC and the Black Awakening of the 1960s*. Cambridge: Harvard University Press.

Carter, Lawrence Edward Sr., ed. 1998. *Walking Integrity: Benjamin Elijah Mays, Mentor to Martin Luther King, Jr.* Macon, GA: Mercer Uiversity Press.

Césaire. Aimé. 1972. *Discourse on Colonialism*. New York: MR.

Challenor, Herschell. 1981. "The Influence of Black Americans on U.S. Foreign Policy Toward Africa." In Abdul Said (ed.), *Ethnicity and American Foreign Policy*, rev. ed. New York: Praeger.

Clay, William. 1992. *Just Permanent Interest—Black Americans in Congress, 1870–1991*. New York: Amistad Press, Inc.

Clearer, Eldridge. 1992. *Soul On Ice*. New York: Dell Publishing Group.

Cruse, Harold. 1990. "New Black Leadership Required." *New Politics*. New England: New England University Press.

Curtis, Lynn. 1996. *The State of Families*. Milwaukee, WI: Families International, Inc.

Cutler, John. 1972. *Ed Brooke: Biography of A Senator*. Indianapolis: The Bobbs-Merrill Company, Inc.

Davis, John. 1969. "Black Americans and United States Policy Toward Africa." African Forum: A Quarterly Journal of Contemporary Affairs.

Delany, Martin Robison. 1852. *The Condition, Elevation, Emigration, and Destiny of the Colored People of the United States*. Philadelphia: The author.

Diop, David. 1973. *Hammer Blows and Other Writings [by] David Mandessi Diop*. Translated and edited by Simon Mpondo and Frank Jones. Bloomington: Indiana University Press.

Du Bois, W. E. B. 1900. "To the Nations of the World." Speech delivered to the Pan-African Congress. London.

Du Bois, W. E. B. 1947. *The World and Africa*. New York: Viking Press.

Du Bois, W. E. B. 1968. *The Autobiography of W. E. B. Du Bois*. New York: International Publishers.

Du Bois, W. E. B. 1961. *The Souls of Black Folk*. New York: Fawcett Publications.

Du Bois, W. E. B. 1896. *The Suppression of the African Slave Trade in the United States of America, 1638–1870*. Cambridge: Harvard University Press.

Ebony. 1994. "Black Presidents in Fortune 500 Companies." January (49): 100–108.

Ebony. 1992. "50 Top Black Exceptions in Corporate America." January (42): 108–116.

Edmondson, Locksley. 1971. "Race and Human Rights in International Organizations and International Law and Afro-American Interest." *Afro-American Studies* 2.

Eichler, Margrit. 1977. "Leadership in Social Movements." *Sociological Inquiry* 47(2): 99–107.

Fairclough, Adam. 1987. *To Redeem the Soul of America: The Southern Christian Leadership Conference and Martin Luther King, Jr.* Athens: The University of Georgia Press.

Farmer, James. 1942. "The Race Logic of Pacifism." *Fellowship Magazine* VII, 25.

Federal Bureau of Investigation. 1993. Supplementary Homicide Reports, 1976–1991. (Machine-readable data files.) Washington, D.C.

Foner, Philip S. 1970. *The Black Panthers Speak.* Philadelphia: J.B. Lippincott Company.

Gibbs, Jewelle Taylor. 1988. *Young, Black, and Male in America: An Endangered Species.* Dover, MA: Auburn House.

Glasgow, Douglas. 1980. *The Black Underclass: Poverty, Unemployment and Entrapment of Ghetto Youth.* New York: Vintage Books.

Gordon, Jacob. 1985. *The Black Church: A Guide to the Black Community.* Lawrence: The Institute for Public Policy and Business Research.

Gordon, Jacob. 1991. "Racism and Colonialism in the Modern World." In Woelfel and Trulove (eds.), *Patterns in Western Civilization.* Needham Heights, MA: Ginn Press.

Gordon, Jacob U. and Richard Majors (eds.). 1994. *The American Black Male: His Present Status and His Future.* Chicago: Nelson Hall.

Gottschalk, Louis. 1964. *Understanding History.* New York: Knopf.

Graham, Lawrence. 1999. *Our Kind of People.* New York: Harper Collins Publishers.

Greene, Robert Ewell. 1974. *Black Defenders of America, 1775–1973.* Chicago: Johnson Publishing Company, Inc.

Hamilton, Tullia. 1978. "The National Association of Colored Women, 1896-1920." Emory University. Unpublished dissertation.

Harris, Leonard. 1989. *The Philosophy of Alain Locke: Harlem Renaissance and Beyond.* Philadelphia: Temple University Press.

Hawkins, Walter. 1993. *African American Generals and Flag Officers.* North Carolina: McFarland and Company, Inc.

Hero, Alfred O. 1969. "American Negroes and U.S. Foreign Policy, 1937–1967." *Journal of Conflict Resolution* 8.

Hickey, Neil, and Ed Edwin. 1965. *Adam Clayton Powell and the Politics of Race.* New York: Fleet Publishing Corporation.

Hooks, Benjamin L. 1979. Quoted in the *New York Times* May 18. Reprinted in the *Wall Street Journal,* Centennial Edition 1989, p. B20.

Hughes, Langston. 1940. *The Big Sea: An Autobiography.* New York: Knopf.

Hughes, Langston. 1974. *Selected Poems.* New York: Vintage Books.

James, C. L. R. 1963. *The Black Jacobins: Toussaint Louverture and the San Domingo Revolution,* 2d ed. New York: Vintage Books.

James, Joy. 1997. *Transcending the Talented Tenth, Black Leaders and American Intellectuals.* New York: Routledge.

Johnson, James Weldon. 1933. *Along This Way.* New York: Viking Press.

Johnson, James Weldon, and J. Rosamond Johnson. 1980. *Lift Ev'ry Voice and Sing.* New York: Edward B. Marks Music Corporation.

Johnson, Jesse J., ed. 1974. *Black Women in the Armed Forces, 1942–1974.* Hampton: Hampton Institute.

Johnson, Lyndon B. 1968. Lyndon B. Johnson to Randolph, April 15, *Nightletter,* Johnson to Randolph, May 23.

Jones, Mack. 1981. "The Increasing Irrelevancy of Black Leadership." Paper prepared for presentation at the 1981 Annual Meeting of the National Conference of Black Political Scientists, Baltimore, Maryland.

Lassey, William R. and Marshall Sashkin. 1983. *Leadership and Social Change.* San Diego: University Associates, Inc.

Legum, Colin. 1962. *Pan-Africanism.* New York: Praeger.

Linnemann, Russell, ed. 1982. *Alain Locke: Reflections on a Modern Renaissance Man.* Baton Rouge: Louisiana State University Press.

Lomax, Louis E. 1962. *The Negro Revolt.* New York: Harper.

Marable, Manning. 1983. *How Capitalism Underdeveloped Black America.* Boston: South End Press.

Mays, Benjamin E. 1971. *Born to Rebel: An Autobiography.* New York: Scribner.

Maurer, M. 1990. *Young Black Males and the Criminal Justice System.* Washington, D.C.: The Sentencing Project.

McHenry, Donald. 1974. "Captive of No Group." *Foreign Policy* 15.

McKay, Claude. 1953. *Selected Poems of Claude McKay.* Boston: Twayne Publishers.

Meier, August, and Elliott Rudwick. 1973. *CORE: A Study in the Civil Rights Movement, 1942–1968.* New York: Oxford University Press.

Miller, Jake. 1978. *The Black Presence in American Foreign Affairs.* Washington, D.C.: University Press of America.

Morris, Milton. 1972. "Black Americans and the Foreign Policy Process: The Case of Africa." *Western Political Quarterly* 25.

Morton, D. C., and T. I. Snell. 1992. *Prisoners in 1991.* U.S. Department of Justice: Bureau of Justice Statistics.

Muhammad, Elijah. 1962. "The Muslim Program." *Muhammad Speaks,* July 31.

Myrdal, Gunnar. 1944, 1962. *An American Dilemma: The Negro Problem and American Democracy.* New York: Harper & Row.

National Center for Health Statistics, Health, United States. 1993, 1994. Washington, D.C.: Government Printing Office.

Nevins, Allen. 1938. *The Gateway to History.* New York: Garoand.

Newton, Huey P. 1995. *To Die for he People: The Writings of Huey P. Newton,* ed. Tom Morrison. New York: Writers and Readers Pub.

Orfield, Gary, Mark Bachmeir, David James, and Tamela Eitle. 1997. *Deepening Segregation in American Public Schools.* Cambridge, MA: Harvard Graduate School of Education.

Pan African Congress. 1963. "Report of the 1945 Pan-African Congress." In *George Padmore's History of the Pan-African Congress: Colonial and Coloured Unity, A Programme of Action.* London: Hammersmith Bookshop.

Plummer, Brenda. 1982. "The Afro-American Response to the Occupation of Haiti, 1915–1934." *Phylon* 43.

Posnock, Ross. 1998. *Color and Culture: Black Writers and the Making of the Modern Intellectual.* Cambridge, MA: Harvard University Press.

Putney, Martha. 1992. *When the Nation Was in Need: Blacks in the Women's Army Corps During World War II.* London: The Scarecrow Press, Inc.

Randolph, A. Philip. 1963. "If I were Young Today." *Ebony.* Chicago: Johnson Publication.

Rashad, Adib. 1994. *Elijah Muhammad and the Ideological Foundation of the Nation of Islam.* Newport: U.B.U. Communications Systems.

Rivlin, Benjamin. 1990. *Ralph Bunche: The Man and His Times.* New York: Holmes & Meier.

Robinson, Randall. 1998. *Defending the Spirit: A Black Life in America.* New York: Dutton.

Rout, Kathleen. 1991. *Eldridge Cleaver.* Boston: Twayne Publishers.

Rowan, Carl T. 1993. *Dream Makers, Dream Breakers: The World of Justice Thurgood Marshall.* Boston: Little, Brown and Company.

The Sentencing Project. 1990. *Black Males and the Criminal Justice System.* Washington, D.C.

Schultz, George. 1984. World Affairs Council. Boston.

Seale, Bobby. 1991. *Seize the Time: The Story of the Black Panther Party and Huey P. Newton.* Baltimore, MD: Black Classic Press.

Smith, Jessie Carney. 1994. *Black Firsts.* Detroit: Visible Ink.

Smith, Robert C., and Richard Seltzer. 1992. *Race, Class and Culture: A Study in Afro-American Mass Opinion.* Albany: State University of New York Press.

Smith, Willy De Marcell, and Eva Wells Chunn, eds. 1991. *Black Education.* New Brunswick: Transaction Publishers.

Toffler, Alvin. 1970. *Future Shock.* New York: Random House.

Toffler, Alvin. 1972. *The Futurists.* New York: Random House.

Urquhart, Brian. 1993. *Ralph Bunche: An American Life.* New York: W.W. Norton and Company.

U.S. Bureau of the Census. 1992. *General Population Characteristics of the United States* (1990 Census). Washington, D.C.: U.S. Government Printing Office.

U.S. Department of Labor. 1991. *A Report on the Glass Ceiling Initiative.* Washington, D.C.: Government Printing Office.

U.S. Department of State. 1984. *Realism, Strength, Negotiation: Key Foreign Policy Statements of the Reagan Administration.* Washington, D.C.: Bureau of Public Affairs.

Walker, Julia E. K. 1983. *Free Frank: A Black Pioneer on the Antebellum Frontier.* Lexington: University of Kentucky Press.

Warren, Chief Justice Earl. 1954. "Brown v. Board of Education." United States Reports, vol. 347, pp. 483.

Washington, Booker T. 1896. "Address of Booker T. Washington . . . at the opening of the Cotton States and International Exposition." In New York State Commission's *Report of the Board of Commissioners Representing the State of New York at the Cotton States and International Exposition held at Atlanta, GA, 1895.* Albany, NY: Wynkoop Hallenbeck Crawford Co., pp. 190–201.

Washington, James Melvin, ed. 1986. *A Testament of Hope: The Essential Writings and Speeches of Martin Luther King, Jr.* San Francisco: Harper.

Washington, Johnny. 1986. *Alain Locke and Philosophy: A Quest for Cultural Pluralism.* Westport, CT: Greenwood Press.

Washington, Johnny. 1994. *A Journey Into the Philosophy of Alain Locke.* Westport, CT: Greenwood Press.

Weiss, Nancy J. 1989. *Whitney M. Young, Jr., and the Struggle for Civil Rights.* Princeton, NJ: Princeton University Press.

Williams, Juan. 1987. *Eyes on the Prize.* New York: Viking.

Wittner, Lawrence. 1969. *Rebels Against War: The American Peace Movement, 1941–1960.* New York: Columbia University Press.

Woodard, Michael. 1997. *Black Entrepreneurs in America.* New Brunswick, NJ: Rutgers University Press.

Woodward, C. Vann. 1966. *The Strange Career of Jim Crow.* New York: Oxford University Press.

Index

About the Author

Jacob U. Gordon is Professor of African and African-American Studies and Research Fellow at the University of Kansas in Lawrence, Kansas. He is the editor of the *African-American Male: An Annotated Bibliography* (Greenwood, 1999).